EMOTIONAL DISORDERS OF MENTALLY RETARDED PERSONS

EMOTIONAL DISORDERS OF MENTALLY RETARDED PERSONS

Assessment, Treatment, and Consultation

Edited by

Ludwik S. Szymanski, M.D.
Director of Psychiatry
Developmental Evaluation Clinic
Associate in Psychiatry
Children's Hospital Medical Center, Boston, and
Assistant Professor of Psychiatry
Harvard Medical School

and

Peter E. Tanguay, M.D.
Professor of Psychiatry,
Director of Clinical Services, and
Director, Clinical Research Center
Division of Child Psychiatry
Neuropsychiatric Institute
University of California, Los Angeles

University Park Press
Baltimore

UNIVERSITY PARK PRESS
International Publishers in Science, Medicine, and Education
233 East Redwood Street
Baltimore, Maryland 21202

Copyright © 1980 by University Park Press

Composed by University Park Press, Typesetting Division.
Manufactured in the United States of America by
The Maple Press Company.

Library of Congress Cataloging in Publication Data
Main entry under title:
Emotional disorders of mentally retarded persons.
Includes index.
1. Mentally handicapped—Mental health.
I. Szymanski, Ludwik S.
II. Tanguay, Peter E. [DNLM:
1. Mental disorders—Complications.
2. Mental retardations—Complications.
WM300 M548]
RC451.4.M47E45   616.85'88   80-10714
ISBN 0-8391-1514-8

CONTENTS

CONTRIBUTORS

Bruce Cushna, Ph.D.
Associate Director
Developmental Evaluation Clinic
Children's Hospital Medical Center
and
Principal Associate in Pediatrics
(Psychology)
Harvard Medical School and
Adjunct Assistant Professor of
Special Education
Boston College
300 Longwood Avenue
Boston, Massachusetts 02115

Allen C. Crocker, M.D.
Director
Developmental Evaluation Clinic
Children's Hospital Medical Center
and
Associate Professor of Pediatrics
Harvard Medical School
300 Longwood Avenue
Boston, Massachusetts 02115

Bruce A. Eissner, M.D.
Staff Psychiatrist
Developmental Evaluation Clinic
Children's Hospital Medical Center
and
Instructor in Psychiatry
Harvard Medical School
300 Longwood Avenue
Boston, Massachusetts 02115

Mary B. Hagamen, M.D.
Director of Division of Adolescent
and Child Psychiatry
Nassau County Medical Center and
Associate Clinical Professor
Department of Psychiatry and

Behavioral Science
School of Medicine
State University of New York at
Stony Brook
65 Awixa Avenue
Bayshore, New York 11706

Paul E. Jansen, Ph.D.
Family Counseling Service—
Region West
74 Walnut Park
Newton, Massachusetts 02158

David R. Leaverton, M.D.
Director of Training, Child Psychiatry
Associate Professor of Psychiatry
University of Maryland School of
Medicine
645 West Redwood Street
Baltimore, Maryland 21201

Timothy M. Rivinus, M.D.
Director, Psychosomatic Unit
Department of Psychiatry
Children's Hospital Medical Center
and
Instructor in Psychiatry
Harvard Medical School
300 Longwood Avenue
Boston, Massachusetts 02115

Quinn B. Rosefsky, M.D.
Staff Psychiatrist
Developmental Evaluation Clinic
Children's Hospital Medical Center
Boston and
Instructor in Psychiatry
Harvard Medical School
232 Grove Street
Wellesley, Massachusetts 02181

Ludwik S. Szymanski, M.D.
Director of Psychiatry
Developmental Evaluation Clinic and
Associate in Psychiatry
Children's Hospital Medical Center
  and
Assistant Professor of Psychiatry
Harvard Medical School
300 Longwood Avenue
Boston, Massachusetts 02115

Peter E. Tanguay, M.D.
Professor of Psychiatry
Director of Clinical Services
Director, Clinical Research
  Center for the Study of Childhood
  Psychosis
Division of Child Psychiatry and
  Mental Retardation
UCLA Neuropsychiatric Institute
760 Westwood Plaza
Los Angeles, California 90024

FOREWORD

For almost 20 years professional workers in medicine, psychology, education, and social work, along with legislators, parents, and individuals from the judicial system, have made a concerted effort to redress centuries of neglect in meeting the needs of mentally retarded persons and their families. As a consequence of these efforts, achievements during this period, although still short of national goals, have been remarkable.

These truly significant achievements received their major impetus from President Kennedy's unparalleled and unprecedented message to Congress on mental illness and mental retardation. The appointment of a President's Panel on Mental Retardation and the panel's report on a national plan to combat mental retardation, along with the landmark legislation that followed, provided the foundation and structure for the program that endures to this day. For the first time in our history, the federal government committed the resources of the nation on a large scale to enhancing the well-being of some of its least fortunate citizens.

Gains for retarded persons can be noted on many fronts. Educational programs, buttressed by judicial decree proclaiming every child's constitutional "right to education," are now being extended increasingly to severely and profoundly retarded children. Diagnostic and treatment programs are contributing meaningfully to development and behavior. Vocational rehabilitation services, expanding their goals beyond gainful employment to include independent living, have helped many retarded youth and adults previously regarded as uneducable and untrainable to perform socially useful roles. Students with diverse backgrounds have been trained for service and research careers in the field. Research in mental retardation, long neglected by the scientific community, achieved prominence and respectability through a newly created national network of research centers.

The creation of a special panel to study the needs of mentally retarded persons, apart from those of the mentally ill and emotionally disturbed, recognized significant differences between the two populations. Mental retardation, by definition, originates during the developmental period and, in many of its forms, is chronic and lifelong. Mental illness, by contrast, although it occurs in some forms in childhood, occurs mainly in adulthood, and unlike mental retardation is frequently acute and episodic. While neither group is a pure entity, and there are clear and important areas of overlap in their service requirements, these fundamental differences have important implications for the role and responsibilities of various agencies and disciplines, the organization of the health and social service delivery system, and the planning of these services over a lifetime.

Before 1963, when legislation was passed that provided planning grants to states to develop services for the mentally retarded, the responsibility for mental retardation services at the state level had been in a "single designated state agency." In most cases this agency was the state mental health agency. The 1963 Mental Retardation Planning Amendments allowed for a move away from the more restrictive mental health model, which utilized the traditional "single designated state agency" approach, and instead encouraged the creation of multidepartmental councils. These councils were charged with coordinating services to provide care for mentally retarded persons.

The Mental Retardation Facilities Construction and Community Mental Health Centers Act, also passed in 1963, provided legislation that authorized the construction of research centers, University Affiliated Facilities, and community facilities for retarded persons. This same piece of legislation also established community mental health centers for the mentally ill. Accordingly, this legislation represented a further move to differentiate between mentally retarded and mentally ill persons in the planning and delivery of services to these two populations.

This possibly unforeseen movement toward the development of parallel rather than converging service delivery systems was prompted in large measure by organized parent groups. Based on chronic neglect by society of their mentally retarded children, parents felt, justifiably, that joining forces with mental health constituencies would reduce their national visibility and hard-earned priority status. The decision to pursue an independent course of action was, in retrospect, well founded; the burgeoning programs of the 1960s and 1970s in research, services, and training might not otherwise have been achieved.

With time, however, concepts about the capacities of mentally retarded persons and the philosophy of care and treatment changed; the continued separation of the two service delivery systems became less tenable. We have always been aware that mentally retarded persons, by virtue of their intellectual deficits and the manner in which they are perceived by others, are particularly vulnerable to social and emotional stress. It is not happenstance that early leaders in the mental retardation field, serving as superintendents of state facilities and administrators of mental health departments, were usually psychiatrists. The shift from mental health dominance has had a salutary effect in promoting a more balanced professional approach to the complex and diverse needs of mentally retarded persons and their families. At the same time, the tendency of mental health professionals to concentrate their skills and talents on individuals with psychiatric disorders but normal intelligence has left a huge void in our knowledge and treatment of troubled retarded children and their families. The conventional view that the retarded person could not profit from psychiatric treatment modalities probably contributed to this tendency.

The prevalence of emotional disorders in the United States is high. Approximately 10% of all school age children have such disorders, ranging in severity from mild to severe. Teachers are troubled by their inability to educate these children and school administrators are further concerned about the disruptive impact of their behavior on the education of other students. Parents are, in general, the most affected of all, since it is they who perceive themselves as the cause of their children's disorders, and it is they who must bear the responsibility for their children's care and well-being.

The lower prevalence of emotional disorders among preschoolers and adults, in contrast to those of school age, may be a reflection of the rigorous demands of the school environment for academic achievement and behavior conformity. It is also probable that in some children symptoms of disturbance may appear a long time after the origin of the disturbance. Every child encounters stressful experiences as he moves from the protective setting of the family to an independent status. Most children succeed in this move to independence, but some do not. These who fail and become emotionally disturbed may be congenitally ill-equipped to cope with life's demands, as are children with central nervous system pathology. Others may develop psychiatric disorders because of an overprotective or abusive family that offers little opportunity for social and emotional growth. Still others may have the disorder thrust upon them by unrealistic family and community expectations and unwholesome environments.

All of these factors occur more frequently with retarded than with intellectually normal children. Low intelligence and associated physical handicaps impinge on coping behavior and sorely tax parents' child-rearing skills. The frustrations that occur may tend to breed hostility and aggression and secondary handicaps, which are sometimes more disabling than the intellectual deficit itself. These persons, if mildly retarded, do not "disappear" from service delivery systems when they drop out of school. They populate our institutions for the mentally retarded and mentally ill, or are incarcerated in juvenile or adult correctional facilities, or become dependent upon social welfare benefits.

Current trends in mental retardation, although conceptually, philosophically, and legally sound, may present additional stressful situations to some retarded persons and their families. Many well-intentioned efforts to quickly reduce the populations of institutions for retarded persons, for example, have caught many communities ill-prepared to provide suitable alternative residential arrangements and the essential network of supportive services. Persons who have spent many years in institutional care and are confronted for the first time with the need to make decisions in major domains of living can experience serious adjustment problems.

Keeping children within the mainstream of the educational system is a laudatory goal and enables many retarded children to gain self-esteem and confidence. With tutorial help, a mentally retarded child's academic progress may equal that of a normal child, and might surpass the level that would have been achieved in a special education class. However, it has become apparent that this approach is too competitive for some mildly retarded youngsters and that the sense of failure experienced may generate disturbed and disruptive behavior.

These trends may pose potential stresses to families as well. Parents who have placed their retarded child in an institution after much agonizing and have readjusted their life-style to his absence may encounter serious difficulty upon his return. Similarly, the more widely accepted position that retarded persons should be cared for in their own homes and communities may create guilt and anxiety in parents who are unwilling or unable to assume the burdens involved. Under these circumstances, even if they comply with current trends, distorted parent-child relationships may prove inimical to healthy personality development of the retarded child.

The implementation of deinstitutionalization programs and the fulfillment of mainstreaming and normalization goals demands a comprehensive array of services. The first line of defense is the family. If retarded persons are to realize a sense of fulfillment and become productive members of society to the extent their abilities permit, every effort must be made to strengthen and support the parental role. However, it must be recognized that many parents, particularly those with limited resources or coping skills, cannot carry the burden of care, training, and management of a retarded child unaided. Only as a network of community-based services applying health, social service, and mental health concepts is brought to bear can retarded persons be helped to achieve their rightful place in society.

Professionals and scientists in mental retardation can regard with pride the accomplishments of recent years. Although much remains to be done, the populations of institutions have been reduced greatly, community-based group homes and foster homes have increased greatly, educational opportunities are being extended to the most severely handicapped, and public health and social services of various kinds have become increasingly available to retarded persons and their families. For the reasons stated earlier, however, the mental health aspects of mental retardation have not been sufficiently addressed. There are beginning indications, however, that this gap in the armamentarium of services required by retarded persons may be eliminated eventually. In a recent report by the President's Commission on Mental Health, mentally retarded persons were identified as one of several unserved or underserved groups by community mental health centers.

Responsive to such concerns, mental health practitioners at the local level are beginning to sponsor workshops and seminars to learn more about the special needs of retarded persons and how to serve them more effectively.

The desired convergence of mental health, mental retardation, and other human services requires not only planning and coordination at all levels but communication of the knowledge and content derived from practice and research among the fields involved. This book should help bring about a greater integration of knowledge, skills, and services to foster improved programs and care, which is the objective of a civilized society. In so doing, this book is in the fore of what may be the next revolution for better care—the functional integration of services to meet each family's needs more effectively.

Books such as this one are a step in that direction.

Julius B. Richmond, M.D.
Assistant Secretary of Health
and Surgeon General
Public Health Service
Department of Health
and Human Services

PREFACE

This book is for mental health professionals who work in the field of developmental disabilities. Its goal is to present practical approaches for assessing, diagnosing, and treating mental illness in retarded persons. Many studies have shown that mentally retarded persons may not only develop all of the types of mental illnesses found in the general population but that as many as 50% may, at some time, suffer from some type of diagnosable psychiatric disorder. These disorders are treatable using approaches discussed in this book. Because treatment, care, and habilitation of disabled persons are becoming increasingly interdisciplinary, a major focus of the book is upon the roles and interactions of the various disciplines in the diagnostic and treatment process. The book is also written with an understanding of the changes that have taken place in the care of retarded persons in the past decade, changes resulting from such powerful concepts as mainstreaming and normalization, changes that have led to a renewed concern for the rights and dignity of all individuals, whether or not they are handicapped. Because of the increasing degree to which all handicapped persons are being integrated into the community, there is a secondary emphasis in this book upon the role of the mental health professional as a consultant.

Many of the ideas and programs discussed in this book were developed by a team of professionals with whom we work. In particular, we are indebted to Dr. Allen Crocker (Director), Dr. Bruce Cushna (Associate Director), Dr. Jean Zadig (Director of Special Education), and to the staff of the Developmental Evaluation Clinic at Children's Hospital Medical in Boston. This clinic is a University Affiliated Facility, funded by the United States Department of Health, Education, and Welfare, Maternal and Child Health Service Project Number 928 and Office of Developmental Disabilities grant 59-PO5163. We are also indebted to the faculty of the Mental Retardation and Child Psychiatry Program at UCLA, and to the University Affiliated Facility that is part of that program. We hope that our book is an example of the fine interdisciplinary training that is available at both of these centers.

We extend our thanks to Ms. Cynthia Bates, Ms. Ellen Israel, Ms. Patricia Cooney, Ms. Jeanne Bombardier, and Ms. Anna Gibbons for secretarial assistance.

to
our
wives

PROFESSIONAL ROLES AND TRAINING

Lack of trained professionals is an important obstacle to providing mental health services to retarded citizens. The major reasons for this lack and suggestions on how to overcome it are discussed in Chapter 1. Chapter 2 discusses guidelines for the clinical training of mental health professionals in mental retardation, in the context of two different models of service delivery: one in which mental health and mental retardation services are totally integrated, and one in which the two services are administratively and geographically separate, but have coordinated training programs. Chapter 2 is based on the authors' personal experiences in two such training programs.

As is discussed in Chapter 1, provision of mental health services for retarded persons has been a much-debated question for many years. A number of writers have reviewed this topic (Potter, 1964; Donaldson and Menolascino, 1977). They noted that the relationship between the mental health and mental retardation fields has reflected, through the years, societal attitudes toward retarded persons. This relationship could be seen as an evolution through several phases: 1) An early phase (19th century) in which care of retarded persons was considered the responsibility of mental health professionals, particularly psychiatrists, and in which humanism and education were stressed. 2) A period of therapeutic nihilism and preoccupation with neuropathology, with isolation of retarded persons in large institutions. During this period, which lasted until approximately the early 1960s, the responsibility of mental health professionals was seen to be more administrative than actively therapeutic. 3) A current phase in which attention is focused upon the mainstreaming of retarded individuals into "normalized" community life (Nirje, 1969; Wolfensberger, 1972). Such efforts have involved the concept of the interdisciplinary team of professionals, including mental health specialists.

Mental health professionals in mental retardation may encounter resistance from co-workers and patients alike, often based on the historical image of their respective disciplines. The controversy around the "medical model" as a roadblock to proper care of retarded individuals serves as an example (Potter, 1970). Chapter 2 is designed to help these professionals to understand and overcome such obstacles and to integrate themselves into the interdisciplinary team. Similarly, it may be of help to other professionals in their work with mental health specialists.

REFERENCES

Donaldson, J. Y., and Menolascino, F. J. 1977. Past, current and future roles of child psychiatry in mental retardation. J. Am. Acad. Child Psychiatry 16:38–52.

Potter, H. W. 1964. The needs of mentally retarded children for child psychiatry services. J. Am. Acad. Child Psychiatry 3:352–374.

Potter, H. W. 1970. Human values as guides to the administration of residential facilities for the mentally retarded. In: F. J. Menolascino (ed.), Psychiatric Approaches to Mental Retardation. Basic Books, New York.

Nirje, B. 1969. The normalization principle and its human management implications. In: R. Kugel and W. Wolfensberger (eds.), Changing Patterns in Residential Services for the Mentally Retarded. President's Committee on Mental Retardation, Washington, D.C.

Wolfensberger, W. 1972. The Principle of Normalization in Human Services. National Institute on Mental Retardation, Toronto.

PROFESSIONAL ROLES AND UNMET MANPOWER NEEDS

Bruce Cushna,
Ludwik S. Szymanski,
and Peter E. Tanguay

Chapter 1

Mentally retarded persons, even more than nonretarded, need mental health services. The need is acute, and yet there are many indications that the ability of mental health professionals, and psychiatrists in particular, to deliver such services has been blunted. Why this is so and what may be done about it are discussed in this chapter.

The current philosophy of care and management for retarded persons is one of community placement, with children mainstreamed in public schools and adults living in community residences. Experiences in such "normalized" and unprotected environments exert stress on cognitively handicapped individuals, often resulting in psychiatric disorders—notably, behavior disturbances in younger persons and emotional (mainly depressive) reactions in older ones. In a study of retarded adults living in the community, Seltzer and Seltzer (1978) pointed out emotional instability and behavior problems as important factors in individual failures to adjust to vocational and community placement and in the need to be returned to institutions.

These developments, in the authors' experience, have generated increasing need for mental health services, both for direct clinical diagnosis and treatment and for consultations with educators and staffs of community residences and various service agencies. Thus, the current major challenge for mental health professionals has been helping directly and indirectly to mainstream retarded persons in the community. As pointed out by Dr. Julius Richmond, the Surgeon General, in the Foreword, in the last decade federally assisted training programs, such as University Affiliated Facilities, brought more psychiatrists, psychologists, and social workers into contact with retarded patients on a national basis; however, in a survey of 18 child guidance programs in the Boston area several years ago, we found that many programs still lacked a staff trained to offer clinical services to the retarded children despite the presence of retarded persons among their potential population. Many mental health clinics still categorically exclude retarded people from their services. An additional unmet need is for provision of psychiatric services to large state institutions for retarded persons.

What are the mental health services for which a need exists? At a program-planning level, professionals are needed who can plan for the mental health needs of retarded persons, incorporating into general care programs elements that acknowledge individual psychodynamics and each person's need for emotional support. In addition, mental health professionals must share the responsibility of developing and implementing studies aimed at assessing the impact of the program and its element on patients and clients. At an individual level, professionals are needed to carry out psychiatric assessment and diagnosis and to provide a range of treatments. Appropriate treatment includes behavior therapy, individual and group psychotherapy, pharmacotherapy, and therapeutic assistance to families with retarded children and adolescents.

OBSTACLES TO PROVISION OF MENTAL HEALTH SERVICES

What factors play a role in the relative paucity of mental health services for retarded citizens? There appear to be four main variables that substantially influence the shortage: failure of mental health professional organizations to intervene effectively; failure of professionals, individually, to respond to the need; interdisciplinary disagreements between professions and professionals; and society's and, in particular, retarded persons' attitudes toward mental health professionals.

These dynamic factors may also underlie politically motivated and expeditious bureaucratic policies that fail to provide funding for such services, or that order separation of retarded individuals from centers where such services would be available. Common to all of these factors is ignorance: ignorance of what mentally retarded people are like, ignorance of how effective treatment may be in alleviating their mental health problems, and ignorance of what to expect from professionals. Stereotypes and prejudices feed upon such ignorance and further complicate the problem.

MENTAL HEALTH PROFESSIONAL ORGANIZATIONS

Only the large, professional organizations have sufficient power and visibility to influence public policy or to reverse training deficiencies through their certification power over institutional training programs. Such professional organizations as the American Association on Mental Deficiency (AAMD) do, of course, exert a strong influence on behalf of retarded citizens, but their voice is rarely swelled to a chorus by other professional groups. The American Academy of Child Psychiatry, despite the strong advocacy work of some of its members, and despite its strong statements regarding the mental health needs of retarded children, still does not demand that the training programs in child psychiatry that it accredits must provide adequate training in the care of mentally retarded children and adolescents. The manner in which training programs could accomplish this goal is discussed in Chapter 2, but to date relatively few programs do so. Moreover, few professional organizations speak out against those public policies that deny mental health services to retarded persons. Perhaps this latter shortcoming is largely related to lack of knowledge by individual members about what is needed and what will work.

PROFESSIONAL IGNORANCE AND BIAS

Professionals are not immune to cultural biases and misconceptions prevalent in our society about mental retardation. These are a part of society's prejudice against, and fear of, people whom it does not understand. The immature-for-age behavior of a retarded person may provoke a psychiatrist's (or anyone's) own regressive forces (as pointed out by Cytryn and Lourie, 1975), leading to anxiety and a variety of defensive maneuvers.

The most common source of these biases is ignorance. In spite of calls for training in this field throughout the last two decades (Potter, 1964; Gardner, 1968; Cytryn, 1970), Leaverton and Van Der Heide found in 1975 that only 51% of child psychiatry training programs included any material on mental retardation in their curricula (and that could be only a brief lecture). Many child psychiatrists, including experienced ones, never interviewed and treated a retarded child or adult. They are amazed when given that opportunity and they realize that "a mongoloid child can show feelings" (actual quote from a senior colleague). Child psychiatry fellows entering training programs in the Developmental Evaluation Clinic have been observed regularly to avoid talking with verbally retarded children whom they interviewed, out of conviction that the children would not comprehend the questions and/or would not tolerate the stress of being asked about certain emotionally charged topics, such as their feelings about attending special classes. Professionals stereotypically fail to recognize that there are many forms and degrees of mental retardation and that most retarded persons are not "vegetables" requiring full custodial care.

Another bias is noted in the loose, undefined use of the term *organicity*. Many psychiatrists still tend to dichotomize retardation into "organic" and "nonorganic" types—the former implying "brain damage," an incurable condition that is the cause of disturbed behavior, and therefore not treatable with psychotherapy.

The fallacy of this belief lies in the misconception that the goal of psychiatric treatment should be curing the retardation rather than an associated mental disorder.

Philips (1966) called attention to three misconceptions: 1) that the maladaptive behavior of a retarded child is a function of his retardation rather than of his interpersonal relationships, 2) that emotional disorders in the retarded are different in kind from those in the normal child, and 3) that certain symptoms and specific maladaptive behavior patterns in retarded children are the result of organic brain damage. Menolascino (1977) called attention to "a number of blindspots psychiatrists characteristically exhibit in dealing with the retarded." He listed them as "uncritical acceptance of mental age as an adequate description of a person; treatment nihilism usually based on lack of program knowledge; a myopic view of conceivable, or even available, program alternatives; excessive focus on the severely retarded and their families in contrast to the mildly retarded."

Physicians, including psychiatrists, are trained to cure illnesses, and it is understandable that they may be threatened by a retarded child whose retardation cannot be cured (even if his mental disorder, if existing, can be treated.) Caring for "incurable" retarded patients may lead to intolerable anxiety for some physicians. The most obvious maneuver would be to avoid seeing them. Goodman (1964) suggested that sometimes institutional placement may be recommended by physicians in an attempt to remove the symbol of their "failure." Some professionals may overidentify with such patients instead of being empathetic and compassionate (Beck, 1959; Cohen, 1962).

In summary, awareness and resolution of these biases and misconceptions are necessary prerequisites to working with retarded patients. It is, however, not different in substance from problems of countertransference and misconceptions encountered in one's basic training and practice of any mental health discipline.

PROFESSIONAL RELATIONSHIPS AND THE
CONCEPT OF THE INTERDISCIPLINARY TEAM

Perhaps because of the broad range of services that retarded persons need, all of which must be considered in toto, the interdisciplinary team approach has become mandatory. As would be expected, interpersonal rivalries and personal politics may sometimes impede team function.

Who should be team leader is a frequent concern. The question is often posed in disciplinary terms: Should it be the pediatrician? the educator? the psychiatrist? The question can be very difficult to answer. Mental retardation, being multicausal, having a multisymptom manifestation, and often requiring many simultaneous therapeutic approaches, cannot "belong" to any one discipline.

Review of the literature indicates that recent major papers and studies on care, planning, and service delivery for retarded persons have come from a variety of disciplines, for instance, social work, pediatrics, psychology, and psychiatry.

In addition, no discipline provides comprehensive training in all facets of diagnosis and management of mental retardation. Only training and experience in the framework of a well-functioning interdisciplinary team may prepare a professional to be able to lead such a team. Any interdisciplinary team member can fulfill such a task. On the other hand, some disciplines more than others provide a comprehensive background. A pediatrician with good training in developmental pediatrics and experience in child psychiatry, or a child psychiatrist with good background in developmental pediatrics and neurology, may, by virtue of training in psychological and biological aspects of human behavior, be best prepared to serve as a "generalist" in mental retardation.

Not all interdisciplinary developmental disability teams are alike, of course. A team may encompass an entire clinic staff, or it may involve a small group of professionals meeting to discuss a single case. They may be part of a larger department, such as pediatrics, psychology, or psychiatry, in which case a "host" discipline might dominate the remaining ones. A clinic's director, depending on personal maturity and security, may make his own discipline the dominant one or permit the most aggressive professionals to dominate the team. Some teams may be run autocratically, with the leader as the sole decision maker. On other teams, decisions are made by the whole staff by consensus and compromise. The team in its entirety usually has, and needs, a leader (clinic director) who coordinates, secures funds, represents it to the public, and otherwise administers. In clinical routines, each case may have a different leader or team coordinator assigned to bring various disciplines to joint, comprehensive decisions, facilitating their recommendations and implementing follow-up. Some teams (Stone, 1970) advocate selection of a case coordinator from a discipline most appropriate to a particular situation; others have a rotating system where a team member may choose the patient who offers him most interest or challenge.

Interrelationship of Mental Health
Disciplines on the Developmental Disability Team

There has been much confusion and even hostility generated by the more circumscribed issue of interrelationship among mental health disciplines. Henry, Sims, and Spray (1971), in a thorough study of four disciplines (psychiatry, psychology, social work, and psychoanalysis), suggested that they are actually much more similar to than different from one another and form together a "fifth profession." It is true that many, if not most, of the services delivered by these professionals consist of various forms of psychotherapy learned in clinical training, often all in the same program, regardless of respective disciplinary allegiances. One has to be aware, however, that the field of mental health encompasses more than diagnosing psychological conflicts and treating them with psychotherapy. Although the specific disciplines all are involved in such diagnosis and treatment, each still requires unique expertise; often practitioners view the same issues in different lights based on their respective disciplinary training. Thus, the psychiatrist is expected to look at biological aspects of mental illness and synthesize them with psychological ones (West, 1973); the psychologist may have been trained in research approaches and a variety of psychological and neuropsychological testing techniques; the social worker has a special background in social and public welfare (Henry et al., 1971). A professional degree or certification is not a guarantee of knowledge. Thus, a mental health professional of any discipline may be untrained and inexperienced in treating disturbed retarded patients. Also, a professional's knowledge may not be restricted only to his field. There are social workers proficient enough in psychotherapy to supervise psychiatric residents, psychologists who are experts in psychopharmacology, and psychiatrists who know a great deal about biofeedback.

While these skills are essential in managing such a multihandicapping condition as mental retardation, no discipline can be a priori recognized as "owning" the field or being more important or prestigious than another one. What counts is the professionals' training and competence, not their titles, and this should also be reflected in the respect accorded them, privileges, and pay scale. Competence requires abilities, training, and experience, which in turn are time and money consuming. Administrators in this field will have to recognize this in order to attract able professionals. The professionals will have to mature beyond petty disciplinary power struggles and respect one another's knowledge while recognizing their own shortcomings.

Besides team leadership, another important controversy has arisen in the past decade: the role relationships of the psychologist and the psychiatrist on the interdisciplinary team. Historically, psychiatry and psychology stem from two different roots. When the American Association on Mental Deficiency (AAMD) was founded, psychiatry was oriented toward direct service. With Freudian influence and as medical science became more engrossed in academic standards in the early 1900s, the interaction with psychology began. Before the great post–World War II proliferation of Ph.D.-granting psychology departments, psychology was mainly an academic subject. It was the "logic" of the mental processes. Within the American testing movement and with the military and public school system demands for "testing specialists," a type of technician-level job requirement was created in many bureaucratic systems. These "technicians" needed direction and supervision from more advanced and experienced professionals in the field. Often this was provided intramurally by psychiatrists in institutional circumstances where no doc-toral-level psychologist was available. There was also some lack of differ-entiation between master-level (and sometimes less credentialed) testing technicians and certified professional psychologists who were qualified to carry out a variety of diagnostic and treatment procedures. This confu-sion was furthered by psychologists' prolonged inability to agree on licen-sure standards and a more unified code of applied practice.

It is important to recognize that psychology is a pluralistic field. This recognition occurs gradually in the experience of other mental health pro-fessionals. The differences between clinical and experimental psycholo-gist are fairly obvious, but there are finer subtleties in the differences be-tween school psychology, educational psychology, and developmental psychology. The distinction between approved and unapproved intern-ships creates misinterpretations of certain practitioners' skills and qualifi-cations. National board certification and state licensure have eliminated some of the uncertainties regarding what services a psychologist is quali-fied or prepared to deliver. However, differences in background and spe-cialty still lead not only to confusion in role expectation in the field, but also often to lack of appreciation of the highly developed skills of many psychologists.

Historically, rivalries developed as a result of the "guild" structure that many health-related disciplines adhered to, and bitterness grew be-tween the academically based psychology training departments and the practicum and internship sites in hospitals and clinics. This relationship at times functioned under an uneasy truce. At other times it erupted into subtle and undeclared warfare, sabotage, and other, more passive-aggres-sive, hostilities.

The resolution of such reactions requires that professionals work to-gether. There is much to be done in the mental retardation field. Tremen-dous challenges exist in promoting treatment programs and developing normalized and supportive environments for retarded persons. There is room for a variety of approaches to facing this challenge. In a pluralistic society, a broader perspective is demanded on many social issues. The issue would seem more one of preventing domination struggles from in-terfering with the demands of the task at hand and getting on with the work. Working together requires a team effort. As for the rivalry between psychology and psychiatry, mutual respect will only come through an appreciation of the unique aspects of the potential contribution of each discipline. The magnitude of the task at hand mandates a joint contribution. Since there can be no divorce, the best tactic is an increased effort to build this needed mutual appreciation. Like so many ill-matched combinations, this union appears destined to endure.

Integrating Mental Health Professionals into the Interdisciplinary Team

Successful integration of any mental health professional into a team depends on several factors. If the professional is a psychiatrist, and the team has an antimedical/antipsychiatric orientation, the team may want to limit the psychiatrist to provide advice only on specific issues, such as prescribing medication. Some psychiatrists may prefer this situation, wishing to be traditional visiting mental health consultants and not assuming genuine co-responsibility for the decisions of the team. Mental health professionals often will find it difficult to define clearly their team roles because considerable interdisciplinary overlap exists. If a psychiatrist, psychologist, social worker, pediatrician, and nurse have each interviewed a family and observed a child's behavior, they will not (nor should they) refrain themselves from voicing opinions, whether or not traditionally it would be considered their area of competence. By the same measure, the team members, including the psychiatrist, may and should voice their questions, criticisms, and suggestions concerning assessments done by a professional of any other discipline. Such a merger of different viewpoints enables the team to assess the problem from a much broader perspective than would be possible for a single profession. For instance, the psychiatrist may feel that the child is extremely disorganized, yet psychological testing may show that he functions very well under structured conditions. These conditions, in turn, are explained by the speech pathologist's finding of a severe language-processing disorder. Alternately, the child may produce "psychotic" responses on psychological testing because of anxiety about failing in these school-like "tests"; whereas detailed psychiatric evaluation may show him as not being clinically psychotic. Thus, on a team, the various professionals should work synergistically, not competitively. On a team, a specialist's area of competence is not granted to him by virtue of his discipline and degree, but by training, knowledge, and ability to collaborate effectively with other team members. A specialist may be recognized as having the best, but not exclusive, competence within a specific area. Overlap with other disciplines is acknowledged as desirable and constructive, if professionals involved are ready to work out their differences. This model allows for constructive interdependence, but avoids obliteration of professional role definition.

The psychiatrist's roles in early interdisciplinary teams were discussed by Bolian (1968). He pointed out the need for the psychiatrist to be essentially eclectic, to engage in joint work and open, trusting communication in plain English, without psychiatric jargon, with other team members. Bolian saw specific role delineation between mental health disciplines as unnecessary and even impossible. Often, differences between professional approaches are more apparent than real. Thus, a psychologist or teacher may speak about behavior modification using behavioristic jargon, whereas the psychiatrist may talk about consistency, structure, and limits; yet, in a given situation, all these professionals may actually carry out a similar course of treatment. Bolian concluded that "the primary role of the child psychiatrist among other professional members of the mental retardation interdisciplinary team, is to function interpretively at the interface of biology and behavior," a view close to that of Tisza (1975).

On an interdisciplinary team, frictions of various intensities among the members often surface, as is to be expected in any small group of intensely involved persons. Two sisters, one a psychologist and the other a social worker (Brody and Weithorn, 1967), gave a hilarious account of these hostilities.

The mental health professional may have another, very important function on a team, which is usually not spoken of. This is providing emotional support for the other team members. Working in a closed, small group with retarded patients, whose primitive behaviors are likely to evoke countertransference feelings, may stimulate unresolved conflicts and regressive tendencies (Cytryn and Lourie, 1975) and lead to anxiety. This is rarely perceived as such; rather, projection or displacement results. The mental health professional may be approached for advice, ostensibly about clinical issues, but the colleague's anxiety and confusion may indicate that he is seeking more than concrete advice. An expression of empathy is often sufficient, particularly if one recollects similar episodes from one's own practice. "Permission" to set limits for a manipulative and guilt-provoking family may be necessary as well as, in some cases, continuing consultation or even an offer of taking over a difficult case, if appropriate.

The team's psychiatrist might be approached also with questions about personal problems or requests for referral for psychiatric help. In all these situations, extreme tact is necessary. The psychiatrist must remember that he is a friend and colleague first and a psychiatrist second. Under no circumstances should he get involved in interpretations or asking for unnecessary personal details, because later the colleague may find it difficult to work with a person who knows so much about him. The psychiatrist has to be aware that his temptation to delve into a colleague's problems may be a veiled expression of his own anger and wish for revenge, due, for instance, to a past professional conflict with that colleague.

ATTITUDES OF SOCIETY TOWARD MENTAL HEALTH SERVICES

Conscious stereotypes of mental health professionals as well as unrecognized fears may influence the degree to which there is demand for and use of community mental health services for retarded persons. Some of the stereotypes are based upon actual professional abuses that retarded persons have experienced in the past. Others are based upon the retarded person's anxiety regarding his own limitations.

The term *shrink* epitomizes the popular reactions to these stereotypes. This figurative term reflects the concern that something (presumably the brain) is notably out of proportion. In a more sophisticated rationalization, the term may be rooted in a historic belief that disturbed behavior was caused by cerebral edema. Some theorists trace the colloquialism to social-anthropological interests regarding "head hunters" in the 1950s. However, the term in current popular usage refers to the social demand that certain offensive or objectionable behaviors be curtailed by psychotherapeutic intervention. It is comparable to the educational situation where most teachers beg for psychiatric help to get an acting-out, disturbed child out of the classroom, while more seriously disturbed, withdrawn children receive "social promotions." Treatment from this perspective becomes merely a correctionalist endeavor through which offensive actions are diminished or eradicated, and the remaining "reduced" person is left more socially acceptable. Totally contrary to any attempt at understanding psychiatric symptomatology or the more symbolic interpretations of disturbed behavior, this viewpoint is a distortion of the basic intent of treatment. It substitutes a reductionistic demand for what should be an experientially expanding or constructive process. This should leave many mental health specialists embarrassed. Because it is such a widespread misinterpretation, it must be dealt with carefully and directly by the professional when it appears.

A retarded person is in many ways similar to a withdrawn patient in that he needs a certain degree of ego support, encouragement, and "building up" before he can really confront and begin to resolve some of the more troubling issues in his life. Mildly retarded individuals are usually keenly aware that they are not good competitors. Edgerton (1967) reviewed many tactics and ploys used by such persons to avoid admission of limitations, even hiding from themselves the admission of the degree of their deficiencies. Retarded persons need support in treatment, as they may at times need help in describing and expressing the issues that trouble them. Those who are rejected by psychotherapists, feeling unable to meet a level of low verbal mastery as a challenge, avoid "shrinks." The converse situation, in which a competent therapist meets the challenge with skills to assist a more verbally limited patient in communicating his conflicting feelings in expressed interpersonal reflection, holds the solution to the issue.

The family of the retarded individual is also deeply in need of openness and acceptance by a prospective therapist. The family is under unavoidable stress. This stress causes exaggerated reactions, which can be easily misinterpreted as being characteristic of more serious psychopathology. The fear that their psychic space, already too drastically diminished, may face further shrinkage is a definite obstacle to many families with a retarded member. The desired goal of promoting a healthier acceptance and avoiding stresses in their life is the means of offering the psychotherapeutic help they so often desperately need.

A number of specific stereotypes may lead mentally retarded people and their families to avoid seeking help for psychiatric problems.

Fear of the Professional as Controller and Manipulator

The mentally retarded person may fear losing control to another individual who will "use" him. There may be realistic aspects to the fear. There are subtleties in too many power plays that leave subordinated individuals feeling manipulated and cheated. Double standards, particularly in the economic and tax spheres, leave the general public with a sense of being victimized, unable to do anything to prevent or alter this situation. Families' fears of their retarded member being exploited or taken advantage of are intensified by the reality of inequalities in coping with bureaucratic obstacles in the provision of welfare, food stamps, and other economic subsistence aids as well as in job competition.

Closely related to this is the correlation between economic deprivation and lower mental ability scores. The majority of the children labeled mildly retarded by the educational system come from lower class homes. Poorer children look more mentally limited on all indices, such as sophistication in language and social skills, general knowledge, and personal presentation. Poorer families are disproportionately numbered whenever statistics on mildly retarded children are collected. In many ways poverty contributes to disability and particularly to the larger numbers of poor children appearing in the ranks of the mildly retarded. Although many of these are authentically developmentally delayed and not just unfortunates mislabeled by unreliable test scores, the fear of being manipulated has its correlates in other social and economic realities.

Poorer families have the fewest and poorest mental health resources available to them. Poorer families have the least confidence in "talking doctors," and probably the least trust in medical science in general. The fear that they will be subjected to further manipulation or exploitation is obvious.

The psychotherapist has the means to meet this challenge. He must meet the patient and the involved family on their terms. If undermining suspicions are left unacknowledged and their threat unresolved, there will be no "treatment." If the terminology of the therapist is beyond the family's or patient's comprehension, communication breaks down, making it impossible to proceed. The therapist must learn the symbolic exchange in which the family is involved. It is up to the specialist to master the manner in which this social cluster promotes mutual support and expresses individual needs, the manner in which its members provide alliances to reward one another and acknowledge social contribution toward their common goals. Once this challenge is accepted by the professional, the social world of the patient can be entered and constructive and positive alternatives explored.

Fear of the Omnipotent Father Figure

Although each stereotype bears some semblance to the others, the difference here is that power and overprotective control may be regarded as beneficent or well intended. Often the paternalistic image was promoted by other medical practitioners. The logical fallacy that supports such a wishful myth is apparent. In familial relationships, a too-powerful parent only makes the child feel incompetent. Children need to learn to become independent. Patients in psychiatric treatment need to learn to think through and solve their own interpersonal problems. Retarded patients, more than anyone, need to feel they have the competence to make personal decisions on their own. Feelings of powerlessness are too prevalent in their everyday affairs. "Cure" and the means to a mentally healthier existence lie not in the direction of knowing someone whose all-engrossing wisdom solves every problem. Self-confidence needs to be promoted from within the patient. Morale needs to be built and sustained. The sense of capability and inner strength must be developed. This cannot be accomplished with the implication that someone else has all the answers, no matter how kindly or paternal this figure might be.

Fear of the Authoritarian Figure

Last among the popular stereotypes is the dominating authority figure who has insufficient patience for the chosen life-styles of those who might come to him for treatment. Perhaps this is related to a view of the transference relationship: in becoming truly independent of a perceived parent figure, it is often necessary to transfer some or all of the emotional reactions toward that individual to a third person (possibly a therapist) in order to view these feelings more objectively. In this process, a strong dependency relationship often develops. The issue then becomes whether this dependency is unavoidable or whether there are means within the psychotherapeutic relationship of restricting the degree to which this dependency might disrupt a patient's life.

The retarded person's life is a constant struggle to avoid dependency relationships. From parental overprotection, or the "crate of eggs" syndrome, in infancy to the educational system's tendency to pity, isolate, and create artificial, noncompetitive learning milieux, the retarded person is not offered sufficient risk to derive feelings of competence and self-direction. The challenge to a competent psychotherapist should be to develop a style that allows retarded patients choice, feelings of self-direction, and derivation of a sense of mastery and achievement in the domain of personal and affective relationships. To achieve this objective, concepts about the process of psychotherapy need to be flexible. The psychotherapeutic relationship must be entered into with a freedom to investigate alternate means of promoting sound decisions and constructively exploring human relationships. Ultimately it becomes a matter of establishing a trust or reliance on one's personal decisions. There appears to be some merit in allowing the retarded patient to express many of his concerns first from the perspective of his own preoccupations. In this way the stereotype itself can be dealt with. The popular fear of not being able to cope with a dominating psychotherapist can be reduced to the question of "Who knows better than I do what the problems are that confront me? Why should anyone else tell me what my personal troubles are?" The resolution lies in the skill with which the therapist can assure the patient that he can retain the privilege of settling his own problems. The therapist is there to provide the perspective of alternate choice. The patient must derive the sense of power of choice and the strength developed through constructive decisions. The retarded patient makes this process very explicit.

Patient Advocacy and the Mental Health Professional

A frequently controversial role for a professional in any discipline is one of patient's advocate. Advocacy can be defined broadly as an effort on behalf of a retarded person to secure his rights. These rights have been divided by Crocker and Cushna (1976) into: a) normal rights to be defended or sought (such as family living, education, treatment and habilitation, employment), and b) special rights of particular concern to persons with developmental disabilities (such as guardianship; protection against inappropriate use of psychoactive drugs and behavior modification, counseling regarding contraception). Some professionals claim that they are primarily clinicians and that advocacy should be left to politicians, parents' organizations, and perhaps social workers. Others believe that clinical assessment and recommendations are worthless unless the clinician assumes at least some responsibility for procuring the services he has recommended. Obviously, the truth must be between these two views, since it may be impractical for a highly trained clinician to spend excessive time on advocacy efforts when others need his specialized services. He cannot, however, abdicate totally his advocacy responsibilities.

The mental health professional's specific contribution to patient advocacy may include "educating" other professionals about retarded people's potential for gratifying lives despite their handicaps; helping others realize that retarded people's behavior is not "crazy" or dangerous; and helping retarded people, through mental health intervention, to acquire more socially acceptable behaviors, thus rendering them able to benefit from privileges associated with mainstreamed life.

CONCLUSIONS

The role of the mental health professional in the mental retardation field is varied and in much demand. The challenge of a sound and appropriate life adjustment for a potentially compromised person is one that has need for expanded professional endeavor and coordinated team work. Creative and imaginative programming requires working together. Mutual respect and united team effort are the most effective means of getting the job done.

REFERENCES

Beck, H. 1959. Counseling parents of retarded children. Children 6:225–230.

Bolian, G. C. 1968. The child psychiatrist and the mental retardation "team." Arch. Gen. Psychiatry 18:360–366.

Brody, E. M., and Weithorn, C. 1967. The need for refinements in the techniques of interdisciplinary hostility for social workers and psychologists. Am. J. Orthopsychiatry 37:797–799.

Cohen, P. C. 1962. The impact of the handicapped child on the family. Social Casework 43:137–142.

Crocker, A. C., and Cushna, B. 1976. Ethical considerations and attitudes in the field of developmental disorders. In: R. B. Johnston and P. R. Magrab (eds.), Developmental Disorders: Assessment, Treatment, Education, pp. 495–502. University Park Press, Baltimore.

Cytryn, L. 1970. The training of pediatricians and psychiatrists in mental retardation. In: F. J. Menolascino (ed.), Psychiatric Approaches to Mental Retardation. Basic Books, New York.

Cytryn, L., and Lourie, R. S. 1975. Mental retardation. In: A. M. Freedman, H. I. Kaplan, and B. J. Sadock (eds.), Comprehensive Textbook of Psychiatry. 3rd ed. Williams & Wilkins Co., Baltimore.

Edgerton, R. B. 1967. The Cloak of Competence. University of California Press, Berkeley.

Gardner, G. E. 1968. Training and education of physicians in the field of mental retardation. Clin. Proceed. Child. Hosp. 24:1–14.

Goodman, L. 1964. Continuing treatment of parents with congenitally defective infants. Social Casework 9:92–97.

Henry, W. E., Sims, J. H., and Spray, S. L. 1971. The Fifth Profession. Jossey-Bass, San Francisco.

Leaverton, D. R., and Van Der Heide, C. 1975. Lip service no longer. Paper presented at the American Association on Mental Deficiency annual meeting, Portland, Ore.

Menolascino, F. J. 1977. Challenges in Mental Retardation: Progressive Ideology and Services. Human Sciences Press, New York.

Philips, I. 1966. Children, mental retardation and emotional disorder. In: I. Philips (ed.), Prevention and Treatment of Mental Retardation. Basic Books, New York.

Potter, H. W. 1964. The needs of mentally retarded children for child psychiatry services. J. Am. Acad. Child Psychiatry 3:352–374.

Seltzer, M. M., and Seltzer, G. 1978. Context for Competence. Educational Projects, Cambridge, Mass.

Stone, N. D. 1970. Effecting interdisciplinary coordination in clinical services to the mentally retarded. Am. J. Orthopsychiatry 40(5):835–839.

Tisza, V. B. 1975. Training the child psychiatrist. J. Am. Acad. Child Psychiatry 14:204–209.

West, L. J. 1973. The future of psychiatric education. Am. J. Psychiatry 130:521–528.

TRAINING OF MENTAL HEALTH PROFESSIONALS IN MENTAL RETARDATION

Peter E. Tanguay and Ludwik S. Szymanski

Chapter 2

Although the need for mental health services for mentally retarded people has been stressed by many clinicians in the past, there is evidence that most mental health training curricula still do not include adequate clinical experience with mentally retarded people. This shortcoming is particularly marked in psychiatry, where mental retardation is "the Cinderella" (Potter, 1965) of the field. In 1962, the President's Panel on Mental Retardation cited psychiatric clinics as an important resource for diagnosis and treatment of retarded individuals, and in 1966 the American Psychiatric Association issued a position statement emphasizing the need for psychiatrists to work in the field of mental retardation, and that child psychiatrists in particular must be active in all phases of prevention, diagnosis, and treatment of mental retardation. The statement affirmed that every child psychiatrist should receive sufficient didactic and clinical training to enable him to deal with a retarded individual and his family, and that this training should be received within the framework of approved child psychiatry training centers. The American Psychiatric Association statement recognized that many disciplines are involved in providing services to the retarded and it recommended that each discipline should be involved in the education of the other. It also recommended that education in mental retardation be made a part of all medical student education and be taught to trainees in general psychiatry. The position statement concluded with an affirmation that these principles would be "publicly announced and referred to all appropriate components of the

American Psychiatric Association...for such action and follow-up" as seemed indicated (American Psychiatric Association, 1966).

Despite these exhortations, Leaverton and Van Der Heide (1975) reported that as late as 1975 about 50% of programs in child psychiatry still did not include any training in mental retardation in their curricula, and of those that did, the training was often too brief or was only included as an elective. Echoing these findings, Szymanski reported in 1975 that a survey of 30 University Affiliated Facility (UAF) centers disclosed that only 18 had either full- or part-time child psychiatrists on their teaching staffs. Some centers reported that they had had a good psychiatric program, but it was terminated when the psychiatrist left and another one could not be found to take his place. Given that UAF centers were developed by the National Institutes of Health to be the university-based or university-affiliated interdisciplinary training program for the development of skilled manpower in the field of mental retardation, the absence of child psychiatrists from the staffs of a substantial number of these centers is a telling statistic.

If the goals set by the President's Commission on Mental Retardation are ever to be fulfilled, there must be a radical change in how mental health professionals, and especially child psychiatrists, are trained to practice in the community. This chapter presents guidelines for establishment of training programs in mental retardation for mental health professionals and includes examples of two such existing programs. Although it is based upon the authors' experiences in training psychiatrists, much of the material should be relevant to mental health training programs in general.

TRAINING GOALS

The goals of the training program should always be defined clearly. These goals can be classified under three broad headings: to teach trainees about developmental disability per se, to train mental health professionals to serve the developmentally disabled, and to train each mental health professional to work as an effective member of an interdisciplinary team.

Knowledge about developmental disability should include a thorough understanding of the signs and symptoms of the various diagnostic categories, along with an appreciation of etiological factors that may play a role in their onset. This latter information should be taught within a field theory framework (see Chapter 4), avoiding futile searches for "the" primary cause and the artificial dichotomy of "organic" and "functional" subtypes. Trainees should be aware of the advantages and disadvantages of standard psychometric assessment of cognitive function and should be familiar with the manner in which such tests are administered. Trainees should also be aware of the range of services available in the community for retarded persons, as well as what services need to be developed. They should be aware of the social impact of developmentally disabled (and especially retarded) individuals upon the community, and the manner in which societal prejudices and fears may be dealt with.

Competency in provision of mental health services for developmentally disabled people requires that professionals become adept in the assessment, treatment, and prevention of mental illnesses in this population. They should learn, through actual clinical experience, to assess the person's emotional and cognitive development, specific strengths and handicaps, the presence and degree of psychopathology, and the extent to which the family has adapted to the situation. They must become expert in using information derived from the evaluation to reach a diagnosis and formulate a treatment plan. Treatment experiences should include individual psychotherapy of at least one retarded child and one retarded adult or adolescent. Experience as leader or co-leader of a therapeutic group whose members are retarded is also desirable. It is likewise very important that the trainees become expert in the use of behavioral techniques, as well as develop an understanding of the use and side effects of psychotropic agents in treating certain forms of severe mental illness in retarded people. Knowledge of prevention should include experience in early intervention programs, within which the trainee (along with other members of the mental health team) assesses the strengths of the handicapped child and his family, with a view toward formulating a treatment program aimed at minimizing the future development of psychopathology.

In order to learn *interaction skills* necessary to work within an interdisciplinary framework, trainees should participate as full members of the interdisciplinary team, and not simply as consultants. They must learn to communicate using terms that are understood clearly by all team members, avoiding psychiatric or psychological jargon. Trainees must also become adept at integrating their findings and recommendations with those of other team members as the team strives to develop a comprehensive case formulation and treatment plan.

TRAINING PROGRAMS

The manner in which a training program is organized depends to a great extent on the internal structure of the clinical facility in which the program resides. Two models are presented. In the first, the developmental disabilities clinic was separate from the mental health clinic in the institution, and in the second, it was an integral part of a department of psychiatry.

The Developmental Evaluation Clinic (DEC)

The Developmental Evaluation Clinic, located at the Children's Hospital Medical Center in Boston, is a UAF, supported by the Maternal and Child Health Service Division of the Department of Health, Education and

Welfare. The clinic, an independent unit of the Department of Medicine, was established in 1967 and greatly expanded in 1971 after receiving federal funding as a UAF. It has 41 staff members in 15 disciplines and over 300 full-time and part-time trainees. Since the inception of the clinic in 1967, close to 2,000 patients have been seen for primary evaluations, in addition to those seen for briefer consultations and follow-up.

Currently, five to six children are seen weekly for comprehensive 2- or 3-day evaluations. Their ages range from under 1 to over 20 years, the majority being of early school age. A typical patient is multiply handicapped, presenting problems in several areas of development. These problems may result from a variety of factors. More than half of the patients present symptoms of emotional disorders, ranging from situational reactions to psychosis. In fact, more psychotic children are seen yearly at the DEC than in the hospital's Department of Psychiatry.

Child psychiatry was one of the original disciplines at the clinic. The psychiatric staff consists of one full-time and one part-time child psychiatrist. Members of the Department of Psychiatry provide additional supervision of the trainees.

Trainees from many disciplines (at both graduate and undergraduate levels) are trained at the DEC. Among them are two groups of child psychiatry trainees. The first group consists of the child psychiatry residents in training in the Department of Psychiatry. Rotation of these trainees through DEC is elective, but so far almost all have chosen it. The residents in this group spend an average of 6 hours a week at the DEC for a period of 4 to 6 months. Under supervision, they see one child and his family per week for psychiatric assessment as part of an interdisciplinary evaluation by the clinic's team. Time permitting, they also participate in interdisciplinary seminars and conferences and may follow a retarded child for short-term therapy. The second, and unfortunately small, "group" consists of one full-time psychiatry fellow paid by a DEC grant. He spends 1 year in a combined training program, his time equally divided between the DEC and the Department of Child Psychiatry. At the latter he participates fully in the training program.

The fellow's training program at the DEC cannot be broken down into isolated subjects, but consists instead of intermingled and overlapping themes, which may be described as follows.

Direct Clinical Experience
Diagnostic Experience   This includes individually supervised psychiatric diagnostic assessment of children seen at the DEC as an integral part of their comprehensive evaluation and follow-up by the interdisciplinary team. Since these cases are not preselected as "good" or "teaching" cases, the fellow has an opportunity to see a broad variety of children at all levels of functioning. In some instances he may uncover an otherwise unsuspected emotional disorder. He must assess the develop-

ment of various components of the child's personality, determine the presence of psychopathology, and assess the child's patterns of adaptation to any handicaps he may have. He familiarizes himself with immature patterns of personality development seen in mentally retarded persons and with the family's adaptation to the retarded child. He learns to interpret nonverbal communications and to identify behavioral symptomatology displayed by retarded children and adults. He learns to differentiate abnormal behaviors based on psychopathology from behaviors related to other causes. He is taught to assess both behavior and development along discrete developmental lines, such as have been described by Freud (1965). The fellow presents (and defends, if necessary) his findings and conclusions during case conferences and participates in feedback interviews with the family. In connection with the latter, he learns techniques of effectively communicating the results of the evaluation to the family. Psychiatric recommendations, if suggested, are formulated as part of an overall treatment educational program. The fellow has an opportunity to monitor their effectiveness in follow-up interviews.

Treatment Experience   At the DEC, two to four retarded children are assigned to the fellow for continued psychotherapy. Other children are seen for short-term crisis intervention. The fellow may function as the therapist of the child or of the parents. The psychiatric training is psychodynamically oriented, but in interaction with the clinical team his experience becomes eclectic, and the fellow has an opportunity to learn a variety of therapeutic techniques, including behavior modification and drug therapy.

Interdisciplinary Experience   The fellow is a full member of the clinic's team in all aspects of its functioning (and not only in connection with his assigned cases). He is taught to avoid detached, intellectual psychiatric diagnostic elaboration and to provide instead a clear opinion that takes into account findings and recommendations of other disciplines, and that eventuates in a comprehensive and practical plan of treatment. The fellow interacts continuously with members of other disciplines through formal and informal consultations, case discussions, mutual observation and participation in one another's interviews, joint field visits to community agencies, and participation in interdisciplinary seminars on retardation and child development. Thus, he learns continuously from other disciplines about diagnostic and treatment techniques and ways of viewing the patient or client. At the same time he teaches the trainees from other disciplines about corresponding psychiatric approaches. Other interdisciplinary experiences include coordinating a "drug clinic" (for follow-up of children on psychoactive drugs), a "sex clinic" for mentally retarded adolescents or young adults and their parents, and co-leading groups for retarded adolescents. Also, in informal consultations, he learns to help other team members cope with countertransference feelings and anxieties they may have in connection with their work with mentally retarded and disturbed patients.

Community Experiences The fellow collaborates with teachers, physicians, social workers, and foster families, all of whom participate in the child's care in the community. In doing so he obtains diagnostically important data, participates in joint planning for the child's management, follows up the child's progress, and provides consultations whenever necessary. Fellows also provide group consultations to staffs of institutions for the multiply handicapped, as well as give lectures and demonstrations to special education teachers. Through this they also gather experience in child advocacy.

Psychobiological Experience Multiply handicapped DEC patients usually present problems in cognitive, emotional, and physiological development; so the DEC team includes both psychologically and somatically oriented disciplines. The fellow thus has an opportunity to learn about such phenomena as the behavioral sequelae of neurological changes; the interplay of organic, psychological, and environmental factors in producing psychopathology; and the effects of organic sensory deficits on personality development.

Preventive Experience Since the clinic accepts young children for baseline evaluation, the fellow has a unique opportunity to see children who are at risk for developing emotional maladjustment in the future, because of their handicaps and / or the family's attitudes toward them. The fellow evaluates such factors, assesses the risk, and with other team members plans comprehensive preventive measures. He also monitors the child in follow-up evaluation.

Leadership Experience All DEC staff members and trainees take turns as patient coordinators. The coordinator has an overall responsibility for planning and effecting each child's evaluation, treatment, and follow-up and for leading staff case conferences. He acts as the clinic's representative to community agencies and as liaison to the parents. Thus, the fellow learns to lead and to be a participant in the group process. He is also expected to participate as a member or leader in the clinic's various administrative committees and projects.

Coping with Countertransference Working with retarded children has been recognized as often being anxiety provoking and evoking countertransference feelings. Through individual supervision and in encounters with other team members the fellow learns to recognize and to deal with these feelings.

The Mental Retardation and Child Psychiatry (MRCP) Program

The MRCP program, located at the UCLA Neuropsychiatric Institute, is one of three divisions in the Institute, the others being Adult Psychiatry and Neurology. The program was organized in 1969, under the overall direction of Dr. George Tarjan. It includes a child psychiatry unit, a UAF center, a Mental Retardation Research Center (MRRC), and a clinical research center for the study of childhood psychosis.

Special features were built into the program from the outset. Figuratively speaking, there has been only one door into the child psychiatry clinic, through which all children must pass. No child is turned away because he does not fit someone's model of what a psychiatric patient should look like. Child psychiatry trainees, under the supervision of an interdisciplinary faculty and staff, are expected to evaluate any and all cases who come through this door, whatever the child's diagnosis. When a child psychiatry trainee is assigned a new case in the ambulatory clinic, for example, he has no idea of who he will meet: a multiply handicapped child referred because of school problems, a child with suspected conversion hysteria, a Down's syndrome child whose parents need information regarding special schools, a newly diagnosed autistic child, a manic-depressive adolescent, or an epileptic child whose seizures are interfering with his ability to function outside of the home.

The faculty of the program includes 12 full-time child psychiatrists, 7 full-time child psychologists, 2 developmental pediatricians, numerous educational specialists, an audiologist, a speech pathologist, social workers, nurses, and occupational or rehabilitation therapy specialists. Many neuroanatomists, neurobiochemists, neurophysiologists, geneticists, sociologists, and social anthropologists have their primary appointment in the MRRC, although they teach and consult in all parts of the program.

The goals of the training program are similar to those delineated in the first section of this chapter. There are, however, two additional important goals: to graduate child psychiatrists whose future career will include at least part-time service in public institutions or in health maintenance organizations, and to have approximately 20% of graduating trainees (among whom are seven to nine child psychiatrists) elect an academic career involving teaching and research. This latter goal results from the belief that one of the major reasons for the lack of adequate mental retardation training in the field of mental health (and especially among child psychiatrists) is the dearth of training program directors and faculty who are themselves experts on the subject.

All trainees receive intensive didactic training, organized around a core curriculum of lectures and seminars. A range of topics is presented in the curriculum, including those listed in the first section of the chapter.

In their first year of training, child psychiatry fellows (as do trainees from some other disciplines) spend a 6-month period on one of four inpatient services: adolescent nondevelopmentally disabled, adolescent developmentally disabled, under 12-year-old nondevelopmentally disabled, and under 12-year-old developmentally disabled. Each inpatient ward, which provides care for 16 to 18 patients, has its own individual identity and mix of patients. At the end of 6 months the trainee changes ward assignments and spends a second 6 months on a different ward. The move is arranged so that each fellow receives as diverse experience as is possible. A fellow who begins on an adolescent unit will move to a child service; a fellow who begins on a ward for children of normal intelligence will move to a ward for the mentally retarded and developmentally disabled. In all four services intensive work with the patient's family is stressed. As the fellow's patients are discharged to after-care, he will continue to follow them under supervision. Even if the fellow does not personally treat patients from each and every diagnostic category, he will certainly become familiar with all categories through regular ward conferences, preadmission evaluations, and ward rounds, as well as conversations and discussions with other trainees.

In comparison with child psychiatry training programs elsewhere, the emphasis on inpatient training may appear somewhat anachronistic. Such training has several important advantages, however. First, fellows deal with a more severely disturbed or handicapped group of patients than they might see in the outpatient department. Second, under the leadership and guidance of the ward psychiatrist, the fellow is required to evaluate and treat four or five patients. The fellow can observe children longitudinally and intensely, talk with their teachers in the school, and gain an appreciation of the interaction of the patients and the staff as a group. Third, the fellow's work is under the close scrutiny of staff members from a number of disciplines, and there are several experts available to the fellow should he need help. Fourth, as the fellow gains in expertise and confidence, he is encouraged to act as psychiatric consultant to the nonmedical UAF trainees. In this manner child psychiatry fellows begin to develop the necessary skills to function as members of an interdisciplinary team.

Concomitant with his work on inpatient services, each first-year fellow is assigned a few child patients to evaluate in the outpatient department. Again, these patients represent a wide variety of diagnostic categories. Supervision of the fellow's work is carried out in a team consisting of the child psychiatrist, several child fellows, a clinical psychologist, a psychiatric nurse, a social worker, and an educational psychologist. It is the function of the clinical psychologist to instruct the fellows in administering and scoring a "minibattery" of psychological tests, including the sentence completion test, the draw-a-person test, the Bender-Gestalt, the children's apperception test, the Denver Developmental Screening Test, and the Minnesota Multiphasic Personality Inventory. The educational psychologist presents and discusses educational assessments as they are completed. The psychiatric nurse actively participates in whatever home visits are necessary in the parent training programs that are offered by the clinic. The social worker assists the child fellow in arranging transfers to other care facilities when this is required. A speech pathologist and an audiologist are also available to each team.

Each fellow also has two or more clinical psychiatrists who supervise his work in psychotherapy and play therapy, sometimes through audio- or videotape. These supervisors are all child psychiatrists in private practice, and some are child analysts.

Each fellow also has the additional opportunity of working in specialty clinics in the outpatient department. These clinics include an aftercare clinic for developmentally disabled children, a crisis intervention clinic, and a systematic parent training clinic, which teaches parents to use behavioral approaches to solving family problems. Each of these clinics is run by an expert who can provide the child fellow with a unique learning opportunity.

Second-year fellows, in addition to a continuing experience in the outpatient clinic, are required to function as psychiatric consultants to the pediatric inpatient service in the medical center and to several pediatric outpatient clinics. A child psychiatrist supervises this latter work. Fellows also attend the weekly development rounds in Pediatrics, and they act as consultants to a developmental disability clinic in the pediatric rehabilitation center. Each of the latter activities is supervised by a member of the full-time child psychiatry staff. Fellows are required to take part in a school consultation service run by a member of the clinical child psychiatry staff. They may, if they elect, work with a unique forensic psychiatry team, which specializes in evaluating and counseling children and parents in child custody cases. A specialist in forensic psychiatry supervises them in this latter work. Second-year fellows also take emergency child psychiatry calls in the outpatient department on a rotational basis. Last, second-year child fellows are actively engaged in lecturing to and supervising medical students in their child psychiatry work. As in all of our training programs, approximately 50% of the patients seen by the medical students are mentally retarded or developmentally disabled.

CONCLUSIONS

Despite the need for substantially increased participation of mental health professionals in the care of developmentally disabled individuals, it is clear that most mental health professionals receive little training in this regard. Prejudices and myths that serve as rationalization to avoid working with developmentally disabled (and, in particular, mentally retarded) persons may be responsible for such a situation. A second important reason is the lack of mental health professionals who are themselves expert enough in mental retardation to provide such training. Because of this, it may be unreasonable to expect all training programs to begin to offer training in dealing with developmental disability. From a practical viewpoint, a reasonable goal might be to hope that at least the 5 or 10 largest training centers could begin to do so. The degree to which this is realized will depend upon the seriousness with which professional organizations, and especially those responsible for training program accreditation, demand that such training be introduced. Perhaps, as more such training opportunities are implemented, the effect will be circular: as more people are trained, more will be available to provide training for others, and eventually mental health services will be readily available to all, regardless of level of intelligence or degree of adaptation to their environment.

REFERENCES

American Psychiatric Association. 1966. Psychiatry and mental retardation. Position statement. Am. J. Psychiatry 122:1302.

Freud, A. 1965. Normality and Pathology in Childhood. International Universities Press, New York.

Leaverton, D. R., and Van Der Heide, C. 1975. Lip service no longer. Paper read at the American Academy on Mental Deficiency annual meeting, May 20–23, Portland, Ore.

Potter, H. W. 1965. Mental retardation, the Cinderella of psychiatry. Psychiatr. Q. 39:537–549.

Szymanski, L. S. 1975. Training the prince to find his Cinderella. Paper presented at the American Academy of Child Psychiatry annual meeting, October, St. Louis.

ASSESSMENT

The chapters in this section concern theories of causation and methods of assessment of mental illness in developmentally disabled individuals. Before attempting to diagnose and treat mental illness in such individuals, one should have a good understanding of what mental retardation *means and what factors play a role in producing it. For this reason the section begins with a chapter detailing the history of the use and misuse of psychometric techniques in diagnosing mental retardation (Chapter 3) and is followed by a short chapter outlining recent ideas concerning the usefulness of a field theory approach to understanding "causation" in developmental disability (Chapter 4). Chapter 5 deals with facts and fallacies about the role of biological factors in the etiology of mental retardation and adds depth to the discussion. This chapter may be especially helpful to those professionals whose background is nonmedical.*

Chapter 6 describes psychiatric diagnostic process and Chapter 7 focuses on clinical assessment of cognitive development of retarded persons. Interviewing techniques as well as guidelines for evaluating the clinical findings are described in these chapters. The next two chapters focus on two difficult diagnostic problem areas that are often encountered by mental health professionals in the field of mental retardation. Chapter 8 discusses differential diagnosis of early infantile autism and mental retardation. Chapter 9 focuses on assessment of sexual development, vulnerability, and abuse of mentally retarded persons.

THE PSYCHOLOGICAL DEFINITION OF MENTAL RETARDATION: A Historical Overview

Chapter 3

Bruce Cushna

TERMINOLOGY

The definition of mental retardation in current professional usage is dependent upon a psychologically sophisticated understanding of mental measurement. The phrase *subaverage intellectual functioning* presumes documented (preferably quantified) comparison with established, standardized norms of intelligence. Even when current recommendations are followed and no individual is labeled retarded unless there is concurrent *impairment in adaptive behavior*, measurement of these more social and self-help competencies is also required for objectivity.

HISTORICAL DISCOVERY

Biologically, humankind always has been concerned with disease and the effects of its devastation: defective individuals. In early history the degree of dehabilitation had to be significant enough to earn the afflicted individual a label that set him aside as different from others. Deformity and birth defects were justification for infanticide in as advanced a civilization as the Greek city states. However, mild mental deficiencies were left

Acknowledgment is given to the UAF support of the U.S. Department of Health, Education and Welfare, Bureau of Education for the Handicapped, Grant #PR 451-AH-80344; and Office of Developmental Disabilities, Grant #59-P-05163/1-07.

unnoticed until the competitive aspects of the Industrial Revolution produced a society that was becoming increasingly chagrined with the liability of lesser incompetence. In more concrete terms, throughout history, there has been awareness and concern with "idiots" and "imbeciles." It required the socially competitive aspects of the 20th century to find the largest population of retardates, the "morons." This population went mainly "undiscovered" until social and economic concerns and mental measurement techniques advanced enough to recognize them.

Industrialization and technological advancement meant mass scale and efficient production. They meant that certain degrees of individualistic quaintness had to be abandoned, and our social ordering had to take on a more standardized, assembly line appearance. It was this mass-production society, with its developed need for speedily interchangeable economic participants, that provided the impetus under which institutions for the retarded spread across the nation to attend to social liabilities. Under these historic conditions, Henry Goddard (1910) coined the term, *moron*, now considered an undesirable term, at Vineland in the early 1900s. These increased liabilities were considered a drain upon economic resources. They could not contribute according to standardized expectations. They required special schooling, residences and support. Falling short of social expectations subjected them to ridicule. *Moron*, after all, was an invented term literally meaning the "foolish" simpleton.

THE FEAR OF INCOMPETENCE

However, concerns deeper than the coinage of labels motivated the development of mental measurement techniques. The social dread of incapacity rose drastically under these changes. When institutions originated in the mid-1850s, there was a philanthropic support of caring for those less capable. By the turn of the century there was a frenzy to build institutions. By then the eugenicists had forwarded the slogan "Segregate and Colonize." There should be little doubt that the intent was anything less than to isolate a less capable group from the common social exchange. Studies of families such as the Kallikaks (Goddard, 1912) and the Hill People (Danielson and Davenport, 1912) reported on generations of social misfits who were mildly retarded. Their misbehavior was interpreted as a consequence of their retardation. However, these studies were extremely concentrated on social value judgments. There were "goods" and "bads" in the social context, just as Goddard had combined these two Greek words to form the term *Kallikak*. Bads were the ones who did not contribute economically. Rampant among them were social evils, such as transgressions of familial and sexual mores, neglect of household, and violence toward offspring. It was only a short reach from this position to the American Breeders' Association's cry for sterilization of the retarded. It is not difficult to follow this logically, but it is frightening to witness its effects, such as the rapidity by which the eugenics scare caused so many states to adopt sterilization laws. The crest of this historic wave has passed, but consideration of both professional and popular attitudes toward the retarded and how these developed is essential to the basic understanding of the concept of retardation, as well as being a prerequisite to securing necessary resources and services for this population.

FAMILIAL RETARDATION

The current classification manual of the American Association on Mental Deficiency (Grossman, 1977) lists *familial retardation* as an obsolete term. Before the 1973 Grossman revision of this manual, the term had been rather freely applied to situations where either parent plus one other family member of the retarded individual were mentally limited and where no other more concrete cause could be implicated. In practicality, the assignment of the familial retardation label was done in the absence of a more definitive etiology when the causes were "presumed to be psychologic." The editor of the revised manual was striving to limit the use of the greatest loophole in mental retardation history. It was the easy way out to report that a problem "runs in the family," thus avoiding the effort of looking further for a more precise cause. The revision was a firm attempt to require professionals responsible for classification to do their job.

There are other noteworthy historic trends to be considered. One is that the eugenics movement had been based upon denigrating the lower socioeconomic classes. In the changes of the last half of the 20th century, it is no longer popular to equate *poor* with *bad*. There may be some residuals of that earlier Victorian attitude, but it is currently in bad taste to consider poor people less capable than those of higher socioeconomic strata. However, this is precisely what the IQ score does. This is the primary argument against administering psychological tests to individuals from lower socioeconomic groups.

The socioeconomic correlates with mental ability scores cannot be denied, regardless of any other interacting cultural, ethnic, or racial variables. The correlations, particularly of verbal testing, are highly significant. Language, mainly verbal mastery or vocabulary, reaches extremely high degrees of significance in relation to socioeconomic status. These same subtests or test components correlate with all other parts of the measurement instruments, including nonverbal and mechanical/spatial performance. The language tool itself seems to provide the means of approaching other areas of problem-solving. Perhaps this is aligned with the social-psychological concept of thinking as internalized language. It is not an issue of language form varying among certain subpopulations, but rather that, ultimately, any problem-solving necessitates some type of resymbolization in ways in which the individual must explain the task and the solution-seeking process to himself in order to proceed with facility.

There is also the established fact that children from lower socioeconomic strata advance in motor and spatial problem-solving skills during early childhood periods with some agility. It is only when the language becomes more developmentally strategic (after age 3) that the advantages of higher social status appear. Of course, the definition of social stratification methodologies has several ambiguities. Compounding variables such as two-income families, the growing devaluation of education, and the mobility of the American family are all challenging the established methods of efficiently stratifying these differences among subcultures. However, in the mental retardation movement, no one can deny that the public institutions were packed with poor people. The explanation had been that those people with middle class or better economic means would seek private resources to care for their own family members. The increasing realization that institutions were at worst concentration camps, and at best sublegal attempts at isolated residences where inmates would be deprived of otherwise guaranteed constitutional rights, resulted in these places being unavoidable alternatives for those candidates who had least economic means. Braginsky and Braginsky (1971), in examining the social effects of institutions in the 1960s, found that public institutions had become the means particularly utilized by poor people for abandoning offspring who had passed below the critical level of the "cost/reward ratio." The effect was that institutions were overpopulated with mainly economically deprived individuals. The classification under which a vast majority of these individuals were labeled was either "familial retardation" or "etiology unknown."

The proportion of retarded people classified under unknown etiology is impressive. In institutions this was a matter of about 80% of the mildly retarded population during the 1960s. However, even in community service settings staffed with sound, competent professionals, approximately half of the patients could not be classified by any definitive cause. There was some shyness on the part of professionals to assign a cause where several alternatives might be debatable. There were also ambiguities and uncertainties about the causation at other times. However, the net effect was that mildly retarded persons were less often classified by known cause than their more seriously involved counterparts. Also, persons from poor socioeconomic backgrounds were more frequently classified as mildly retarded.

AMERICAN TESTING MOVEMENT

The American testing movement began with Henry Goddard's literal translation of the Simon-Binet instrument in the early years of this century. Goddard's intent, of course, was to secure a measurement of mental functioning for the residents of the Vineland Training School. The Binet mental age concept and the literally translated tasks proved extremely useful in classifying or categorizing this population for various programming levels. The successful stratification of the residents at Vineland was an heuristic achievement. The accomplishment of programmatically grouping these individuals was immediately professionally heralded. However, the success stood in contrast to the ill-fated attempts to administer this same instrument to the school children of the town of Vineland. This was the first failure of the testing movement. The school children, of course, looked remarkably dull in the face of the measurement standards alteration effected by a much more academically oriented form of English used in the translation from French. This became the first proof that standards are relative. In this instance, when the language was advanced by translation, the sample of New Jersey school children appeared to function below expected age norms derived from the French instrument. This was a definite example of the effects of the culture-bound influence of language.

The immediate lesson was somewhat refocused with the provision of better normative data in Terman's (1916) empirical endeavors. Consequently, once new maturational norms had been obtained in the United States, with their basis for comparison steadied by sampling across geographical and economic dimensions, a new credo was established. The belief in the potential measurement of ability spread easily among an American public that wanted to be convinced of the universal availability of opportunity for personal and economic advancement. The American dream that success was available to all those possessing the ability to pursue it was embodied in the rapidly spreading application of mental measurement instruments among school age populations.

Involvement in World War I brought a need for mass scale processing of military recruits. The sorting and assignment of military personnel was greatly enhanced by the derivation of mental measurement instruments for young adults, the Army Alpha and Beta tests. The necessity of wartime expediency and the overall ideological commitment to rise to a cause put this powerful tool to the test. The efficiency and effectiveness of military assignment upon evidence supplied by these instruments moved the American public forward in the conviction that testing was the means to allow those with ability to advance socially and economically. This national application of early tests at this critical time in history convinced large numbers of its future value and also conditioned the nation for greater application among other subpopulations.

The Derivation of Infant and Preschool Scales

In the years following the war, these techniques were applied to increasingly younger populations of children. The belief in an unchanging ability factor led researchers to seek earlier and earlier applications of testing methods. Pediatric baby tests, such as the Gesell Developmental Schedules, which were based upon advancing chronological age expectations, were combined with downward extensions of mental measurement instruments, such as Psyche Cattell's (1947) attempts with the Stanford material. The preschool materials were considered unique from the beginning. This was part of the American educational bias. The three R's were not applied until the child had reached the somewhat magical age of 6. Certain conceptual processes were considered unripened before that stage of pedagogical birth. Consequently, the more play-like approach to the materials of preschool testing incorporated a strong visual processing performance and fine motor contamination into the preschool instruments.

Although the attempt of downward extension was made, the recognition of the basic difference of type of test task was never obliterated. Preschool tasks were always considered to involve basic differences from those administered to older children. Even Maude Merrill (Terman and Merrill, 1973) admitted that test administration had to be somewhat modified. She rationalized this deviation upon the basis of the special necessity to maintain rapport with the preschool child. This became, of course, a second very clear problem in longitudinal assessments. The types of tasks varied greatly as the child advanced in age. The proportionate representation of motoric and later visual processing problem-solving tasks through the early years of life were contrasted to the older, more language dependent, more verbal-conceptual types of testing tasks. These differences led Nancy Bayley (1955) to conclude that there was no reason to "continue to think of intelligence as an integral (or simple) entity or capacity which grows throughout childhood by steady accretions." She cited Hofstaetter's (1954) three basic factors in preschool testing: 1) sensorimotor alertness, 2) persistence, and 3) manipulation of symbols. This stand was presented in opposition to the prevalent search for a unifying or "g" factor. This search incorporated the belief that one singular measurement would explain or predict all components of mental functioning. It was a simplistic, logical reduction, brought about not by scientific research efforts to be parsimonious in explanation but rather by the popular demand. Differences in social and economic accomplishment, which in childhood included schooling, needed to be explained on a basis that either denied or failed to recognize social difference. The unchangeable or constant IQ reflected that popular societal wish.

Sampling Problems

The Stanford-Binet Intelligence Scale in the 1938 L and M revisions failed to incorporate any blacks into the testing sample. The 1960 revisions merely reused the 1938 sample, submitting it to factor analysis. This neglect led to the clamor for new tests that could be applied to nonwhite populations. However, racism claims only obscured the issue. The inappropriateness of cross-cultural application of a verbal instrument was proved in Goddard's first unproductive attempts to extend his instrument beyond the walls of the Vineland institution. Once the instrument was no longer in French, it was invalid. Language itself appears to be the crucial issue. Too formalized or academically oriented language will effectively produce performance differences among age level, socioeconomic, or cultural groups. In these instances, there is no valid comparison with the original normative sample, and future predictions are rendered unreliable. It should be noted that Terman's normative standards were those of normal, middle class, white school children, advancing in the accepted standard educational public school curriculum of the first half of the century. Even as time progressed, it was found that these standards did not represent the public school children in the 1970s. The latest revision of the Binet (Terman and Merrill, 1973) tended to downgrade the early norms of that instrument toward earlier achievement levels.

Components of Intelligence

David Wechsler (1958) demonstrated well that adults varied in areas of problem-solving capacities. His subtest components provided new avenues of assessing various capabilities and mental speed. However, in the intercorrelations of subtests and in the factor weightings that established the interrelationships within his test, it is again self-evident that the power of language usage was central to the instrument. The vocabulary measurement became the best predictor of scores of any other subtest as well as the composite scores in verbal and performance areas and the so-called full scale IQ.

Language facility has long been recognized as the central and basic key to doing well on all tests. Even when nonverbal tests, the so-called culture-free, pantomime tests for the deaf or hard of hearing, and the symbolic-performance type instruments were administered, it was found that they all correlated very highly with such simple verbal instruments as word definition vocabulary or picture recognition vocabulary. Test designers were unsuccessful in trying to originate novel indicators of mental functioning that were relatively free of the basic and intrinsic correlation to verbal skill. In fact, the antithesis to their attempts became more highly probable by their efforts. It became increasingly evident that the greatest indicator of future mental competence was an individual's demonstration of verbal prowess.

The nonverbal instruments in all variations of design appeared to have one common and important characteristic: They all correlated very highly and were all interdependent to some degree upon how well the individual to whom the test was being administered could use words. Even when spoken language was not utilized in test administration or design, the correlation to other tests of that individual on verbal skills was always incredibly high. This led to some interesting contradictions. Individuals from subgroups who did not use language as well as the original validity samples, or individuals who developmentally or culturally were not able to acquire language skills as rapidly, did significantly poorer on test performance. They also seemed to be at a particular disadvantage in educational or competitive economic situations. The question then arose of whether tests were supporting a system of inequity. Arguments were strongly presented that the instruments themselves set certain cultural groups at a disadvantage in competing for recognition, school admission, and privilege that might be based upon the opportunities provided through a higher score on the instruments.

Language itself appeared to have a compounding relationship with socioeconomic status. Poor people for many reasons do not use their language as fluently or as skillfully as people who have greater economic and social advantages. Word definition vocabulary itself was shown by Wechsler (1958) to have the highest socioeconomic correlations. People at all age levels appeared to advance in word mastery, particularly vocabulary skills, at significantly greater rates if they belonged to a higher social status. Wechsler Vocabulary-Full Scale correlations as high as 0.83 (Wechsler, 1955) were striking evidence that the application of mental testing instruments across social class lines incorporated many injustices when ability was the claimed object of measurement.

The Wechsler instrument itself was tested for validity by correlation to the Stanford-Binet. In fact, all mental measurement instruments based their validity studies on that correlated comparison. This renders the validity basis of all current instruments as being that of the prediction of middle class elementary school achievement. Against such a comparison, there should be no argument about the predictive meaning of current instruments. There is no rationale or support for calling their measured artifact an "ability predictor." Socioeconomic differences stand as the most clearly substantiated argument within the mental measurement field for concluding that psychological tests do not measure "ability." They are good predictors of how well a child will use language. They can show which children will progress well within the standard educational curriculum. They can show us which children will most likely fail in schooling. If the measurements are deviant enough, within probability error ranges, they reveal which children should be considered by a review board as eligible for services for the retarded.

Projective Tests

Projective tests or those instruments that objectify human affective orientation are at times questioned regarding appropriate application to the retarded population. Projective tests generally are viewed as beginning with Rorschach's (Beck, 1962) attempts to quantify emotive investment in the interpretation of symmetrical ink blots. Complex and well-developed systems have stemmed from the interpretations of the descriptions of the 10 standard cards chosen shortly before the turn of the century. Academic schools have developed around systems of interpreting these descriptions, including a respectable body of literature concerning children's responses and the changes that occur during the maturational years. Yet, it seems justifiable to state that most efforts with the Rorschach have involved testing adults with psychiatric problems. Developmental changes have produced methodological difficulties in interpreting the children's protocols. Similarly, with retarded individuals, testing affective responses requires special experience and background in interpreting the protocols. It is not surprising to find more concrete or a limited number of responses among the protocols of retarded persons. Certain immaturity in content or preoccupation with details as opposed to holistic interpretations of the cards is common. The treatment of color as an indicator of difficulties in emotional control is similar to procedures used in middle childhood. Rigidity in the denial of color is also an important indicator. Movement, shading, and vista or depth projection are revealing of feigned retardation or "playing dumb." Distortion of percepts can follow some of the developmental patterns of childhood or can be more directly related to cognitive deficits. Each addition of clinical data through these procedures provides new considerations and other opportunities for building a better and more comprehensive review of the patient's ability to meet emotional demands and resolve potential conflicts. However, simplistic generalizations can only be used as a few isolated examples to attest to the fact that there are a growing number of clinicians using Rorschach techniques with retarded persons and developing methods for more objective interpretation.

Probably of more common usage are the thematic or tell-a-story tests, such as the Thematic Apperception Test (TAT) (Murray, 1938) or the Tasks of Emotional Development (TED) (Cohen and Weil, 1971). With these instruments, the unique quality of the retarded person's responses needs to be considered carefully. They offer a wealth of information on family and social relationships, which may be particularly important. The structure of the TED focuses upon many developmental issues. The ambiguity of many of the higher numbered TAT cards offers opportunity for revealing deeper psychopathology, but it may be too difficult a task for severely deficient patients.

If the retarded person's communication skills are poor, it may be well to restrict test administration to writing or drawing tasks. The Draw-A-Person and House-Tree-Person tests are good examples of methods that readily reveal troubling interpersonal concerns or areas of conflict. Interpretation of such drawings follow conventional methods, but allowances need to be made for perceptual-motor deficits, differences in levels of delayed development, and unusual experiential or environmental circumstances. However, these allowances need not be any more extreme than those made for urban/rural differences or conditions of isolated personal background.

The Bender-Gestalt (Bender, 1938) is an excellent test for retarded individuals. Because it provides a good maturational check for reliability comparison with other areas of cognitive functioning, it can be judged by the examiner for developmental appropriateness. Both Bender's and Koppitz's (1964) criteria for emotional indicators may be used, but it is helpful to have an atlas of examples, such as that provided by Clawson (1962). In all drawing tests, the criteria for emotional indicators become controversial; their order of reliability is low. Nevertheless, various indicators of emotional conflict, such as release of frustration seen in emotional (uneven) line quality, confused order of presentation, figure "collision," and "edging," offer valuable information on the personal orientation and concerns of the retarded person. They also provide a link to the neuropsychological information that may be needed to understand the behavioral reactions associated with deficient perceptual-motor performance.

Other nonverbal tests may also be of great value. The Missouri Children's Picture Series (Sines, Paulker, and Sines, 1966), a pictorial type of Minnesota Multiphasic Personality Inventory, has been used experimentally in many settings over the past 10 years. It is hoped that its designers will soon complete the standardization and present it commercially. Its potential with nonverbal and verbally limited children is considerable.

In their various forms, projective tests offer valuable information to assist in the understanding of a retarded person's adjustment and emotional conflicts. Minor adaptations may be necessary in their administration and interpretation, but these are slight in comparison to the returns offered in obtaining information in this area of concern.

The Misuse of Psychological Tests

The most common misuse of psychological tests has been their inappropriate and invalid administration to individuals from minority groups. This practice has led to a popular demand for test restriction in some of the more progressive states, where even individualized testing by highly qualified and well-trained testing specialists is being challenged. The popular demand reflects the attitude that the instruments themselves are a social evil. To examine the full ramifications of that challenge we must look both at what the instruments are and consider the historical attributes that brought these instruments to their current stage of development.

Psychological tests are, after all, merely instruments. They are the working tools of professionals. They were designed to give an objective comparison of the individual to whom the test is being administered with standardized norms from an established population. The measurements of these instruments are valid only when the individual being measured can be compared validly to the population from which normative standards have been derived. The main misuse of mental measurement instruments has been inappropriate application. Individuals from minority groups or subcultures, individuals who have had a markedly deviant course in acquiring their developmental accomplishments, and others who have been deprived of visual or auditory sensory input in critically formative years have all been inappropriately compared, in violation of what the test designers initially set as their validity criteria.

The mentally retarded population is a subculture. Even the vast majority of this population, the mildly retarded, are expected to achieve only minimal academic skills. It remains sufficient to recognize their academic potential as being so far deviant from the normal population that as a group they become eligible for specialized educational services when they validly derive scores more than 2 standard deviations below expected age means. However, statistical limitations must be recognized. Qualitative distinctions between an IQ of 2 and an IQ of 10, for example, are blatantly absurd. Even the importance of the differences between an IQ of 30 and an IQ of 40 may be somewhat questionable. The inappropriateness of item tasks when presented to severely and profoundly retarded individuals must immediately be recognized. Besides, at the extremes of the IQ distribution, other variables become more contributory. At the lower extreme, physical and sensory limitation become more significant. This is self-evident; it is probably more productive to examine the lesser degrees of retardation at this point.

Educational Applications

Within the educational setting, test administration easily fell into practices of misuse. Theoretically, screening tests were intended to detect candidates for special services; individual tests were intended to confirm eligibility. However, the negative views of special services soon negated this intent. Instead of seeking candidates for assistance, the tools became the detecting devices for excluding large groups of children from the standard curriculum.

The nomenclature of the labeling process reflected this negative course of action. Whereas Terman (1916) had originally intended a 10-point range to be called the borderline between dull-normal and mildly retarded, the entire first-to-second standard deviation (Wechsler Score 70 to 84; Binet Score 68 to 83) became in educational practice "borderline retarded." Before the laws on education for all the handicapped, any child found to have a score in that range could be excluded from a regular graded classroom. Misuse of this possibility became rampant. Especially in poorer schools, the troublemakers were quickly selected by their teachers for psychological examination. Sometimes this was direct vengeance against those children who the teacher had most difficulty in understanding: those who spoke English as a second language, those who came from unusual or socioeconomically different backgrounds, those who had been conditioned to variant expressions of emotionality or control of aggression. In other instances, exclusion became almost a necessity to maintain order or direction in poorly controlled and troubled urban districts. Actual exclusion from the regular classroom became widespread.

Probably the best documentation of this practice was provided in a Boston study, *The Way We Go to School* (Jones, 1970). The task force found that the school system had labeled nearly 4,000 children mentally retarded in 1969. Over 1,000 of these were on waiting lists for special class placement. The theoretical estimate by the Department of Mental Health was that there were only 1,500 mentally retarded children in the city. The task force found that special classes were being used as a "dumping ground" for many kinds of problem children, to the detriment of the children most in need of the services and for whom the services had been designed. Understandably, this challenge was quickly followed by litigation and a sizable class action suit against the school system and the director of special education.

It is interesting to note differences in relation to the degree of retardation. It had been long recognized that the social class distribution between educable and trainable special classes was significantly different, the trainables having greater proportions of middle class children. This was originally interpreted as a probable effect of the strains of childbearing or greater risks of physical injury and, consequently, more significant brain involvement among women further removed from physical, manual, or servile work. Another explanation was that this might be the effect of voluntary delay in childbearing among better educated women. However, the differences gradually were seen as the effect of the higher proportion of poorer children being pushed into educable classes in combination with the exclusion principle.

Exclusion meant that many children received no schooling at all. The estimates in Boston were that between 7,000 and 15,000 children were actually not going to school in the 1969–1970 academic year. Such data were powerful evidence in promoting the laws on education for all the handicapped persons. The clear intent of these laws (which vary by respective states but that have mandated standards under PL 94-142) is to reverse the exclusion principle. In its place, the basis for services was to be upon the positive footing of searching for pupils whose needs required special services. However, segregating these children from the mainstream would occur only as a last resort, and even then the child would be protected with an educational plan that would lead back toward an integrated placement in the standard curriculum. Again, the emphasis on *all* handicapped people meant just that: without exception. Thus even the extremes of physical handicaps and the severely/profoundly retarded children were brought under the mandates of equal educational opportunity. The simplistic IQ score excuse for exclusion was clearly dismissed.

Of course, the transgressions against mandated standards for test administration deserve some scrutiny. Many low IQ scores were assigned by poorly trained or even blatantly unqualified test administrators. Children were tested under all sorts of adverse conditions that would render test results invalid. These conditions included such problems as improper ventilation, inadequate lighting, cramped testing quarters (the testing room/ broom closet dual assignment), and subjecting the children to undue emotional duress as well as neglecting to recognize those children too upset or emotionally distraught to be tested at that time. Sometimes the score was "leaned upon" to please the school administration. That is, not always was a false score fabricated or substituted, but points were lost in harsh or overly strict scoring procedures—much to the detriment of the child. In these instances, the instruments were not the social evil, but they were involved in a complicity that certainly deprived many children of their rightful opportunities. The only answer to such wrong doing was to initiate protective review bodies to prevent this occurrence. The power of exclusion was too great to invest in any one measurement technician or professional. A review board was necessary, composed of professionals having access to several assessment procedures from varying sources. This was the only means to assure just decisions and due process. A review board was needed for the protection of children who might otherwise be too easily denied educational opportunity.

The Way Out of the Morass

The greatest fallacy of the testing movement was the underlying assumption that what was being measured was some constant or unifying life principle. Early measurement specialists were searching for an immutable IQ or some basic, unalterable personality traits rather than an impression of some aspect of an organismic entity captured at one point of time in the life history of a growing and changing person. The constant IQ or the predestining personality traits are perhaps better seen now for what they are: historical attempts to crystalize a concept so that it might be studied more effectively. Test measurements have a predictive reliability. They can serve as indicators of what to expect. However, we have learned that on the negative side they also can serve as self-fulfilling prophesies. They do bias expectations to the degree that practitioners, teachers, or parents modify goals and consequently may undermine the quality of services offered an individual.

What is operating here is involved in the manner in which we deal with more dependent individuals in other social situations. Caring for retarded persons does not differ greatly from other social relationships, particularly human family relationships. What professionals do in caring for their own children is often reflected in their relationships toward their patients or clients. Children are similarly in a more dependent relationship upon the adults who care for them. The analogy only goes so far, however. The difference is that the professional as a parent expects his child to grow and to learn. In this way the parent graduates the steps to move a child toward independence. This was not always true with the retarded patient or client, and perhaps this is what is needed. In fact, in the past the converse was more likely the situation. Too little consideration was given to the possibilities of potential total independence, to the degree that graduated steps toward that goal were often not even considered or were pitifully neglected.

The way out involves a vastly expanded professional viewpoint regarding possibilities of advancing independence training, for advocating for least restrictive environments, for recommending every possible mainstreaming effort. Retarded individuals, like all other living beings, continue to grow mentally throughout their lives. They need opportunities not only in school but in their homes, their neighborhood communities, and recreational and prevocational facilities as well. Rather than the constraints of self-fulfilling prophesies, retarded persons need to be recognized for eligibility for increased services. They need to be guided toward greater availability of alternatives. There must be choice of activities. There must be selection, and the support afforded by having some voice and some control in their own life decisions. These are the foundations of a mentally healthy existence. These attitudes must be accepted by professionals working with retarded individuals in order that the tools they use are employed appropriately.

ACKNOWLEDGMENTS

I am indebted to the valuable suggestions and support of the staff of the Developmental Evaluation Clinic at Children's Hospital Medical Center, particularly Drs. Allen C. Crocker, Hayden Duggan, Ludwik Szymanski, and Jean M. Zadig; my wife, Elizabeth Ryan Cushna; Mr. Edward Connolly; and Ms. Cynthia Bates.

REFERENCES

Bayley, N. 1955. On the growth of intelligence. Am. Psychol. 10:805–817.
Beck, S. J. 1962. Rorschach's Test. Grune & Stratton, New York.
Bender, L. 1938. A Visual Motor Gestalt Test and Its Clinical Uses. The American Orthopsychiatric Association, New York.

Braginsky, D. D., and Braginsky, B. M. 1971. Hansels and Gretels. Holt, Rine-
hart & Winston, New York.
Cattell, P. 1947. Cattell Infant Intelligence Scale. Psychological Corporation,
New York.
Clawson, A. 1962. The Bender Visual-Motor Gestalt for Children. Western Psy-
chological Services, Beverly Hills, Cal.
Cohen, H., and Weil, G. R. 1971. Tasks of Emotional Development Test. D. C.
Heath, Lexington, Mass.
Danielson, F. H., and Davenport, C. B. 1912. The Hill Folk. Cold Spring Harbor,
Eugenics Records Office, Long Island, N.Y.
Goddard, H. H. 1910. Four hundred classified by the Binet method. J. Psycho.-
Asthen. 15:17–30.
Goddard, H. H. 1912. The Kallikak Family. Macmillan Publishing Co., New
York.
Grossman, H. J. (ed.). 1977. Manual on Terminology and Classification in Mental
Retardation. American Association on Mental Deficiency, Washington, D.C.
Hofstaetter, P. 1954. The changing composition of intelligence. J. Genet.
Psychol. 85:159–164.
Jones, H. E. (ed.). 1970. The Way We Go to School: The Exclusion of Children
in Boston. Beacon Press, Boston.
Koppitz, E. M. 1964. The Bender Gestalt Test for Young Children. Grune and
Stratton, New York.
Murray, H. A. 1938. Explorations in Personality. Oxford University Press, New
York.
Sines, J. O., Paulker, J. D., and Sines, L. K. 1966. The development of an objec-
tive, nonverbal, personality test for children. Paper presented at the meetings of
the Midwestern Psychological Association, Chicago.
Terman, L. E. 1916. The measurement of intelligence. Houghton Mifflin Co.,
Boston.
Terman, L. E., and Merrill, M. A. 1973. Stanford Binet Intelligence Scale.
Houghton Mifflin Co., Boston.
Wechsler, D. 1955. Wechsler Adult Intelligence Scale. Psychological Corporation,
New York.
Wechsler, D. 1958. The Measurement and Appraisal of Adult Intelligence. Wil-
liams & Wilkins Co., Baltimore.
Wolfensberger, W. 1972. Normalization: The Principle of Normalization in Hu-
man Services. National Institute on Mental Retardation, Toronto.

SUGGESTED READINGS

Kanner, L. 1967. A History of the Care and Study of the Mentally Retarded.
Charles C Thomas Publisher, Springfield, Ill.
Koocher, G. P. (ed.). 1976. Children's Rights and the Mental Health Professions.
John Wiley & Sons, New York.

A FIELD THEORY APPROACH TO UNDERSTANDING DEVELOPMENTAL DISABILITIES

Chapter 4

Peter E. Tanguay

By now, most professionals in the mental health field are aware that searching for single "causes" of developmental disability is futile and unproductive. A simple cause-and-effect model is rarely adequate as an explanation for most human phenomena. Even in medicine and surgery it has been found increasingly necessary to invoke a holistic model of disease causation in order to understand, treat, and prevent illnesses effectively. Thus, while it may be true that a virus or a particular strain of bacteria plays an important role in the development of pneumonia, or that a specific carcinogen may provoke development of cancer, these factors alone are insufficient in most instances to "cause" the pathology in question. Many factors influence the development of an infection such as pneumonia: the virulence of the bacteria or virus, the state of health of the individual, the person's environmental and socioeconomic situation, and the person's genetic susceptibility to the bacteria or virus. "State of health" is an extremely complex system of biochemical, endocrinological, and physiological mechanisms that seek to remain in homeostatic balance with each other. Extreme conditions in any one part of the system or "field" may increase the likelihood of contracting illness. Such conditions may be a result of a particularly virulent organism, malnutrition in the host because of poverty or ignorance of nutritional facts, unsanitary living conditions, injury to a particular target organ, general systemic debility because of other illnesses, and suppression or failure of immune mechanisms. The development of a cancer may be influenced by genetic susceptibility of the host, presence of carcinogens in the environment, or abnormality in cellular DNA and RNA production. Factors may exert

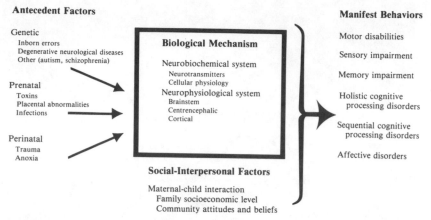

Antecedent Factors

Genetic
  Inborn errors
  Degenerative neurological diseases
  Other (autism, schizophrenia)

Prenatal
  Toxins
  Placental abnormalities
  Infections

Perinatal
  Trauma
  Anoxia

Biological Mechanism

Neurobiochemical system
  Neurotransmitters
  Cellular physiology
Neurophysiological system
  Brainstem
  Centrencephalic
  Cortical

Social-Interpersonal Factors

Maternal-child interaction
  Family socioeconomic level
  Community attitudes and beliefs

Manifest Behaviors

Motor disabilities

Sensory impairment

Memory impairment

Holistic cognitive
  processing disorders

Sequential cognitive
  processing disorders

Affective disorders

Figure 1. Model illustrating a field theory approach to understanding developmental disabilities.

their effects alone or, more often, may interact in a synergistic way to increase or decrease the likelihood of illness.

If a holistic systems theory approach is crucial to understanding physical illnesses, how much more important it must be to understanding human behavior and its development. A model illustrating a field theory approach to understanding developmental disabilities is given in Figure 1. Biological mechanisms, themselves the product of millenia of genetic evolution, depend upon myriad factors for their proper operation. A striking example of this dependence is shown by the manner in which visual input (both the amount and type of stimulation) directly affects the manner in which neuroanatomical and neurophysiological connections develop between the retina, the lateral geniculate body, and the visual cortex (Hubel and Wiesel, 1970; Spinelli and Jensen, 1978). Another relatively direct influence of the environment upon neurobiological development is illustrated by certain inborn errors of metabolism, including phenylketonuria. The genetic defect in phenylketonuria results in the absence of an important enzyme, phenylalanine hydroxylase. The absence of the enzyme does not, however, lead directly to mental retardation, but requires that the environment provide a supply of the amino acid phenylalanine if symptoms are to develop.

A somewhat different form of interaction, this time between environment and perinatal factors, appears important to the outcome of high risk status in infancy. *High risk* infants are identified early in life by prematurity, low birth weight, or signs of mild neurological impairment. Such children are considered to be *at risk* for later cognitive and psychiatric disorder. As Eisenberg (1977) pointed out, however, many studies have shown that the eventual intellectual status and emotional status of high risk children are strongly correlated with family socioeconomic status. High risk infants living in middle class families are much less likely to develop impairments than are those living in lower class homes. The important variables in the latter situation appear to be decreased post-natal medical care, poorer nutrition, and lack of sufficient infant and childhood linguistic and nonlinguistic stimulation.

Even when neurobiological development is within normal limits, however, environmental factors remain crucial in determining the degree to which cognitive and emotional development will be normal. In the great majority of instances of mild mental retardation, it is the learning environment that appears to be at fault, either because it is intellectually impoverished or because the child's intellectual explorations are not rein-forced.

Given the complexity of the sociobiological system, and the pro-longed nature of its development, it stands to reason that the manifest behaviors that result from a specific pathological factor may be quite variable. Focusing for a moment on the biological side of the equation, adverse factors that impair brain development very early in life are likely to have quite different effects from those that act mainly in the second or third year. Some systems in the brain may be particularly vulnerable to certain types of adversity at a particular time. In the auditory system, for instance, the cochlear nucleus appears to be particularly vulnerable to anoxia during early gestation (Hall, 1963) compared to later in life. Be-cause of this, conditions leading to anoxia in the first months of gestation might result in cochlear abnormalities, whereas the same conditions oc-curring later might produce an entirely different effect (e.g., damage to cortical auditory centers). Such abnormalities could, depending on their location in the auditory system, have different but equally important ef-fects on language development. In the same way, a relatively minor ab-normality in auditory processing that occurs in adulthood might have only minor effects on the comprehension of speech; the same abnormality occurring in childhood might disrupt language acquisition altogether.

Therefore, three points must be kept in mind when it comes to under-standing the development of a developmental disability: the interaction between adverse factors, the specific loading for each factor, and the time within the life of the organism that each factor exerts its effect. The first of these points is particularly important to the discussion of the role of biological factors in Chapter 5, and the third forms the basis for a hypoth-esis that is proposed in regard to the etiology of early infantile autism in Chapter 8.

REFERENCES

Eisenberg, L. 1977. Development as a unifying concept in psychiatry. Br. J. Psy-chiatry 131:225–237.

Hall, J. G. 1963. On the neuropathological changes in the central nervous system following neonatal asphyxia. Acta Oto-laryngol. 188(suppl.):331–375.

Hubel, D. H., and Wiesel, T. N. 1970. The period of susceptibility to the physiological effects of unilateral eye closure in kittens. J. Physiol. 206:419–436.

Spinelli, D. N., and Jensen, F. E. 1978. Plasticity: The mirror of experience. Science 203:75–78.

THE BIOMEDICAL COMPONENTS OF MENTAL RETARDATION

Chapter 5   *Allen C. Crocker*

Biomedical approaches to the problems of mentally retarded persons include: a) a search for possible "specific" elements in the etiology of the cortical handicap, b) assistance in clinical management of special liabilities and complications in these situations of human exceptionality, c) provision of informed primary health care and support for the involved individuals, and d) implementation of prevention programs where current knowledge permits. Although it is true that undue use of the "medical model" (including hospital environments) for the study of mental retardation can be constraining, pediatricians, neurologists, and other medical specialists can nonetheless provide valuable contributions to the interdisciplinary team actions on behalf of the retarded individual. When an important degree of mental handicap is present, thoughtful medical participation, both early and late, is a significant element in the "right to treatment" composite. Early in life, identification of developmental deviation is often a pediatric responsibility; following this, clinical assistance is usually sought regarding the apparent mechanism of the cortical dysfunction.

SCHEMES OF "CAUSATION" IN MENTAL RETARDATION

Parents and professionals who encounter a child with a major developmental disorder share an urgency to seek the *cause* of the child's atypicality. Many different considerations motivate this urgency ranging from the intellectual "need to know" to anger about not knowing the cause and fear about repetition. Almost every major professional group or center involved in developmental disabilities has organized its own schema listing the "causes" of mental retardation, reflecting interpretative variance and sample differences.

The classifications of the causes of mental retardation have been plotted according to such varying reference points as the degree of handicap (mild, moderate, severe), the adaptive or behavioral implications, biological versus environmental backgrounds, and the nature of the impinging force, independent of the timing of action (trauma, toxins, infections). A useful plan may be one that analyzes events by the developmental sequence (hereditary/preconception, postconception/prenatal, perinatal, childhood).

When one seeks statistical information, however, there are sources of confusion on two levels. First is the issue of producing an overly simplistic scheme whereby the apparently dominant factor is listed as "the" cause, while, in fact, the cause is probably multifactorial. For example, a child with prenatally caused congenital anomalies will often prove unusually vulnerable to perinatal complications or postnatal adverse forces. A child with subtle polygenic hereditary liabilities may be prone to later complications. Obviously, where the weight of alleged causation is assigned in such a complex setting becomes a highly arbitrary matter. The role of nutritional limitation, repeated infection, or suboptimal social supports becomes obscured in the situation of certain "special" children. Second, assigning absolute importance to specific historical events in the backgrounds of children with (even discrete) handicaps can be difficult. The most notable circumstance in this regard relates to events in the perinatal period. Do we possess the knowledge to seize upon the record of a somewhat lowered Apgar score and defend its pertinence to later delayed psychomotor development? Is the issue of maternal preeclampsia, or of modest prematurity (or a small-weight-for-dates status), enough to relate to subsequent functional mediocrity? The limitations in answering these questions are a function of imprecision in the state of the art.

Analysis of the events by developmental sequence seems to be a good system for recording the apparent etiology of mental retardation (as well as other functional disorders). The major categories for consideration are:

Hereditary factors The influences are programmed even before the conception of the child, existing as genetic characteristics of the parents, transmission of which will follow specific formulas.
Early influences on embryonic development Of critical importance may be changes in the egg or sperm, or the just-fertilized ovum, or modification in the rapidly developing embryo during the first trimester of pregnancy.
Other pregnancy problems and perinatal morbidity Special concern exists for support of the baby in the uterus as he grows in size and ma-

turity during the last two-thirds of pregnancy and during adaptation
to birth and the newborn period.

Acquired childhood diseases

Environmental and social problems Knowledge is slowly increasing regarding the role of general environmental factors (sensory experiences, nutrition) and interpersonal relations in the support of the
growing human. These issues cut across the whole developmental period, but often come to clinical expression most notably in late childhood or early adult life.

Hereditary Factors

Genetic factors, in a direct sense, are a relatively rare cause of mental
retardation. Best known among such situations are the *inborn errors of
metabolism*—diseases with biochemical abnormality that affect brain development, such as phenylketonuria (PKU), Tay-Sachs disease, Hurler's
disease, and galactosemia.

In addition to the inborn errors of metabolism, there are hereditary
diseases, such as neurofibromatosis, tuberous sclerosis, and the various
muscular dystrophy syndromes, which may or may not be accompanied
by subnormal intellectual function. Predictions of developmental disability in such instances are hazardous.

Early Influences on Embryonic Development

Spontaneous changes in the chromosomes of fetal cells are puzzling biological events and may produce developmental disability. The most frequent example of this is the child with Down's syndrome, in whom abnormalities occur either as a result of a trisomy of chromosome 21 or, in
3%-4% of the cases, as a translocation chromosome alteration. The
former represents a spontaneous change in a chromosome, and the latter
is hereditary.

Babies with unusually small heads (microcephaly) or large heads (as
in hydrocephaly), with changes in the heart or urinary tract, or with abnormalities of the hands and feet (fused fingers, absent bones, club feet)
are usually assumed to derive their handicaps from forces that alter the
developing tissues and organs early in pregnancy. Sometimes the changes
are subtle, such as relatively minor modifications in the position or structure of the ears, the external characteristics of the eyes, the shape of the
nose, the size of the lower jaw, or even the patterns of the fingerprints or
the skin markings of the palms. Such anomalies may sometimes be a result of prenatal infection (e.g., maternal rubella), use of certain medications during pregnancy (e.g., thalidomide), or life habits (e.g., fetal alco-
hol syndrome). Only in a minuscule percentage of such cases can one
make a reasonable assignment of probable causative factors.

When one is reviewing congenital anomalies and querying the mechanism of mental retardation or developmental delay per se, one can legitimately ask: Does the central nervous system (CNS) have a special vulnerability, which suggests that when other areas of the body are involved in "embryodysgenesis" processes, the brain is particularly likely to be impinged upon? In other words, if one finds signs of developmental delay in a child who also has anatomical alteration in his phenotype, can the retardation be assigned also to prenatal influence? The answer often appears to be yes, based on generic and experiential considerations. First, the nervous system is the most elaborately structured section of the body, and its development and maturation occur throughout fetal and early life. Second, it is common to find that some degree of mental retardation (with or without small head size or other evidence of CNS malformation) accompanies many multiple congenital anomaly syndromes. These issues are being studied further.

Late Pregnancy and Perinatal Problems

Once the basic processes of cell migration, tissue differentiation, and organ formation (embryogenesis) are completed, by the beginning of the second trimester of pregnancy, a long period of fetal growth and maturation begins. Sustained supports are needed for the fetus during these last two trimesters of pregnancy, but knowledge is incomplete regarding critical thresholds. The term *fetal nutrition* is used to describe the nutrients necessary for the baby's growth that are derived from the mother's circulation through the placenta. Deficiencies can reflect mediocrity in the mother's diet (calories, protein, calcium, vitamins) or, more frequently, some compromise in the anatomical or functional capacity of the vasculature of the placenta, which modifies the transfer of materials to the fetus. A striking example of this can be found in multiple pregnancies (twins, triplets) where unequal segments of placental support may be established for individual fetuses, with grossly visible differences in fetal size resulting. The placenta may develop vascular malformations, infarction, or varying degrees of premature separation (with vaginal bleeding). In single-child pregnancies, there may be on occasion a correlation between identifiable placental pathology and the delivery of a small-weight-for-dates baby. Other factors in the maternal environment that may be relevant to fetal pathology include toxemia of pregnancy, urinary tract infections, other maternal infections, and drug use.

Premature onset of labor, with the delivery of an immature (and undersized) infant, is a critical event. Artificial life support systems for premature babies involve further risk of limitations in CNS development. The premature infant is particularly vulnerable to the specific stresses of delivery, wherein all obstetrical hazards have an exaggerated potential for pathology.

Birth injuries represent another significant early-life risk. Other factors leading to a complicated or high risk delivery include placenta previa, difficult breech delivery, and prolonged labor (cephalopelvic disproportion) with eventual cesarean section. On a child-by-child basis, it is very difficult to find good correlation between the occurrence of moderate obstetrical difficulties and later developmental progress. Furthermore, when used retrospectively, obstetrical records (and even early pediatric notes) may provide an incomplete picture of the functional implications of the events in that difficult period.

In the first few days of life, major threats to the fetus include:

Hypoxia, as in atelectasis or in respiratory distress syndrome

Hyperbilirubinemia, as in Rh or blood group incompatibility, or accompanying sepsis

Hypoglycemia, usually of obscure origin, sometimes accompanied by convulsions

Infection after prolonged rupture of the membranes, during delivery or from sources in the nursery

Intracranial bleeding, from traumatic delivery or in relation to asphyxia

Surgical emergencies, from congenital anomalies (such as intestinal obstruction)

In all of these instances, there is opportunity for injury to the brain, although the degree of handicap is difficult to predict.

Acquired Childhood Diseases

Once the child is past the newborn period, infections represent the greatest threat to development. Although bacterial meningitis is technically a treatable disease, such an infection may cause harm to the CNS. The degree of postinfection morbidity correlates significantly with delay in starting effective antibiotic treatment. Children of very young age or those with congenital anomalies of the nervous system are more vulnerable to complications from infections. Viral meningitides or encephalitides have a broad spectrum of sequelae, as do the encephalitic aspects of the common viral communicable diseases (measles, mumps, chickenpox). Long periods of slow, gradual recovery of function may be seen following encephalitis, during which time thoughtful support and freedom from stress are needed. Motor function handicaps, seizures, behavioral alterations, cognitive difficulties, and perceptual handicaps are possible complications of intracranial infections.

Endocrine diseases are rare causes of acquired mental retardation. Thyroid deficiency in infants and young children is usually a result of a congenital abnormality.

The problem of exposure of children to so-called toxins is a complex one. For practical purposes, only lead poisoning has emerged as having a reasonably well-charted risk. Lead poisoning, or, more often, an increased lead burden, stands as a continuing background threat to childhood development.

Head trauma from accident or abuse is an occasional cause of discrete CNS pathology. Most commonly, regional pareses, such as hemiplegia, may result. Intracranial tumors are rare, but occasionally devastating, causes of mental handicap.

ROLE OF THE PEDIATRICIAN

Pediatricians in developmental disability may function as *primary care pediatricians* (providing screening, referral, health supervision, advocacy, and support to families), *pediatricians who are allied with treatment and educational programs in the community* (giving consultation to clinics and schools), and *specialists for the handicapped child* (carrying out definitive assessment studies, education, research).

The Description of Human Exceptionality

Evaluation of unusual physical features in the child or adult calls for the same type of objective analysis that is given to measurements of intelligence. The modern growth of "syndromology" (or, as McKusick calls it, "nosology") has begun to require more precision in analysis of human physical characteristics, but there is still a tendency in the currently available syndrome atlases and textbooks to record traditional instead of freshly considered functional interpretations. For example, if an individual has features associated with an inborn error of mucopolysaccharide metabolism (facial alteration, change in body form and growth), he may be handled with diminished educational expectations even though this is unjustified in some of the syndromes (such as Maroteaux-Lamy disease). It is still difficult to procure open-minded prognostic planning for persons with sex chromosome aberrations. The presence of various externally evident congenital anomalies (head size and shape, for example) generates a public rejection that may have painful effects on functional outcome. Facial and body atypicality is linked with "looking retarded" in our culture. It is to be hoped that pediatricians will develop behaviors of careful observation, coordinated interpretation, thoughtful counseling, and positive public guidance. Biological or physical anthropologists can provide invaluable assistance regarding the meaning of unusual phenotypic features, especially identification of whether or not these involve "sporadic" (prenatal malformation) occurrence or genetically determined traits.

The Use and Misuse of Medical Diagnoses

There are special dynamics involved in the vigorous pursuit of a specific syndrome diagnostic name to use for the clinical dilemma of a given child.

Preoccupation with such names has been aptly dubbed "the Rumpelstiltskin phenomenon" by a colleague, Dr. Mary Anne Whelan, referring to the urgency to get the name right, which is the turning point of that fairy tale. The need to seek apparent causation for developmental disorders was discussed in detail in the first portion of this chapter, but comments about the use of diagnostic names should also be listed.

For the family, the placing of a specific "disease" name can often relieve some of the tension that existed previously. The coping process can begin more earnestly when there is a seemingly discrete entity to adjust to. A component of guilt and fantasy may be modulated, and there is a sense of alliance with some body of knowledge about the child's difficulties. If credibility has been established, the inclination may be modified to seek more clinics for additional studies.

The medical facility that forms a specific diagnosis for the child has an intellectual gratification. In particular, the presence of an eponymic disease (Williams' syndrome, Cornelia de Lange syndrome) clarifies the status of the patient to some degree and may expedite the counseling process.

There are inherent dangers in this naming process, however. The risk exists of stereotyping. Medical diagnostic names have a series of positive and negative implications, usually somewhat inaccurate when too generally accepted. The name may tend to reinforce the child's abnormalities and obfuscate the personal traits and real needs of the young person. Much pathology-oriented medical terminology is unkind and unjust. Hence, specific disease or syndrome names may be used in the organizational stages of the clinical relationship, but should be minimized thereafter.

Intervening for Prevention

The potential for prevention of mental retardation is vastly more extensive than is commonly appreciated, especially in the biomedical sphere. Examples of opportunities in this area are present in the following outline. The most significant achievements have been in improved genetic services, control of infection, and enhanced obstetrical and perinatal management. Improved support systems for handicapped young children and their families are preventing complications and loss of human resources.

Prevention of Mental Retardation or Its Complications

I.   Prevention Activities—Specific Goal
     A.   Vaccination to prevent intrauterine infection, e.g., congenital rubella

      B.   Carrier detection in high risk groups for genetic disease, e.g., Tay-Sachs disease

      C.   Genetic counseling on personal or pedigree experience, e.g., Crouzon's syndrome, tuberous sclerosis

      D.   Prenatal diagnosis by amniocentesis or fetoscopy, e.g., Down's syndrome, Hurler's syndrome, neural tube defects

      E.   Detection in newborn infants of treatable metabolic disease, e.g., PKU, hypothyroidism, galactosemia

      F.   Childhood protection against complications from infection, e.g., measles, Haemophilus influenzae infection

      G.   Childhood protection from environmental hazards, e.g., lead poisoning

II.   Prevention Activities—General Goals

      A.   Public education regarding risks during pregnancy, e.g., specific medications, excessive alcohol or smoking, advanced maternal age

      B.   Medical supervision of the progress of pregnancy, e.g., toxemia, urinary tract infection, anticipation of problems at delivery

      C.   Improved perinatal management and obstetric-neonatology interaction, e.g., fetal distress, newborn asphyxia, prematurity, respiratory distress syndrome

      D.   Environmental and social supports for children, e.g., psychosocial deprivation, child abuse

III. Prevention Activities—Intercession in Ascertained Situations

      A.   Early identification programs, e.g., early stages of developmental disorder, sensory handicap

      B.   Early intervention and stimulation programs, e.g., multiply handicapped infants and young children

      C.   Support systems for families, e.g., families of handicapped children

The Pediatric-Mental Health Partnership

It can be anticipated that a mutual reinforcement and enrichment of functions will occur when a continuing alliance exists between the pediatrician and the psychiatrist, or other mental health worker, on behalf of the mentally retarded person. This can take place in interaction on the interdisciplinary team or in specific contacts or consultations in clinic or community.

The special needs for a mental health professional provided by the pediatrician include: 1) sound descriptive and diagnostic information on the patient, with data about the expected evolution and/or behavioral aspects of the medical state, if known; 2) comments on the apparent cause of the handicap, especially as this affects family perceptions of the situation (including genetic factors, if pertinent), and 3) management and intervention plans, as these impinge on course and adjustment.

The special needs for a pediatrician provided by the psychiatrist or other mental health worker involve: 1) analysis of the dynamics of client and family in this exceptional situation, for improved understanding, 2) guidance regarding roles in management, to provide maximal support (sometimes with specific therapy planned), and, on rare occasions, 3) assistance in the employment of psychoactive medications where such are appropriate. It is assumed that both professionals would act in concert at times of special crisis or complicating behavioral deviation, including as advisers to other components of the management team.

PSYCHIATRIC DIAGNOSIS OF RETARDED PERSONS

Chapter 6 | *Ludwik S. Szymanski*

INCIDENCE OF MENTAL DISORDERS
AMONG MENTALLY RETARDED PERSONS

Incidence of mental disorders in the mentally retarded population is difficult to assess on the basis of existing studies because of differing interpretations of the diagnosis of retardation, biased selection of samples that
were studied, and lack of uniform use of psychiatric diagnostic classification. Not all researchers have adhered to the standard definition of mental
retardation, and often the chief reliance has been on IQ as measured by
psychological tests, disregarding the degree of the individual's adaptation. Reliability of past records and tests often was taken for granted.
Populations studied were often biased since they were usually not selected
at random, but on the basis of attendance at a clinic, day, or residential
program. This method of case finding may be unreliable (Wing, 1963).
Public residential institutions generally contain severely retarded individuals with gross neurological deficits and behavioral disorders (which
prompted admission to the institution), and the institutional prevalence
rates do not reflect those in a community-based population (Reid, 1976).
Even knowledge that there is a psychiatrist on the staff of a developmental disabilities clinic may generate a disproportionate number of referrals
of disturbed retarded patients. Evaluation of all retarded persons in a
community, following the techniques of Rutter, Graham, and Yule (1970)
in the Isle of Wight survey, might be optimal, but it has not been done.
Identifying retarded adults may be another problem (Gruenberg and
Kiev, 1967; Gruenberg and Turns, 1975), since their number seems to
"drop" with age, perhaps because of better adaptation in the labor
market than in educational settings. In summary, the existing studies have

to be evaluated critically and not accepted at face value. Most researchers agree, however, that there is a high incidence of psychiatric disorders in the retarded population.

Philips (1966) assessed 170 children referred for diagnostic study and evaluation of retardation and concluded: "It was uncommon...to see a retarded child who presented no emotional maladjustment of moderate to severe degree as part of his clinical picture." Menolascino (1965, 1966) found diagnosable psychiatric disorder in 31% of 616 children referred with suspicion of retardation. Of this sample, 24.5% were both mentally retarded and emotionally disturbed. Both of these researchers were based in psychiatric settings, which could have influenced the type of cases referred to them. Webster (1970), who also reviewed pertinent literature and reported on 159 children, from 3 to 6 years of age, referred to a day nursery for retarded children. Nonambulatory children were excluded. All were diagnosed as having a degree of disturbance in emotional development, and thus as emotionally disturbed. In that study, intellectual impairment and learning disability were seen as "basic features in the primary psychopathology." (By this definition, all retarded persons would be diagnosed as disturbed, with which most workers would disagree.) Eighteen percent were classified in that study as "psychotic" (no definition was given). Chess (1970) and Chess and Hassibi (1970) described behavior disorders in a group of 52 mildly and borderline retarded children of middle class families who were living at home. They were divided into the following categories: no psychiatric disorder (21), reactive behavior disorder (18), neurotic behavior disorder (1), behavior disorder caused by neurological damage (11), and psychosis (1). In follow-up studies 6 years later (Chess, 1977), 40% of the children still presented symptoms of some type of behavior disorder (four of them were diagnosed as psychotic).

Philips and Williams (1975) reported retrospective evaluations of records of 100 children referred to a psychiatric clinic for assessment of their retardation. The following diagnoses were assigned: psychotic symptoms, 38%; neuroses, 5%; personality disorders and certain other nonpsychiatric disorders, 16%; behavioral disorders, 26%; transient situational disorders, 2%; no psychiatric disorder, 13%. The symptoms did not differ in kind from those found in a control group of nonretarded children referred to the same clinic (of whom 18% were diagnosed as psychotic). The behavioral symptoms seemed to be more troublesome when the children entered school. Szymanski (1977), in evaluating 132 children referred to a developmental disabilities clinic in a general pediatric hospital, found that among the retarded children in that sample, 46% were well adjusted within the limits of their retardation, in 24% emotional difficulties were the main reason for the child's maladjustment and a cause for his referral, and in 30% they played a secondary role, but still required specific intervention.

UTILIZATION OF PSYCHIATRIC DIAGNOSTIC NOMENCLATURE

Professionals in the fields of retardation and mental health often use a variety of terms such as *mental illness, mental disorders, psychiatric disorder (problem, condition), emotional disorder, behavioral disorder.* These "labels" often reflect the psychological theoretical background of the person rather than a specific category, and in fact these terms are usually used interchangeably. The term *emotional,* strictly speaking, and as reflected in *DSM III* (1980), should be used only for affective conditions. The term *behavioral,* as pointed out by Spitzer and Wilson (1975), should include both ideation and affect.

Fuller discussion of the classification and definition of mental disorders is beyond the scope of this chapter; interested readers are referred to comprehensive reviews by Spitzer and Wilson (1975), Rakoff, Stancer, and Kedward (1977), and *DSM III* (1980). Diagnosing psychiatric disorders is particularly difficult with pediatric populations where one has to consider the child's age when assessing the pathological significance of a symptom. In a retarded pediatric population this is even more difficult, because chronological age does not reflect developmental level. Only comprehensive knowledge of a retarded person's development, cognitive and sensory abilities, and past experiences may help to decide whether a particular behavior is an expression of psychiatric disorder, or an appropriate adaptation, or a learned response. Since the clinician must consider the multiple factors of an individual's development and functioning, summarizing the behavior in a single diagnosis may be impossible. A more appropriate approach would be assessment along several discrete parameters, such as Anna Freud's (1965) concept of the developmental lines. Rutter et al. (1969) developed the concept of a triaxial diagnostic system, which ultimately was developed into the multiaxial system of the *DSM III* (1980). The axes in the *DSM III* are: I—clinical psychiatric syndromes and other conditions, II—personality disorders and specific developmental disorders, III—physical disorders, IV—severity of psychosocial stressors, V—highest level of adaptive functioning the past year. This classification provides also for multiple diagnoses in each axis, as necessary. Another most important feature of this system is specific description of diagnostic criteria for each disorder.

The clinician using the multiaxial system should evaluate the significance of what the clinical symptoms represent, e.g., a specific clinical syndrome or a nonspecific adaptational reaction, understandable in light of the retarded child's personality traits, cognitive level, specific developmental disorders, environmental support, and associated physical deficits. Each one of these will also be recorded on the appropriate axis, thus providing a comprehensive picture.

Two diagnostic classes relating often (but not exclusively) to retarded persons have caused much confusion and have been used indiscriminately. The first, the "psychotic" disorders, are dealt with extensively in Chapter 8. The second class is referred to as *organicity* or *organic brain damage*. One might argue that such broad terms are meaningless. All psychological processes can be seen as depending on brain function (*DSM III,* 1980). Extending this concept to the extreme, one could speak of changes on a hypothetical molecular level that must occur when a memory of a traumatic experience is stored, as well as suppressory neurophysiological mechanisms that prevent this information from reaching consciousness. Clements (1962) pointed out that demonstrable structural and/or physiological changes are necessary for justifying the use of the label *brain dysfunction.* Woodward, Jaffe, and Brown (1970) pointed out two tendencies of psychiatrists: to make psychiatric diagnosis in terms of either organicity or nonorganicity (thus denying the possibility of a mixed clinical picture), and to consider any child with evidence of brain damage unable to benefit from psychotherapy.

Such "organic" labels are often unfounded and unscientific. For example, it is not uncommon for a child's mental retardation to be "explained" by a difficult delivery, even if there are no neurological physical signs. Another child with an identical clinical picture, but with a history of normal delivery, will not be diagnosed as "organic." However, a third child, who has normal intelligence, might have had the most traumatic birth of all! Thus a careful, comprehensive assessment in all spheres is necessary before brain pathology is demonstrated and appropriate specific diagnosis is assigned. Even if the retardation can be ascribed definitely to such pathology, the patient's psychopathology may not; in fact, as pointed out by Philips (1966), it is usually related to "delayed, disordered personality functions and interpersonal relationships with meaningful people in the environment." *DSM III* (1980) discusses the criteria for diagnosis of various organic brain syndromes.

In summary, the following points are important: 1) the same psychiatric diagnostic categories can and should be used with both retarded and nonretarded persons, 2) formal psychiatric diagnosis should include the diagnosis of mental disorder, not only of the retardation, 3) multiple and multiaxial diagnoses utilizing *DSM III* criteria are helpful, and 4) vague and unfounded statements referring to organicity should be avoided.

INTERDISCIPLINARY APPROACH TO THE PSYCHIATRIC DIAGNOSTIC ASSESSMENT OF RETARDED PERSONS

The adaptive behavior of any person, including a retarded one, is a function of biological, sociocultural, and psychological factors (Garrard and Richmond, 1965). In various fields of medicine, including psychiatry, the physician's task in the process of health care delivery can be seen as "one

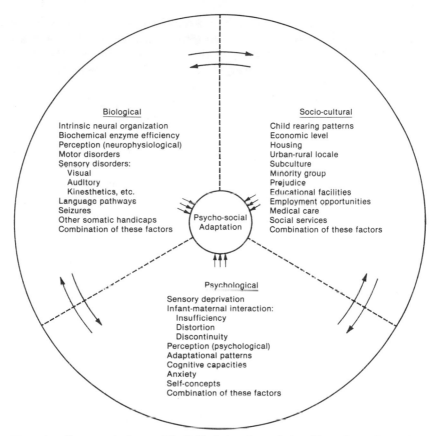

Figure 1. Conceptual scheme of the field of mental retardation. (From Garrard and Richmond, 1965, "Mental Retardation without Biological Manifestations," in C. H. Carter (ed.), *Medical Aspects of Mental Retardation*. Courtesy of Charles C Thomas, Publisher, Springfield, Ill.)

of integrating his knowledge of biology with his knowledge of the social, psychologic and physical environment of the patient" (Richmond and Garrard, 1966).

However, psychiatrists often satisfy themselves with "medical clearance" of their patients by an internist or general practitioner and focus only on their psychological problems. This approach, which in a sense denies the unity of the human psychobiological organism, is inappropriate when working with retarded persons because considerable interdependence exists between cognitive, emotional, motor, and sensory aspects of their development and environmental forces. Particularly helpful is the conceptual scheme developed and adapted for the field of mental retardation by Garrard and Richmond (1965) (Figure 1). Thus, psychiatrists cannot focus, for instance, on evaluating a patient's neurotic conflict as an isolated entity, but they must assess the total level of his development as a psychobiological organism, as well as his life situation and the mutual impact of his various handicaps, the family's attitudes, and the community's attitudes.

Menolascino and Bernstein (1970) pointed out that psychiatric assessment of a mentally retarded child has meaning only if it is part of a general diagnostic procedure, leading to understanding his total functioning in all areas. Most psychiatrists are not competent enough to be solely responsible for doing medical-neurological, psychological, audiological, speech, and language examinations, but they should review previous assessments of the patient's functioning in all pertinent spheres, interpret these data competently, and integrate them with their own formulations.

Whenever doubt arises about whether the past diagnosis of retardation has been justified, referral for comprehensive assessment is indicated. Psychiatrists may be expected to assess clinically the patient's cognitive and neuropsychological functioning. However, it may be prudent not to base the diagnosis of retardation solely on such clinical assessment. Since retardation usually includes developmental delay in multiple areas, and since it carries such important prognostic weight, its diagnosis should not be seen as a province of any one specialty, but of an interdisciplinary team.

OBJECTIVES OF DIAGNOSTIC ASSESSMENT

Psychiatric diagnostic evaluation of retarded persons (or of anyone) should be a goal-oriented process. Menolascino and Bernstein (1970) advised that "the examiner should always ask himself why he has been asked to see a particular retarded individual." They stated two common motives: "...that 1) the referral source does not know what to do next, and 2) there are magical expectations that the psychiatrist will find something (and do something!) that has not been found and done yet!" Szymanski (1977) divided the motives (or questions) that lead to the referral into manifest and latent. The former usually reflect conscious concerns and needs of the referring person or agency. A frequent question is whether an "emotional block" is the cause of the retardation or contributes to it. Disturbing and socially unacceptable behavior, usually of an aggressive type, is another frequent cause for referral. Teachers, counselors, and caregivers may ask whether the patient is retarded or psychotic or whether he may be dangerous to other children in the classroom, and they may demand that drugs be prescribed in order to control him. Older patients may be referred because of any psychiatric symptom, particularly if it interferes with a patient's performance in his work or rehabilitation program.

The latent concerns are usually emotionally charged and often subconscious, and they may be the main reason for the referral. The referring person may feel helpless and guilty, e.g., for not educating the patient enough or not being able to control his behavior. Some parents hope to have the diagnosis changed from mental retardation to emotional disorder, which is seen as treatable. A child previously diagnosed as retarded may be brought for a "second opinion" with the hope that he will be labeled only "slow" or "disturbed." Some parents may hope for a diagnosis of "brain damage," if the diagnosis of emotional disorder evoked guilt feelings for having caused it. A parent overwhelmed by a child's behavior may hope for the doctor's permission to put the child in a residential school.

Recognizing latent and manifest questions and answering them at the completion of the diagnostic process are necessary in order to prevent further "shopping" for a more satisfactory opinion.

During the diagnostic process the psychiatrist has to function in multiple roles (Szymanski, 1977). He may be the first one to suspect previously undiagnosed mental retardation in a child referred because of behavioral disorder. His important contribution as a professional team member, besides providing psychiatric input, is "synthesizing" the opinions of various specialists who might have seen the patient, and interpreting them for the parents and helping them to overcome their resistance to accepting the diagnosis. He may serve as a diagnostician-behavioral management consultant to staffs of special schools and as a rehabilitation and resource-finding consultant to pediatricians.

Patient advocacy is often necessary during the diagnostic process. Retarded persons (like nonretarded children) are usually brought to the psychiatrist by their parents or other caregivers. Sometimes they complain about the patient's behavior, which is disturbing and threatening to them, even if such behavior is developmentally normal. For instance, the staff may regard a curious and active resident in a residential facility as aggressive, and will thus reward abnormally dependent and passive behavior. Developmentally normal sexual curiosity may be seen as threatening and dangerous. Psychiatrists have to be careful in order not to give diagnostic opinions and recommendations that will be convenient to the caregivers, and to the retarded person's detriment. They should try to reconcile the caregiver's manifest and latent concerns with the patient's needs. Another aspect of their role as advocates is working toward securing for the patient the services essential for implementing the recommendations. Finally, psychiatrists might be asked to perform diagnostic evaluation to establish a person's competence, e.g., for the purpose of giving consent for medical procedures, including sterilization. Essentially, such competence examinations should not be carried out by psychiatrists alone, but by an interdisciplinary team. In any case, psychiatrists will have to act as patient advocates to prevent abuse of patient rights.

IMPEDIMENTS TO THE DIAGNOSTIC PROCESS

Szymanski (1977) divided factors interfering with the diagnostic process into three categories:

1. *Biases of the professional*   These are described in more detail in Chapter 1; they include lack of experience with retarded persons, guilt for not being able to "cure" them, rejection, and overprotection.

2. *Reactions of the families*   The family of a retarded patient may arrive for the psychiatric interview considerably anxious, often because of unresolved guilt feelings (e.g., for having a retarded child, for causing his behavioral disorder by improper management, for angry and rejecting feelings toward him). These feelings may be projected onto the professional and result in hostility, defensiveness, and uncooperativeness. It is important to realize that the parents' anger may be based in reality and caused by unsatisfactory experiences with professionals who failed to provide needed services or who limited themselves to advising on institutionalization for the newborn retarded child (although the latter practice has been disappearing lately, as pointed out by Pueschel and Murphy, 1977). In these cases, direct support to the parents through empathizing and tactfully exploring the reasons for the family's attitude may be in order. For example, the professional may inquire whether the parents have gone through a "normal" period of feeling that they had something to do with their child's handicap.

3. *Reactions of the patient*   The psychiatric interview may be as anxiety provoking for a retarded patient as for a nonretarded one (although not necessarily for the same reason). The retarded patient's defenses may be more primitive and fragile, and if he does not have the language capacities for verbalizing his feelings, he may act them out. The interview may be seen as a "test" that he may fail. Careful explanation of the interview's purpose and procedure is most helpful. When the patient has no receptive language, the professional must rely on nonverbal communication of support and empathy. In the presence of overwhelming separation anxiety, he may have to see the patient and caregiver(s) together. In general, unless contraindicated (e.g., if an older patient opposes it), valuable observations can be made if they are seen both jointly and separately. In the joint interview, the professional can observe how the parents (or caregivers) handle the patient's anxiety, whether they offer him support, whether they exert pressure on him to "perform," whether they overcontrol him or set no limits, how they play with him, whether they encourage or discourage independent behavior, and what the general tone is of their relationship and interaction. Valuable information may be obtained

from comparing the child's behavior in the presence of and in the absence of his parents. The techniques of the family interview with older and verbal individuals are similar to those employed with nonretarded patients.

STRATEGY OF THE INTERVIEW WITH THE PATIENT

The techniques of interviewing retarded patients are basically the same as those employed with nonretarded ones, except for modifications in communication patterns and in interpretation of data.

For the convenience of discussion, the strategy of the interview can be divided into the following stages: introductory, observational, exploratory, and closing. In each stage, certain themes are particularly prominent, although they are not necessarily limited to that stage.

In the *introductory stage,* two main tasks have to be accomplished: assessing the patient's communicative abilities and "tuning in" to his level, and establishing rapport. Addressing a patient in language too simple for him may be perceived as insulting. On the other hand, if he is addressed on a level too advanced for him, he may not understand the interviewer and may be too embarrassed to admit it. "Sizing up" of the patient may be aided by questions on neutral issues, such as whether he has ever been in this hospital or clinic before. Explanation of the diagnostic process is given at this stage, including reassurance, if necessary, that it is not a test, does not involve shots, and so on. Limits, if they are necessary, are set in a clear, unequivocal way. Periods of silence should be avoided because retarded patients find them anxiety provoking, and fear that the doctor dislikes them or expects something unknown of them. Play materials may be pointed out, but at first no pressure should be exerted to use them, to enable free choice. Verbal interchange at this stage should avoid emotionally charged subjects. The patient should be given an opportunity to demonstrate his strengths, e.g., in talking about what he is most successful in. With nonverbal patients, the tasks of this stage have to be accomplished through communicating acceptance and support through body language, affective expression, the offering of toys, and the like.

By the *observational stage,* the interviewer and the patient will have developed rapport and started to communicate effectively, some general limits will have been set, the patient will feel oriented in the office, and he will see the interviewer as a friendly, noncritical, and empathetic person. Thus, he may be less inhibited about engaging in verbal and nonverbal tasks, such as play, which should be suggested, but not forced. In this way, the professional may observe the patient's creativity, independence in choice of activities, and handling of multiple stimuli. There should be no pressure to focus on emotionally charged subjects (unless they are brought up by the patient). The main focus is on observing the total spontaneous output of the patient's behavior, verbal and nonverbal, play, interpersonal relatedness, and motor and perceptual capacities.

In the *exploratory stage,* it is assumed that in most cases the patient has already demonstrated at least some of his spontaneous and creative behaviors and has developed good rapport with the interviewer. Emotionally charged subjects are explored now more actively, with support and empathy given as necessary. Ability to accept limits and frustration is tested, e.g., requiring the patient to sit down and concentrate on a verbal topic or play task. Verbal reinforcement should be given liberally, tactfully, and nonpaternalistically to older and brighter patients and more openly, perhaps with tangible rewards as well, to lower functioning ones. A frequent and basic mistake is to underestimate a verbal patient's capacities for, e.g., verbalizing feelings, problems, and worries.

In the *closing stage,* toward the end of the interview, the interviewer returns to less charged topics and expresses support and empathy. The goal is to help the patient leave the office still regarding the interviewer as a friendly and understanding person, rather than feeling stressed because of revealing painful feelings. Some feedback should be given, when appropriate, depending on the patient's cognitive and language skills. This could be a general statement summarizing his problems, abilities, and options for remedial actions, for example: "You seem to be unhappy about not having friends and about your troubles learning to read, but you are a nice and friendly person and can draw very well. I think that talking about your troubles made you feel a little better. Would you like to do it more often with a person like me? Maybe we could find out what you can do to make friends." Besides showing support and understanding, the professional can thus test the patient's reaction to planned recommendations.

SOME SPECIFIC INTERVIEWING
TECHNIQUES USEFUL WITH RETARDED PERSONS

Directiveness

Directiveness may be difficult for a traditionally trained psychiatrist accustomed to assuming the role of a passive observer. Nevertheless, it is essential, both in diagnostic and psychotherapeutic interviews, and this has been highlighted in the literature (Jakab, 1970; Menolascino and Bernstein, 1970; Szymanski, 1977).

Mentally retarded persons have reduced cognitive, conceptual, and communication abilities; they are conditioned to expect failure on tests and criticism from others, are often passive and dependent, and thrive on support and reinforcement. Thus, they require direction, structure, and support. Without these they tend to produce little during the clinical interview. There is a positive side to this as well, as pointed out by Webster (1970): "If [the patient] is helped to conceptualize in simple terms his emotional problems, the therapeutic results can often be even more dramatic than with some of his nonretarded peers."

However, because of their suggestibility and wish to please others, leading questions should be avoided. If the interviewer must ask a structured question, he should give two opposite, possible answers to choose from; otherwise the patient may answer yes to the first possibility he hears. "Are you unhappy or are you happy in your (special) class?" is preferable to "Are you happy there?" However, the interview should be in part nondirected and unstructured to permit spontaneous productions as well.

Nonverbal Techniques

Nonverbal techniques are essential because retarded persons often have difficulty in verbal communication. Directiveness may also be necessary. With younger patients, play interviews are helpful. It is better to select a few appropriate toys rather than present the patient with a confusing array. Toys permitting symbolic and expressive play are preferable to those inviting perseveration. A dollhouse with small, flexible dolls is very useful. The diagnostician should not be afraid of participating actively (for example, setting up situations for the patient to solve), but he should avoid leading to the solutions. When pointing to a mother doll, asking "Who is this?" is preferable to asking "Who is she?" or "Is this a mother?" When the patient puts the doll family to sleep, the diagnostician may make the baby doll "get up" or "cry," and then ask the patient why the baby woke up and what is going to happen. Setting up a doll's classroom may be very revealing as well. The professional should observe the ability for symbolic play, its content (which may be reflecting the patient's experiences and concerns), and the patient's ability to handle an emotional response to charged issues or sexual roles identification. Drawings are also useful. Besides being a projective technique, they offer an opportunity to assess perceptual-motor and spatial abilities. The patient's relatedness, maturity of defenses, social behavior, attention, and self-control must also be observed. Some of the questions to answer are (Szymanski, 1977): How are ego defenses used to handle the anxiety aroused by the interview situation? Does the patient regress to dependency or temper tantrums? Does he relate indiscriminately to the interviewer, does he "size him up" first, or does he not relate at all?

Interviews with severely retarded, nonverbal persons are, of necessity, more limited. Because they depend greatly on routine and familiar environment, office interviews are not necessarily representative of their usual behavior. Office interviews may show the patient's response to, and regression under, stress. Preferably the professional should see them jointly with caregivers familiar to them, or better yet, in situ, in their home, classroom, or institution. Observation during normally structured, as well as unstructured, periods may be necessary for fuller understanding of their behavioral repertoire in various situations.

Interviews with Retarded Adults

Retarded adults (except for severely retarded ones) are acutely aware of, and sensitive to, being treated as eternal children. However, the other extreme of addressing them on an inappropriately high level in language above their comprehension abilities should also be avoided. Remarks and praise should be appropriate, for example, volubly admiring a mildly retarded adult's ability to dress without help is as inappropriate as admiring a doctor's ability to feed himself. Play materials should be offered carefully, perhaps just by making them visible. Surprisingly, even older individuals may look at them longingly and use them enthusiastically when face-saving permission is given, such as "I like to play this game myself." The interviewer should explore verbal persons' awareness of social expectations for people of their age and their reactions to being unable to meet them. Usually, (perhaps because of social deprivation) they are very eager to talk about their lives, concerns, and feelings.

Interviews with Families and/or Other Caregivers

The interview with the family and/or caregivers is important, regardless of the patient's age, since they will have to provide much of the history the patient is unable to give. Also, retarded persons are much more dependent on their caregivers than their nonretarded peers, including implementing the recommendations of the diagnostician. In order to understand the patient's psychopathology and to develop a realistic treatment program, the interviewer must have insight into the relationship between the family and community and the patient, their acceptance of his handicap, and their potential for giving him constructive support. Understanding the role that the handicap plays in the context of the family structure and dynamics is important. The interviewer must explore parental past and present psychopathology, as well as strengths; the marital situation; environmental stresses; the availability of support (e.g., from the extended family); the perinatal "emotional climate"; the parents' ability to see the child's strengths as well as deficits; and their ability to derive gratification from him. Factual knowledge about mental retardation should be assessed as well. Many parents, even well educated ones, are ignorant in this respect, believing that a diagnosis of retardation means that the child is a "mongol," totally unable to learn, cannot talk, and will become a vegetable. Bearing in mind the ubiquitous guilt feelings of the parents of retarded persons, the interviewer should be careful not to see the parents a priori as patients whose psychopathology caused the child's maladjustment. Thus, when inquiring into their personal problems and histories, the relevance of these issues to the child's current problems should be made clear.

REPRESENTATIVE EMOTIONAL PROBLEMS OF RETARDED PERSONS AT VARIOUS DEVELOPMENTAL STAGES

The stresses upon and the needs of a retarded individual and his family are not static, as pointed out by Richmond and Garrard (1966): "We can regard the family as facing the challenge of a series of adaptations rather than making a single adaptation. Thus, there are predictable periods of crisis in the family with retardation." A number of such developmental crises, or transitional periods, can be delineated. The mental retardation handbook of the American Medical Association (1965) lists 12 crisis points: first suspicion of retardation, final diagnosis, school entrance, rejection by peers, sibling relationships, acute illness, general family crises, puberty, vocational adjustment, marriage, decision on placement, and separation following placement.

Infancy and Early Childhood

Children in infancy and early childhood are more often sent to a developmental disabilities clinic than referred specifically for a psychiatrist's evaluation. Developmental delay is the main complaint, and appropriate specialists are usually involved. Psychiatric examination may be requested if the child is autistic-like, or the psychiatrist may see these children if he is part of an interdisciplinary evaluation team or a consultant to an early intervention program. Because of increased awareness of the need for early intervention and availability of preschool programs for special needs children, such services are offered early.

As pointed out by Eisenberg (1958), cognitive and emotional development are interdependent. This is well evidenced in young, retarded children. Retardation may influence emotional development directly, through basic disturbance in cognitive development, as well as indirectly, through modifying the environment, particularly parental attitudes. The child's slow responsiveness and phenotypic abnormalities, if any, may be factors interfering with the process of child-mother bonding (as noted by Emde and Brown (1978) and discussed in detail in Chapter 11). Some retarded children, however, may have quite normal early development and attachment (Cytryn and Lourie, 1975). Delayed acquisition of skills like walking, toilet training, and speech will delay development of independence, separation-individuation, and sense of mastery. How early the diagnosis of retardation is made and how it is conveyed to the family are crucial. Early diagnosis that is explained thoroughly, stresses the child's learning potential, and gives the parents an active role in promoting his development is essential. In reverse situations, parents may be told that their child will not be able to learn and there is nothing they can do for him. Decathexis or overprotection of such "hopeless" infants often follows, resulting in disorders such as withdrawal, depression, absent or exaggerated stranger anxiety, and poor or indiscriminate relatedness. If the diagnosis is delayed or equivocal, parents may be confused about their child's abilities and may overstimulate him beyond his capacities. Older toddlers may perceive parental dissatisfaction with them, thus laying the foundation for low self-esteem and sense of failure. Childhood autism may first be noticed at this age as severe developmental delay (Ornitz, 1973). The psychiatric evaluation in these cases has to focus considerably on exploring the existence and nature of child-parent bonding, availability of appropriate stimulation, and appropriateness of expectations. If retardation is diagnosed, the psychiatrist must assess the parents' potential to accept the diagnosis of the child's disability, and to accept and participate in education-rehabilitation plans. The mental health professional has here a rare opportunity for preventive work, since he is in a position to recognize children and families "at risk" for future maladjustment and design appropriate intervention.

School Period

Learning difficulties, behavior disturbances, and social maladjustment are leading complaints that bring retarded children to mental health clinics. A child may or may not be already conditioned to expect failure. The retardation may first be noticed and/or diagnosed during the early school years, particularly in the 75%–85% of cases that are only mildly retarded. At this stage the child faces a set of formidable challenges: separation, establishing peer relationships, academic learning, postponing gratification, learning self-control, tolerating frustration. A retarded child perceives his parents' dissatisfaction with his achievements (or lack of them) early and may interpret it as rejection. Parental overprotection and/or overstimulation and inappropriately high expectations may further handicap the child's development. Defects in cognition, concept formation, and motor skills handicap the child in his interactions with peers, who may reject and tease him, or at best accept and treat him as a younger child. The sum total is development of low self-esteem, expectation of failure, and dependency. These are compounded by society's (including the family's) view of the child as incompetent, which may become a self-fulfilling prophecy. The current practice of mainstreaming a retarded child in regular classes provides him with exposure to normal peers as role models, but also exposes him to rejection and confrontation with his own inadequacies. Regression to (or fixation in) safer early behavior patterns is a frequent defense. A variety of symptoms may bring these children to a mental health professional: chronic depression, school phobia, impulse disorder, dependency, lack of motivation, poor peer relationships, and socially inappropriate behaviors.

Adolescence and Adulthood

The age-appropriate and socially expected developmental challenge of adolescence may be insurmountable for one who has not accomplished tasks appropriate for an earlier developmental age. Since pubertal development is normal in most cases (especially with the mildly retarded), there is an anxiety-provoking discrepancy between somatic maturation and lack of psychological readiness, at times complicated by changes in neurological status, such as emergence of seizures. Increase in physical strength, if an individual is aggressive, may be anxiety provoking to the caregivers. The quest for autonomy is compromised by the lack of skills, dependency, ambivalence about separation, and cognitive and communication deficits, but the individual is often aware of what society expects of one his age. He may employ destructive defenses, such as acting out (antisocial, sexual, aggressive) or regression. Some go through pseudoadolescence, focusing on external adolescent behavior rather than on appropriate developmental tasks; they are often exploited by unscrupulous normal peers whom they yearn to emulate. Lack of friends and social isolation add to feelings of loneliness. Sexual ignorance is the rule, although sexuality may be seen (particularly by females) as one open avenue to proving one's normalcy. The failure of the struggle to develop a sense of identity will reaffirm an individual's low-self image. Parents must realize that retardation is permanent, and they need to plan for the child's future care in light of their own advancing age. They may feel perplexed and helpless. However, with appropriate resources and support, retarded adolescents may succeed surprisingly well and develop into adults with good vocational skills and considerable independence, who adapt well to normalized life in the community within their limitations (Edgerton and Bercovici, 1976; Birenbaum and Re, 1979). Floor et al. (1975) reported that about half of 54 married couples of retarded persons sustained marriage for several years with "a reasonable degree of competence," and they stressed the need for comprehensive services for this population. Social isolation remains a considerable problem for many retarded adults, however, especially if they live alone rather than in a community residence.

Retarded adolescents and adults can be afflicted with any form of mental disorder, as can nonretarded adolescents and adults. Depression is seen frequently. Psychotic decompensation may occur. This author has even treated anorexia nervosa in a 33-year-old female with Down's syndrome. Disturbed retarded persons of this age are frequently referred to mental health facilities because of behaviors disturbing to others in places of employment or in community residences where they live. Usually, behavior modification techniques have been unsuccessful and the psychiatrist may be asked only to prescribe psychotropic drugs (as a measure of last resort).

ASSESSMENT OF SYMPTOMATOLOGY AND FORMULATING THE DIAGNOSIS

A common mistake committed especially by psychiatrists is focusing excessively on diagnosing the retardation and neglecting the diagnosis of the patient's mental disorder. To be effective, the diagnostic formulations should focus on the patient's ego strengths as well as his deficiencies. The psychiatrist should not attempt to create an artificial dichotomy of "is he retarded or disturbed," but should assess to what degree binding the patient's psychic energy through inefficient defenses prevents him from maximally utilizing his cognitive abilities. The diagnostician should neither deny the presence of retardation (labeling it instead an emotionally based learning disability) nor lump all mental disorders under the rubric of retardation (Philips, 1966) and consider disordered behavior as part of retardation. In some instances, a trial treatment program including psychotherapy, education, environmental support, and drugs, is necessary for an accurate diagnosis.

Another common mistake is to assess the psychopathological significance of patients' symptomatology in the same way it would have been done with nonretarded patients of the same mental age. Mental age is not a concrete feature, but an artificial construct, averaging the level of functioning in various areas. A retarded 15-year-old adolescent with a mental age (MA) of 5 years is not like a 5-year-old child in physical development, self-image, life experiences, or expectations imposed on him. On the other hand, it may be permissible to see the "overactivity" of a 6-year-old with an MA of 3 years, who has recently started to walk, as the exploratory curiosity of a toddler. The pathological significance of a particular behavior is measured by the degree of its interference with the patient's functioning and self-fulfillment. A stereotypic mannerism could be an expression of deprivation as well as of psychosis, a neurological deficit, or depression. This topic is discussed extensively by Chess and Hassibi (1970) and Chess (1977). Chess and Hassibi (1970) stated ". . . youngsters whose overall adaptation is organized and pertinent, may exhibit behaviors that in an intellectually normal child of the same mental age would be an indication of serious psychopathology." They also discussed assessment of various behavior patterns noticed in a sample of 52 retarded children. Fifty-eight percent were considered overactive by their caregivers and teachers, but in many cases this did not reflect an abnormal degree of movement, but reflected inappropriate timing and context of the activity or even mere restlessness, if one considered the child's mental age. Aimless, repetitive motor activity (such as jumping, rocking) may occur often and need not be a sign of cerebral dysfunction or psychosis; it may be associated with otherwise positive adaptation. Such self-stimulatory and stereotypic behaviors are often reinforced by caregivers, who react by giving attention. In fact, some repetitive behaviors (e.g., bedtime rituals) could have been reinforced in order to facilitate the daily routine. For persons with reduced adaptive flexibility and cognitive ability, such routines may be a source of security through making the task more familiar. A variety of speech and language deviations from patterns expected for the chronological age can be noticed. Delays in speech development and articulation disorders are frequent. Retarded children often use the third person when speaking of themselves. This usually is not evidence of autistic disorder or other psychopathology, but rather of an early stage of language development. Sometimes parents treat their child as if he were much younger, and they actually encourage such use of personal pronouns. Echolalia and egocentric speech (such as asking questions of oneself and answering them, describing one's own current actions) usually represent the developmentally normal speech of younger children and may provide practice with newly acquired language skills or even imaginary companionship, if a real companion is hard to obtain. The language and thought processes may often reflect simplicity of emotional life (Webster, 1970), difficulties in conceptualizing, and lack of social experience. However, as pointed out by Rutter (1975), there is no evidence of mental retardation being associated with a particular personality type.

In summary, the diagnostician has to differentiate between the aspects of symptomatology related to physical handicaps that may be associated with retardation (e.g., "blindisms" of the blind); cognitive deficiencies; stimulation, education, and expectations that the patient has experienced; intrapsychic conflicts; and reactions to environmental stress and deprivation. The clinical manifestations should be interpreted in the context of the "reality of the patient." Withdrawn behavior may be a reaction to rejection by peers rather than part of a basic depression or psychosis. Primitive defenses employed by mentally retarded persons may be a function of their poor ability to conceptualize rather than evidence of essential psychopathology. Autistic behavior in severely retarded, multiply handicapped patients may be part of the autistic stage of development or a function of sensory deprivation, e.g., in a blind-deaf-retarded child, rather than a symptom of psychosis. Inability to follow the topic of the conversation may be because of primary attentional disorder rather than thought disorder or resistance. The following vignette illustrates these problems of differential diagnosis.

A mildly retarded 14-year-old boy talked during psychological testing about a girl in his head who "controlled" him. He was diagnosed as psychotic, but in a psychiatric interview no evidence of thought disorder was found. The boy told, with a smile, how the girl in his head was, of course, not real but that he had to invent her since, not having any friends, he needed someone to talk to.

SOME SPECIFIC DIAGNOSTIC PROBLEMS

Certain mental disorders may be more difficult to diagnose if the patient is mentally retarded. Psychosis may create diagnostic problems; this is discussed in Chapter 8. Another problematic area is the major affective disorders. It is now recognized that manic-depressive illness can occur in early adolescence (Carlson and Strober, 1978) and in retarded persons (Reid, 1972, 1976; Naylor et al., 1974; Rivinus and Harmatz, 1979). Reid (1976) pointed out that the clinical symptoms may be modified by the presence of retardation. Thus, manic wit may be lacking; flight of ideas may be rudimentary; the feelings may be acted out as aggression or self-abuse rather than being manifested directly as mood state or verbalized; and delusions may have a naïve content. With severely retarded persons, diagnosis of major affective disorders may be more difficult, but is possible with careful and prolonged observation of general behavior and physiological parameters. Reid and Naylor (1976) also described "short cycle" retarded patients with cyclical mood changes every 4 to 9 weeks. Accurate diagnosis of manic-depressive illness is important because it can respond to treatment with lithium (Adams, Kivowitz, and Ziskind, 1970; Naylor et al., 1974; Rivinus and Harmatz, 1979). Diagnosis of depression may be difficult if feelings are not verbalized, or if the primary manifestations are apathy, lack of motivation for learning and work, irritability, acting out, or eating and sleeping disorders.

Reid and Aungle (1974) and Reid (1976) drew attention to dementia in older retarded persons, which may be seen increasingly because of greater life expectancy (resulting from better medical care). For instance, Down's syndrome patients may show early neuropathological changes of Alzheimer's disease (Burger and Vogel, 1973). Careful history of functional deterioration, neurological examination, and EEG and CT studies may help in establishing the diagnosis.

The guidelines for formulating therapeutic recommendations should be clear from the foregoing discussion. Unfortunately, even now, therapeutic nihilism is prevalent in mental health clinics. It is based on the false belief that retarded persons cannot benefit from psychiatric treatment. This is based, in turn, on several misconceptions: 1) that all retarded persons should be put in one category (whereas, as pointed out by Potter (1964), mildly retarded persons have more in common with the nonretarded than with the severely retarded); 2) that psychiatric treatment means primarily verbal, individual, insight-oriented psychotherapy; and 3) that psychiatric disorders of retarded persons are irreversible parts of the retardation and are caused by "organicity" (Philips, 1966). Enough evidence has been accumulated in the literature concerning suitability of retarded persons for psychotherapy. The principle of a comprehensive, interdisciplinary approach discussed earlier applies to formulating the recommendations as well. They should take into account the total clinical picture (not merely the mental disorder) and recommendations of all relevant disciplines. Individual, group, or family psychotherapy, when warranted by the clinical picture, is appropriate for a retarded person (who may, in fact, benefit from it even more than a nonretarded one would). The existence of disturbed behavior should not, however, lead to an automatic recommendation of specific mental health intervention. In many cases, an environmental manipulation (casework with the family and appropriate educational, habilitative, and social support) is sufficient and more realistic. The diagnostician should be familiar with all relevant therapeutic approaches (such as behavior modification, pharmacotherapy, group therapy) in order to make an informed recommendation. The recommendations should be realistic, taking into account the family's financial situation, the availability of services in the patient's community, and attitudes of staffs of the schools and other agencies. Many mental health clinics will not offer psychotherapy to a person labeled retarded. The diagnostician may have to become an advocate to secure such services (if he has no possibility of providing them himself) and even an ad hoc consultant to train personnel not experienced with retarded persons. He should be familiar with the existing resources in his community, special education laws in his state, agencies like the Association for Retarded Citizens, mental retardation area boards, and state bureaus of mental retardation. Close work with the school and other pertinent agencies is necessary. Often the diagnostician coordinates their efforts and creates an ad hoc interdisciplinary team, if he is the best available person for this purpose.

It should be kept in mind that the patient will continue to encounter adaptational crises in subsequent developmental periods. The recommendations should always include appropriate preventive measures, such as long-term program planning and anticipatory guidance for the patient and his family.

REFERENCES

Adams, G. L., Kivowitz, J., and Ziskind, E. 1970. Manic depressive psychosis, mental retardation and chromosomal rearrangement. Arch. Gen. Psychiatry 23:305–309.

American Medical Association. 1965. Mental retardation: A handbook for the primary physician. JAMA 191:183–232.

Birenbaum, A., and Re, M. A. 1979. Resettling mentally retarded adults in the community—Almost 4 years later. Am. J. Ment. Defic. 83:323–339.

Burger, P. C., and Vogel, F. S. 1973. The development of the pathologic changes of Alzheimer's disease and senile dementia in patients with Down's syndrome. Am. J. Pathol. 73:457-468.

Carlson, G. A., and Strober, M. 1978. Manic-depressive illness in early adolescence: A study of clinical and diagnostic characteristics in six cases. J. Am. Acad. Child Psychiatry 17:138-153.

Chess, S. 1970. Emotional problems in mentally retarded children. In: F. J. Menolascino (ed.), Psychiatric Approaches to Mental Retardation. Basic Books, New York.

Chess, S. 1977. Evolution of behavior disorder in a group of mentally retarded children. J. Am. Acad. Child Psychiatry 16:5-18.

Chess, S., and Hassibi, M. 1970. Behavior deviations in mentally retarded children. J. Am. Acad. Child Psychiatry 9:282-297.

Clements, S. D. 1962. Minimal Brain Dysfunction in Children. DHEW, NINDB Monograph No. 3, Washington, D.C.

Cytryn, L., and Lourie, R. S. 1975. Mental retardation. In: A. M. Freedman, H. I. Kaplan, and B. J. Sadock (eds.), Comprehensive Textbook of Psychiatry. Williams & Wilkens Co., Baltimore.

Diagnostic and Statistical Manual of Mental Disorders (DSM III). 1980. American Psychiatric Association, Washington, D.C.

Edgerton, R. B., and Bercovici, S. M. 1976. The cloak of competence: Years later. Am. J. Ment. Defic. 80:485-497.

Eisenberg, L. 1958. Emotional determinants of mental deficiency. AMA Arch. Neurol. Psychiatry 80:114-121.

Emde, R. N., and Brown, C. 1978. Adaptation to the birth of a Down's syndrome infant: Grieving and maternal attachment. J. Am. Acad. Child Psychiatry 17: 299-323.

Floor, L., Baxter, D., Rosen, M., and Zisfein, L. 1975. A survey of marriages among previously institutionalized retardates. Ment. Retard. 13:33-37.

Freud, A. 1965. Normality and Pathology in Childhood. International Universities Press, New York.

Garrard, S. D., and Richmond, J. B. 1965. Diagnosis in mental retardation, and mental retardation without biological manifestations. In: C. H. Carter (ed.), Medical Aspects of Mental Retardation. Charles C Thomas Publisher, Springfield, Ill.

Gruenberg, E. M., and Kiev, A. 1967. The age distribution of mental retardation. In: J. Zubin and G. A. Jervis (eds.), Psychopathology of Mental Development. Grune & Stratton, New York.

Gruenberg, E. M., and Turns, D. M. 1975. Science of human behavior: Quantitative experimental and research methods in psychiatry. In: A. M. Freedman, H. I. Kaplan, and B. J. Sadock (eds.), Comprehensive Textbook of Psychiatry. 3rd ed. Williams & Wilkins Co., Baltimore.

Jakab, I. 1970. Psychotherapy of the mentally retarded child. In: N. R. Bernstein (ed.), Diminished People. Little, Brown & Co., Boston.

Menolascino, F. J. 1965. Emotional disturbance and mental retardation. Am. J. Ment. Defic. 70:248-256.

Menolascino, F. J. 1966. The facade of mental retardation. Am. J. Psychiatry 122:1227-1235.

Menolascino, F. J., and Bernstein, N. R. 1970. Psychiatric assessment of the mentally retarded child. In: N. R. Bernstein (ed.), Diminished People. Little, Brown & Co., Boston.

Naylor, G. J., Donald, J. M., Le Poidevin, D., and Reid, A. H. 1974. A double blind trial of long term lithium therapy in mental defectives. Br. J. Psychiatry 124:52-57.

Ornitz, E. M. 1973. Childhood autism—A review of the clinical and experimental literature. Calif. Med. 118:21-47.

Philips, I. 1966. Children, mental retardation, and emotional disorder. In: I. Philips (ed.), Prevention and Treatment of Mental Retardation. Basic Books, New York.

Philips, I., and Williams, N. 1975. Psychopathology and mental retardation: A study of 100 mentally retarded children. I. Psychopathology. Am. J. Psychiatry 132:1265-1271.

Potter, H. W. 1964. The needs of mentally retarded children for child psychiatry services. J. Am. Acad. Child Psychiatry 3:352-374.

Pueschel, S. M., and Murphy, A. 1977. Assessment of counseling practices at the birth of a child with Down's syndrome. Am. J. Ment. Defic. 81:325-330.

Rakoff, V. M., Stancer, H. C., and Kedward, H. B. (eds.). 1977. Psychiatric Diagnosis. Brunner/Mazel, New York.

Reid, A. H. 1972. Psychosis in adult mental defectives. I. Manic-depressive psychosis. Br. J. Psychiatry 120:205-212.

Reid, A. H. 1976. Psychiatric disturbances in the mentally handicapped. Proc. Royal Soc. Med. 69:509-512.

Reid, A. H., and Aungle, P. G. 1974. Dementia in ageing mental defectives: A clinical psychiatric study. J. Ment. Defic. Res. 18:15-23.

Reid, A. H., and Naylor, G. J. 1976. Short cycle manic depressive psychosis in mental defectives: A clinical and physiological study. J. Ment. Defic. Res. 20: 67-76.

Richmond, J. B., and Garrard, S. D. 1966. Some current concepts of mental retardation. In: I. Philips (ed.), Prevention and Treatment of Mental Retardation. Basic Books, New York.

Rivinus, T. M., and Harmatz, J. S. 1979. Diagnosis and lithium treatment of affective disorder in the retarded: Five case studies. Am. J. Psychiatry 136: 551-554.

Rutter, M. I. 1975. Psychiatric disorder and intellectual impairment in childhood. Br. J. Psychiatry 9:344-348.

Rutter, M. I., Graham, P. J., and Yule, W. 1970. A neuropsychiatric study in childhood. Clin. Dev. Med. 35-36.

Rutter, M. I., Lebovici, S., Eisenberg, L., Sneznevskij, A. V., Sadoun, R., Brooke, E., and Tsung-Yi, L. 1969. A tri-axial classification of mental disorders in childhood. J. Child Psychol. Psychiatry 10:41-61.

Spitzer, R. L., and Wilson, P. T. 1975. Nosology and the official psychiatric nomenclature. In: A. M. Freedman, H. I. Kaplan, and B. J. Sadock (eds.), Comprehensive Textbook of Psychiatry. 3rd ed. Williams & Wilkins Co., Baltimore.

Szymanski, L. S. 1977. Psychiatric diagnostic evaluation of mentally retarded individuals. J. Am. Acad. Child Psychiatry 16:67-87.

Tisza, V. B., Irwin, E., and Scheide, E. 1973. Children with oral-facial clefts. J. Am. Acad. Child Psychiatry 12:292-313.

Webster, T. G. 1970. Unique aspects of emotional development in mentally retarded children. In: F. J. Menolascino (ed.), Psychiatric Approaches to Mental Retardation. Basic Books, New York.

Wing, J. K. 1963. Survey methods and the clinical psychiatrist. In: P. Sainsbury and N. Kreitman (eds.), Methods of Psychiatric Research. Oxford University Press, London.

Woodward, K. F., Jaffe, N., and Brown, D. 1970. Early psychiatric intervention for young mentally retarded children. In: F. J. Menolascino (ed.), Psychiatric Approaches to Mental Retardation. Basic Books, New York.

COGNITIVE DEVELOPMENT: Neuropsychological Basis and Clinical Assessment

Chapter 7

Peter E. Tanguay

Traditionally, and with good reason, the intellectual capacity of the mentally retarded or developmentally disabled child has been assessed using standardized psychometric tests. Despite their well-known shortcomings, such tests do provide a statistically reliable means of judging a child's performance in relation to that of a relatively large number of other children in his age group. In the hands of an experienced psychologist, such assessment can provide a wealth of information, not only about what the child can or cannot do, but about the manner in which sociocultural, emotional, and motivational factors may influence his performance. All too often, however, the clinician who sees the child (especially at the time of the initial visit) is given little more than a stark set of psychometric test scores to guide his understanding of the child's personality and behavior, and at times he may receive no test data at all. Clinicians are not only interested in what a child cannot do, but *why* he cannot do it. Clearly there is a need for good *clinical* methods of assessing cognitive development: methods that are open ended and flexible, can be used in the office or playroom, do not require elaborate and costly materials, and are fun for the child to experience. Most veteran clinicians have developed their own idiosyncratic approaches to the task, many of which may be ingenious and useful. Such clinical methods are not meant to supplant standardized psychometric testing, any more than a standard psychiatric assessment of mental and emotional status is meant to supplant projective testing or the Minnesota Multiphasic Personality Inventory (MMPI). Each form of assessment provides a particular set of data about a patient, data that are complementary and necessary for an overall understanding of the person.

THEORETICAL FRAMEWORK

In order to carry out assessment, clinicians must begin with a clear understanding of the phenomena to be measured. Such an understanding may range from a set of data outlining the limits of normal function to complex theoretical models (as in the case of psychoanalysis) that map the internal structure and organization of the phenomena in question. For cognitive development, there exists only one comprehensive model, that of Swiss psychologist Jean Piaget. Piaget's model is especially relevant to clinical work because of the unique clinical approach that underlies its development. Although Piaget's first formal experiences in psychology were with the pioneering psychometrician Simon in Paris, he soon found that he was more interested in why a child failed a test item than he was in the child's specific test scores. Later, at the Burgholzli clinic in Zurich, he observed clinicians using flexible, nondirective interview techniques. The patient was allowed to lead the interview into areas of psychological importance, while the interviewer closely followed his statements and his behavior, hypothesizing their dynamic or diagnostic meaning, and testing these hypotheses with incisive questions at the appropriate moments. Piaget at once realized the exciting possibilities that the method held of learning about how children think. His adaptation of the clinical method was the cornerstone upon which much of his subsequent work was built. Although this work was begun around 1920 and has touched upon numerous epistomological and philosophical issues, the part that remains of greatest interest to practicing clinicians is his earlier work, in which he explored the stages in which cognitive development takes place.

Stages of Cognitive Development

Although initially Piaget's findings were looked upon with some suspicion by the then-reigning experts in psychological research because of his unorthodox methodology and because his conclusions were not based upon statistical analyses of data, subsequent investigations have largely supported his overall statements regarding the stages of cognitive development and their content. Work during the 1970s may have suggested some modifications of his viewpoints, but the stage theory remains intact. Readers wishing a more detailed understanding of Piaget's work than can be given in this chapter are urged to consult a general textbook on Piaget's earlier ideas (e.g., Flavell, 1978), an anthology of his writings (e.g., Gruber and Voneche, 1977), or Piaget's original books, many of which are now available as English translations in paperback. The titles of a number of these books are given in the final section of this chapter (A Selection of Piagetian Tasks).

Piaget described cognitive development as taking place across three periods. The child's cognitive functions within each period are quantitatively and qualitatively different. The young child understands the world not as an ignorant adult, but as a person who uses an entirely different form of reasoning to solve problems and understand events.

Periods, in Piaget's framework, differ along two dimensions. The first involves whether the child's cognitive operations are carried out *externally* or *internally*. External operations, which are the sole mode of cognition in very young children, involve trial-and-error learning through motor manipulation under the guidance of sensory feedback. Internal operations, in contrast, are carried out entirely in imagination. The second dimension involves whether the cognitive activity concerns ideas, objects, or events that are *concrete* or *abstract*. Piaget used *concrete* to mean something that has a real (as opposed to a hypothetical) existence and *abstract* to imply the possible or that which can be hypothesized.

Period of Sensorimotor Operations (Birth to 18–24 Months)   At the end of the sensorimotor period the child must be relatively competent in dealing with concrete objects using external operations (or *schemata*). The period is further subdivided into six stages. In Stage 1, which extends from birth to approximately 1 month, the child's behaviors are largely reflexive, albeit that from the first day of life these reflexes have begun to "adapt." A good clinical example of adaptation has been given by Call (1964). Initially, the sucking reflex is primarily elicited by preoral stimulation, and it unfolds as a relatively stereotyped series of movements. Very soon after birth, however, through exercise of the reflex on whatever objects are given to the child to suck, the reflex begins to be elicited by a wider variety of stimuli and the child's sucking behaviors change to better conform to the shape of the object. This adaptation is greatly facilitated during Stage 2 (stage of primary circular reactions), when the infant appears driven to exercise all of his reflex schemata repetitively and continuously, seemingly for the sheer pleasure such exercise gives him. Because of this behavior the schemata will by chance come to be exercised upon many different objects and situations in his environment, thus increasing the likelihood that useful adaptations will take place. By the fourth month the infant begins to exhibit behaviors of Stage 3 (stage of secondary circular reactions). No longer is the infant content to merely exercise his schemata as schemata; he now appears to be especially interested in using the schemata to "make things happen" around him. Each success he achieves in this appears to prompt further exercise of the schema in a repetitive, circular fashion. The infant, for instance, is no longer content to grasp and release his rattle in a repetitive manner for long periods of time, but wishes to shake it and listen to the sound, bang it on hard surfaces, or wave it within his field of vision. By 8 months of age such combinations of motor and audiovisual schemata become more and more complex. During Stage 4 between 8 and 12 months, development and combination of schemata continue to the point at which, by 12 months, children are capable of solving problems involving multiple sensory cues. Between 8 and 12 months children also begin to show evidence of more complex memory stores: they can recognize strangers and can anticipate events. Thus, when mother puts on her coat, the child may begin to cry, indicating he know this to be a sign of her imminent absence.

During Stage 5, between 12 and 18 months of age, the child's behavior again undergoes a gradual change in overall goals. Where the child had previously been content to "make things happen" in a relatively unvarying and repetitive fashion, now he begins to systematically vary certain behaviors, while watching closely the effect this will produce. Previously, the child may have been delighted to keep dropping a ball from his high chair for the sheer pleasure of watching it bounce; now he will vary the dropping behavior, first to the left, then to the right, onto the carpeted portion of the floor, onto the floor next to the carpet. The child carefully watches to see the results each time. He may experiment in a similar manner with other persons, varying his behaviors and observing their responses. Such experimental behavior, while conducted entirely at a sensorimotor level, obviously has the potential to dramatically increase the child's understanding of the world of people and objects.

At some point in the second half of the second year, during Piaget's Stage 6 of the sensorimotor period, a new and totally different order of cognitive function becomes possible. For the first time the child shows clear-cut evidence that he can solve problems *internally,* using thought. This event marks the end of the sensorimotor period and the beginning of the period of concrete operations.

Period of Concrete Operations   This period is divided into two different subperiods, the preoperational (lasting until 6 or 7 years of age) and the operational (which continues from age 6 or 7 to approximately age 11). The main task that the child must accomplish during the period of concrete operations is to learn to deal with *concrete* reality using *internal* cognitive schemata.

During the preoperational subperiod, the child displays a curious form of cognitive endeavor, which Piaget termed *synchretic* thought. As Piaget described it, synchretic thought was not logical, it could not deal with cause-and-effect relationships, it was not reversible, and it was inflexible. It was as if the child equated objects and events on the basis of what accidental qualities each might have in common, or on the basis of their contiguous relationship. Asked what makes the water flow in a river upon whose banks he is standing, a 3½-year-old child may reply with great confidence that it is the boulders on the river bed that are responsible for the flow, or the sunlight that reflects off the water. Young children are *egocentric* in their thinking, acting as if their personal thought is all that exists, or as if others think exactly as they do. This makes it very difficult for 2- and 3-year-old children to have many meaningful exchanges of information as they play together. When a material is transformed before their eyes in one way or another (such as when a liquid is poured from a tall, narrow glass to a short, wide one), they will tend to *centrate* on one particular aspect of the situation (such as the height of the old column or the width of the new one) in arriving at a decision on whether the quantity, weight, or volume of the material has remained constant. This example shows the child's inability to reverse the operation in his mind, or to reason that if one subtracts from one dimension but adds equally to another, the transformations sum to zero.

Beginning around 5 or 6 years of age, however, children start to show greater flexibility in their thinking and an ability to learn to reason in a protological manner. The next few years are cognitively very exciting ones for the child as he begins to understand how objects and events relate to each other, or how they can be classified into systems that make clear the logical relationships between the various objects or events.

Period of Formal Operations   Between 10 and 12 years of age, children undergo a final transformation in their cognitive capacity. This transformation relates both to the level at which solutions are sought and the manner in which problems are attached. For the first time children begin to deal with abstract as well as concrete reality. They are able to learn the abstract meaning of proverbs and to understand problems involving laws of chance. Moreover, they no longer rush impulsively to seek a solution, compounding variables and confusing relationships in the process, but are more likely to step back, cast hypotheses of what the solutions might be, and then systematically attempt to test each hypothesis. An example of the above is given by an experiment in which four flasks of colorless liquid are placed before the child. Flask A contains dilute sulphuric acid; flask B, water; flask C, oxygenated water; and flask D, thiosulphate. A small bottle containing potassium iodide (KI) is also placed before the child. The mixture A + C + KI yields a yellow color. Adding B to the mixture will not change the color, but adding D will bleach the color. The subject is given one glass containing A + C and another containing B. The experimenter demonstrates the effect of adding a few drops of KI to each. He then invites the child to reproduce the yellow color using the four flasks of liquid and the KI. Preoperational children will attempt to solve the problem by randomly mixing solutions, soon confusing themselves in the process and failing to find an answer. Older children, those who are capable of concrete operations, will mix the solutions one by one, learning the effects of certain combinations, but failing to grasp the overall combination scheme. Only those children who have reached the stage of formal operations will plan their attack: working out a logical system of combinations that will include all permutations and combinations of solutions. Even more important, when faced with an unexpected event (e.g., combination of A + C + D will prevent formation of a color when KI is added), they will be able to reflect upon this, hypothesize various "if...then" explanations, and work out ways of testing each of the latter hypotheses in turn.

Neuropsychological Factors in Cognitive Development

Why is it that there are qualitatively different stages in development, and how are we to explain individual stage characteristics? It is not simply a lack of adequate instruction, because attempts to train a preoperational child to solve problems using operational schemata invariably end in failure. Although the child may learn the rote answer to any one specific problem, further testing will reveal that the solution fails to generalize to other similar problems. It is as if the child lacks a capacity for certain types of cognitive operations, this lack being a result of developmental immaturity.

Neuropsychological studies within the past few decades have led to the development of certain models and theories that may bear upon the subject. Ontogenetically, the model that Luria (1973) proposed is of particular interest. Luria's model was clinically derived, and it treats brain-and-behavior issues from a relatively global viewpoint. Luria conceives of the brain as composed of three parallel systems, each with its own internal hierarchical organization, and each closely interactive with the other. The phylogenetically oldest system is the "system for the maintenance of cortical tone," responsible for many autonomic and vegetative functions, for short-term memory, for emotional and appetitive phenomena, and as a central mechanism in determining state of consciousness along the sleep-wake continuum. The system is located in the brainstem, in the centrencephalic regions, and in medial cortical areas (including the limbic circuit). The second and third systems are located on the lateral convex surfaces of the hemispheres. The second, or analyzer, system includes the primary analyzer regions of each sensory modality, as well as secondary and tertiary analyzer systems, which correspond to what other investigators have referred to as the association cortex. The third system, which is responsible for the organization of behavioral output, is found in the frontal cortex. It is also organized into primary, secondary, and tertiary subsystems. The tertiary level is located in the prefrontal cortex, and in man is very important for the production of complex behavioral responses, including speech. Luria contends that it is in man that the tertiary analyzer and tertiary organizer systems reach their highest development, considerably surpassing that found in even the higher primates. Borrowing from the work of his Russian colleagues, Luria (1973, p. 87) asserts that the tertiary cortex undergoes considerable development after birth. In the case of the tertiary organizer cortex, the rate of increase in area of the prefrontal cortex rises sharply from birth to 2 years of age, continuing to develop at a less accelerated rate until approximately 6 years of age. Luria also contends that there are two distinct peaks in maturation of various types of cells in this part of the brain: one around 2 years of age and a second around age 7.

Parallel to this and of equal importance to understanding cognitive development, there arises in the human brain the additional phenomenon of *hemispheric specialization*. Although first described by degree to which receptive and expressive speech mechanisms were found in the temporo-parietal and inferior prefrontal areas of the left hemisphere, considerable work within the past two decades has suggested that the left hemisphere is in fact specialized for "sequential" decoding and encoding operations, of which speech (in which information is coded in a sequential code) is only one example. The right hemisphere, in contrast, appears specialized for "holistic" processing of information, as exemplified by such tasks as recognizing forces, solving block design puzzles, and the like. The ontogeny of hemispheric specialization is only partly understood. It is known that even at birth certain features of the left temporal region are consistently different from those of the right temporal region (Rubens, Mahowald, and Hutton, 1976; Yeni-Komshian and Benson, 1976), and that by 4 to 5 years of age the left hemisphere is already specialized for processing speech (Kimura, 1963; Piazza, 1977).

Based upon Luria's model, and upon the work of neuropsychologists in the field of hemispheric specialization, one may speculate on what neural organization may underlie the observations of Piaget and other psychologists regarding periods in cognitive development. It is tempting to consider that maturation of tertiary analyzer and organizer systems, which ontogenetically are relatively immature until at least 18 months of age, may underlie transition from sensorimotor to internal problem-solving operations. Such maturation in all probability does not involve only tertiary cortical regions, but extends to all subcortical systems (in the thalamus or basal ganglia) that may be closely linked to the tertiary cortex.

Beyond 2 years of age, further development of the tertiary cortex of the left hemisphere (development that is perhaps not complete until 6 years of age) may be necessary before children can learn internal operational schemata, characteristic of Piaget's second subperiod of the period of concrete operations. The degree to which this development permits the emergence of sequential information processing operations is especially relevant to Piaget's model. Holistic processing appears to be quite similar to "synchretic" thought, while the ability to carry out "sequential" operations could well underlie the "reversibility" and "flexibility" of thought that Piaget described as characteristic of children's cognition after 5 or 6 years of age.

Clinical Assessment

The informal clinical assessment of a person's level of cognitive development need not necessarily involve administration of specific tests, but can, in a rough sense, be based upon observation of the person's everyday behaviors. Specifically, one wishes to note evidence of cognitive behaviors characteristic of one or more of the stages or periods described previously. The manner in which very young children interact with others and deal with objects in their environment should be observed over a period of time to provide a general estimate of their level of development. The way in which somewhat older children are able to solve problems without engaging in trial-and-error methods and the extent to which they can engage in representational play will provide information about their capacity for internal thought. With children or retarded adults who are at least at a late preoperational subperiod, specific tasks can be included in the evaluation, or the interviewer can ask questions and observe the responses. A small sample of such tasks, derived from the writings of Piaget, are outlined in the next section. The aim is to identify the highest level at which the person can function, realizing that at all stages of development (including formal operations), cognitive behaviors belonging to lower stages may normally be in evidence. It must also be emphasized that the clinical opinions reached as a result of such informal assessment procedures can never replace psychometric testing, nor can they be used alone to establish a diagnosis of mental retardation.

A further series of warnings must be given in regard to informal cognitive assessment. The clinician must always be looking for *why* a person behaves as he does when attempting to deal with his environment. The specific conclusions that a person reaches and the strategies he may use in solving problems are important insofar as they *suggest* the level of functioning, but the degree to which this suggestion may be accepted as true must always be verified by further questioning. Asking the person to explain why he answered as he did, asking for proof of the answer in question, and, above all, seeming to be genuinely puzzled (and perhaps also a bit dense) as the person explains his conclusions are strategies that the clinician may often find useful, especially when the person being tested has not yet reached the stage of formal operations. After the interviewer is fairly certain of the cognitive level at which the person is functioning, he may need to ascertain how close the person is to functioning at the next higher level. This can be done by making suggestions, giving clues, or by otherwise trying to lead the person to the next higher level. Conversely, it may be important to identify how well a person has gained a foothold at a particular level. This may be revealed by asking, for example, about perceptually confounding information ("But look at how *high* this column of water is in comparison to that one") and noting his response. Above all, the clinician must guard against the beginner's common mistake of asking leading questions, which may force the person being studied into giving a particular answer. The clinician should not ask, for instance, "Do you think that this glass has *more* water in it than that one?" but rather, "Do you think this glass has the same, more, or less water than that one?" The question could even, for good measure, be repeated later with the possibilities presented in a different order.

Although in the author's experience the estimated level of cognitive function, when expressed as an estimate of mental age, will be roughly similar to that identified by formal psychometric testing, there are certain differences between the findings of informal cognitive testing and psychometric assessment in retarded or psychotic individuals. These differences are largely because most psychometric tests measure both rote knowledge and the person's problem-solving abilities. A 12-year-old retarded child who has received extensive educational treatment may have developed a vocabulary and have learned the correct answers to certain questions, so that cursory examination of his overall IQ score indicates he may be only mildly retarded. Examination of his problem-solving abilities may sometimes reveal that he is barely able to use concrete operations at the 7- or 8-year-old level. Inhelder (1968) found that while retarded children follow the same order of stages in the Piagetian scheme, they did so at a slower rate. Severely retarded children may cease development while still in the sensorimotor or early preoperational period, whereas moderately retarded people will at best only reach the earlier stages of concrete operations. Mildly retarded people should be able to use concrete cognitive operations to solve even the more difficult "classification" tasks, which is given in the next section. Christ (1977) found that many autistic children could not perform at a level higher than Stage 5 or early Stage 6 of the sensorimotor period, even when they were in late childhood or early adolescence. Schmid-Kitsikis (1969), studying a higher functioning group of psychotic children (most of whom were probably autistic and all of whom were verbal), found remarkable inconsistencies in their thought processes, to the extent that the children often simultaneously denied and accepted a concept as true.

A SELECTION OF PIAGETIAN TASKS

A very brief selection of tasks used by Piaget is given below. The selection is meant to provide typical examples of the Piagetian approach. It is biased in the direction of being primarily useful with persons who are functioning in the late preoperational and early concrete operational subperiods. Clinicians who wish to become expert in using Piagetian tasks and those who wish to test higher and lower functioning persons must consult specialized sources (Flavell, 1973; Gruber and Voneche, 1977), where they will find Piaget's tasks described in much greater number and detail than is possible in a single chapter of a general text. The ages at which children deal with the tasks in specific ways are included below, but clinicians must realize that as they use the tasks and become expert in how children think, they will develop a "feel" for what is cognitively normal or abnormal in children and adults. Idiosyncratic methods of using the tasks may shift the age norms given below to some degree, which is not important if the clinician learns through experience how individuals perform when *he* administers the task.

In addition to assessing a person's cognitive level, the clinician should remain alert to many other important factors that influence the results: the degree of motivation and effort expended by the person, his discouragement or confidence in approaching the task, the persistence with which a solution is sought, and so forth. All of these are essential to interpreting the person's results.

Task 1:   *Conservation of Quantity of Liquid*

Source   Piaget, J. 1965. *The Child's Conception of Number.* W. W. Norton & Co., New York. pp. 3–24.

Materials   Two tall, narrow glass containers of equal size; one smaller, wider glass container; several small glass containers.

Method   Fill partially one tall glass container with water and ask the child to fill the identical container with the same amount or as much water. When he has done this and agrees each container holds an equal amount, divide the water from one of the two containers in various ways: 1) pour all of it into the smaller, wider container, 2) pour it into several small glass containers, or 3) pour some into one or more small containers and leave some in the original container. Each time ask the child whether he thinks the liquid (in the wide, shallow container, in the several small containers, etc.) is the same amount as is present in the remaining tall, narrow container. Ask him to justify and explain his answer.

Results   *Stage 1 (ages 4–5):*   Children believe that the quantity varies according to the number or size of the container. They may explain that there is less water in the wide, shallow container because it is less high.

Stage 2 (ages 6–7):   As children move into the period of concrete operations, they become capable of mentally reversing an operation they have just witnessed and seeing the relationship between complementary operations and such. They are then able to solve the problem correctly.

Task 2:   **Conservation of Distance**

Source   Piaget, J., Inhelder, B., and Szeminska, A. 1960. *The Child's Conception of Geometry.* Basic Books, New York. pp. 71–89.

Materials   Two small figures; a set of blocks that can be stacked into various sizes of barriers; a thin cardboard barrier.

Method   Place the two figures approximately 20 inches apart on a table. Ask the child, "Are they near to each other?" or "Are they far apart?" It is important to avoid using reference to movement or distance traveled, and the figures should remain in the same place throughout the task. When the child has replied that the figures are near or are far apart, place the thin cardboard barrier between the objects, and ask the child whether they are still as near or as far apart, and press him to give a reason for his answer. Next, replace the screen with a series of barriers (some broad, some narrow) built from the wooden blocks. Each time question the child as described.

Results   *Stage 1 (age 5):*   Children believe that the distance changes when a barrier is introduced between the two figures. Most think the interval is less. Once the barrier is introduced, children appear to lose all understanding of an overall distance between the two figures.

Stage 2 (age 6):   At first children recognize the overall distance between the two figures, but believe that it is less when the screen is introduced because the space taken up by the screen itself must be subtracted.

Stage 3 (age 7):   Conservation of distance is achieved.

Task 3:   **Concepts of Time, Age, and Growth**

Source   Piaget, J. 1971. *The Child's Conception of Time.* Ballantine Books, New York. pp. 219–250.

Materials   None.

Method   Begin by asking the child his age. Then inquire about brothers, sisters, or friends (their age, are they younger or older than he is, were they born before or after he was, when he grows up will they be younger or older than he (and by how many years). Ask for justification for his answers. Next inquire about his mother and father (are they older or younger than he is, born before or after him, when he grows up will they be younger or older than he, do they continue to get older). Then inquire about his grandparents (are they younger or older than his parents, were they born before or after his parents). Finally, ask whether trees, small dogs, flowers, or stones grow older.

Results   Preoperational children are not at all adept at logical, sequential thought, and as a result they have static and almost discontinuous ideas of aging and the passage of time. They may equate growing in size with growing old (and, in keeping with this, may say that older people do not grow old), and may fail to grasp that age differences between people remain constant.

Stage 1 (ages 4–5):   Children may believe that age is independent of order of birth, and that age differences may be modified by time. Some children may not know if they were born before or after their parents, or may claim that they will be as old as their parents when they grow up.

Stage 2 (ages 6–7):   Two types of understanding may be seen: either children believe that age depends on order of birth but that age differences do not remain constant, or that age differences are maintained but do not depend on birth order.

Stage 3 (age 8):   Duration and succession become coordinated, and children can deal correctly with concepts of aging and the order of births.

Similarly, until 7–8 years of age, children confuse ideas of aging of plants, animals, and so on, with size, believing that aging ceases when maximum size is attained.

Task 4:   ***Complementary Classes: The Singular Class***

Source   Piaget, J., and Inhelder, B. *The Early Growth of Logic in the Child.* Routledge & Kegan Paul, London, 1964, pp. 125–129.

Materials   Four large red squares, four small red squares, three large red circles, four small red circles, one large blue circle, one large blue square, one small blue circle, one small blue square.

Method   Show the subject all of the material except the large blue square, the small blue square, and the small blue circle. Proceed through the following questions: 1) Ask the subject to classify the objects as he likes ("Arrange them in some order," "Put together what goes together," "Put together what is alike," "Put the same things together"). If he fails to do this correctly, ask him to divide the objects into two groups. 2) When he has finished making his first groups, ask him to redivide them, using another criterion ("Do you have any other ideas on how these objects could be divided?" "Can you divide them up in a different way?") 3) When he has done this, ask him to divide them using a third criterion. 4) If the child has not yet classified by color, add the three additional blue objects (large square, small square, and small circle), and again ask him to divide the objects using a third criterion.

Results   Children have considerable difficulty in admitting that there is such a thing as a singular class. At 5 or 6 years of age, children may have difficulty constructing even two classes in the exercise, and it is only by 7 or 8 years that they begin to construct all three classes, and initially they do so only after the additional blue objects have been added to the group.

Task 5: **Understanding of Movement and Speed**

Composition of Displacement: Train on parallel tracks.

Source   Piaget, J. 1970. *The Child's Conception of Movement and Speed.* Ballantine Books, New York. pp. 81–100. (This task is an adaptation rather than a copy of the original task.)

Materials   Pencil and paper; small blocks or other markers.

Method   Draw two parallel tracks on paper to represent two railway lines. One track (A) has several railway stations, the other (B) has a station at either end. There is one train on each track, represented by a marker.

The train on track B makes a journey from one end to the other without stopping. It then returns without stopping to its starting point. Ask the child: "Did the train travel farther on its initial or return journey, or did it travel equal distances?" Curve the paper so that the first half is an upward slope and the second half is a downward slope. Repeat the journey, and then repeat the question. Next have the train on track A carry out a journey stopping at each station, while train B travels again nonstop. Ask: "Did one train travel farther than the other?"

Results   For most young children, an upward journey represents a farther distance than a downward one, and a journey with several stops is farther than a nonstop one. By ages 6–7 children begin to give correct answers, showing a decrease in centration (decrease in synchretic thought and beginning of logical operations).

Task 6: **Classification by Shapes and Colors**

Source   Inhelder, B., and Piaget, J. 1964. *The Early Growth of Logic in the Child.* Routledge & Kegan Paul, London. pp. 60–74.

Materials   Red squares, blue squares, and blue circles.

Method   Present child with a randomly arranged series of red squares, blue squares, and blue circles. Ask him first to name the objects. To check perception and memory you may ask him to reproduce the row, doing so with the original series visible or hidden. To check his understanding of class inclusion, ask the following series of questions: 1) "Are all the circles blue?" 2) "Are all the red ones square?" 3) "Are all the blue ones circles?" 4) "Are all the squares red?" Depending on child's answer, you may ask, "Are *some* of the red ones circles?" and so on. Be flexible in questioning in order to explore the child's ability to deal with the interaction of the two classes in question: shape and color.

Results   As would be expected, children's ability to solve class inclusion problems is relatively poor around 5 or 6 years and becomes relatively good by age 9 or 10. (Sample results for a group of children are shown on page 63 of the source.)

Younger children tend to give inconsistent answers, with correct and incorrect intermixed. Look for facility and alacrity in answering these questions and whether child has overall facility for quickly solving the problem.

Task 7:   *Seriations with Visually Perceived Elements*

Source   Inhelder, B., and Piaget, J. 1964. *The Early Growth of Logic in the Child.* Routledge & Kegan Paul, London. pp. 250–261.

Materials   Ten rods ranging in length from 9 to 16.2 cm in increments of 0.8 cm. These can be constructed of cardboard strips or (preferably) from $1/8$- or $1/4$-inch wooden dowels, obtainable at most home improvement centers and lumber shops.

Method   Randomly scatter the set of rods in front of the child. Then say, "Try to arrange these sticks from the smallest to the largest. Can you guess what that will look like? Try to draw what it will look like on this sheet of paper." (This is done to test the child's ability to anticipate the result.) When he has finished his drawing, ask the child to actually arrange the rods from the largest to the smallest. Watch how he does it.

Results   Visual seriation using this type of material does not develop until 7–8 years of age.

Stage 1 (ages 3–4 years): Children cannot anticipate the series in their drawings, nor can they construct it. They may draw a few uncoordinated pairs or, occasionally, a series of unrelated lines.

Stage 2 (ages 5-6 years):   Children can depict the correct seriation in their drawings—occasionally after two or three tries, but sometimes immediately. However, their performance of seriation using the actual rods may be only approximate and is by trial and error. (The solution of the latter problem implies reversibility of thought: finding the smallest element, then the smallest element among those that remain, always checking to see that a given element is both longer than those already in the series and shorter than those to follow. The drawing itself is carried out by simply constructing a series of longer and longer lines, without any need to make a comparison between pairs.)

Stage 3 (ages 7-8 years):   Children not only complete the drawing correctly, but carry out the seriation task with assurance and alacrity.

Task 8: **Moral Judgment, Attribution of Blame**

Source   Piaget, J. 1965. *The Moral Judgment of the Child.* The Free Press, New York. pp. 121–138.

Materials   None.

Method   Tell the child that you have a number of stories you would like to tell him. Here are some suggested ones (although any similar stories may be substituted):

There was once a boy named John. One night his mother asked him if he would help her set the table for supper. He got up to get some dishes out of the cupboard, but when he opened the cupboard door, a stack of cups fell right out, and before he knew it, 15 cups lay broken on the floor! There was another boy named Charles, and one day when he was in the kitchen alone with nothing to do, he decided to play with some cups on the kitchen table. Now his mother had told him never to do this, but Charles did do it anyway, and before he knew it, one cup fell on the floor and was broken.

Ask the child at this point to repeat the main ideas in the story. Then say, "If you were the mother of John or of Charles, what would you say to them?" Ask the child to justify his answers, and keep exploring them until you are satisfied that you understand his reasoning. If the child fails to consider motive, you might prompt him in this regard to see if his reasoning can accommodate such ideas.

Once upon a time there was a boy named Bill who liked to swim. One day, when he had a cold, his mother said to him, "You may go play with your friends at the local swimming

*pool, but you must not go into the water.'' He promised her
he would not. But while he was playing near the swimming
pool, one of his friends fell into the water and would have
drowned if Bill had not jumped in and saved him.*

Again, be sure the child understands the main idea of the
story. "Now," you continue, "if you were Bill's mother,
what would you say to him when he came home all wet?"

Results   The purpose of this task is not to evaluate superego
strength or actual moral behavior of the child, but to evaluate the child's cognitive understanding of the problem and
its possible solution. You are looking for the child's ability
to decenter from the immediate and flamboyant facts ("Im-
agine, *15 cups* lay broken on the floor!") and consider the
interrelationship between these and other factors in the total
situation.

Task 9:   *Child's Concept Regarding Movement of Clouds and
Heavenly Bodies*

Source   Piaget, J. 1969. *The Child's Conception of Physical
Causality*. Littlefield, Adams & Co., Totowa, N.J. pp.
60–86.

Materials   None.

Method   The best way to begin questioning the child, in order
not to suggest an answer, is to begin with vague questions
and to take advantage of every answer by adding, "Why do
you say that? How does that happen?" Do not be satisfied
with any answer until you have verified it by requestioning in
several different ways. The art of questioning children requires patience above everything else.

Begin by ascertaining that the child is aware of clouds, the
moon, and the sun. Ask: "You have seen the clouds mov-
ing—why do they move?" Keep questioning, following the
child's lead, always looking for the degree of preoperation-
ality (especially synchretism) in the child's answers. Later,
ask why the moon moves, why the sun moves. Ask: "What
does the moon do when we walk along? Why does it do
this?" (If child has answered that the moon follows him,
ask: "What would happen if I were to pass you, walking in
the opposite direction? Would the moon follow you or me?
Why?" and so on.)

Results   *Movement of clouds:*   There are several stages. Initially, around 5 years of age, the explanation is magical and
synchretic ("We make the clouds move by walking"). Later
(age 6), clouds move because man or God makes them move.

By age 7, children believe that clouds move by themselves, but they say little about how the movement is effected. They may say that it is the sun or moon that makes the clouds move, perhaps by commanding them to move. By age 8, children connect the wind with cloud movement (cause-and-effect, logical, or sequential thinking), although they may have erroneous ideas about where the wind comes from or what it is. By age 9 they may offer a correct solution, a result of having the capacity for cause-and-effect thinking and having been taught the proper facts by others.

Movement of the sun and moon: The stages are similar to those described above. Initially, the information is magical, next it is artificial, and then the artificiality is transferred from man to clouds, night, or rain by moral (the clouds demand the sun to move) as well as physical ways. Later, the child advances purely physical cause-and-effect reasons, these being more or less correct in accordance with what he has learned in school.

Task 10:   ***Child's Concepts Regarding Origin of Sun and Moon***

Source   Piaget, J. 1965. *The Child's Conception of the World.* Littlefield, Adams & Co., Totowa, N.J. pp. 256–284.

Materials   None.

Method   Begin with such questions as "How did the sun begin? Has there always been a sun?" Using the child's answers, keep questioning. The goal is not to simply record the child's answers as such, but to observe the type of reasoning he uses. Does the child show synchretic reasoning, irreversibility of thought processes, centration? Ask about the origins of the moon and the changes in the moon's appearance. Ask the child to provide an explanation of sunrise and sunset, the heat from the sun, and the sun's light. Ask him what stars are, how they began, where they go during the day, why the sun moves, and why the moon moves.

Other questions concerning artificialism include the origins of trees, mountains, rivers, lakes, wind, the sky and its nature, and clouds and their nature.

Results   *Stage 1 (ages 6–7):*   The sun and moon were made artificially; various synchretic explanations are adduced to explain the behavior and appearance of the sun, moon, and planets.

Stage 2 (ages 7–8):   The origin of the sun and moon are partly natural, partly artificial. Children may state that the sun was made by a natural process but of substances of artificial origin, (e.g., planets come from clouds, but clouds are produced by smoke from chimneys).

Stage 3 (ages 9–11):   Children do not resort to artificial explanations. (School instruction must play an important role in this, although Piaget claims that children come to develop a naturalistic explanation, and often an incorrect one, independently.)

REFERENCES

Call, J. 1964. Newborn approach behavior and early ego development. Int. J. Psychoanal. 45:286–294.

Christ, A. E. 1977. Cognitive assessment of the psychotic child. J. Am. Acad. Child Psychiatry 16:227–237.

Flavell, J. 1973. The Developmental Psychology of Jean Piaget. Van Nostrand Rheinhold, New York.

Gruber, H., and Voneche, J. 1977. The Essential Piaget. Basic Books, New York.

Inhelder, B. 1968. The Diagnosis of Reasoning in the Mentally Retarded. John Day Co., New York.

Kimura, D. 1963. Speech lateralization in young children as determined by an auditory test. J. Comp. Psychol. 56:899–902.

Luria, A. R. 1973. The Working Brain. Basic Books, New York.

Piazza, D. M. 1977. Cerebral lateralization in young children as measured by dichotic listening and finger tapping tasks. Neuropsychology 15:417–425.

Rubens, A. B., Mahowald, M. W., and Hutton, J. T. 1976. Assymmetry of the lateral (sylvian) fissures in man. Neurology 26:620–624.

Schmid-Kitsikis, E. 1969. L'examen des Operations de l'Intelligence. Delachaux & Niestlé, Neuchâtel, Switzerland.

Yeni-Komshian, G. H., and Benson, D. A. 1976. Anatomical study of cerebral asymmetry in the temporal lobe of humans, chimpanzees, and rhesus monkeys. Science 192:387–389.

EARLY INFANTILE AUTISM AND MENTAL RETARDATION: Differential Diagnosis

Chapter 8

Peter E. Tanguay

In 1943, in a somewhat obscure journal (which ceased publication within a few years), an article appeared by a well-known and very respected American child psychiatrist, Leo Kanner. The article was entitled "Autistic Disturbances of Affective Contact," and it began: "Since 1938, there has come to our attention a number of children whose condition differs so markedly and uniquely from anything reported so far, that each case merits—and, I hope, will eventually receive—a detailed consideration of its fascinating peculiarities..."

The hallmark of the condition was, in Kanner's estimation, the "extreme autistic aloneness" shown by the children and their failure to develop normal interpersonal relationships. The children did not develop social responses within the first 6 months of life, they did not respond to overtures of affection from parents or other significant individuals, they did not establish normal social eye contact, and, as they grew older, they seemed to be living in a world of their own, which excluded contact with others. Their language handicaps were equally striking and unique. Although they developed the ability to use words and phrases, they used them in an echolalic manner, devoid of any genuine communicative process. In addition, many children displayed bizarre motor activity (such as flapping and whirling themselves) and unusual perceptual behaviors (including fascination with lights or with spinning objects, and exploration of their environment by smelling, touching, or mouthing objects). In con-

Preparation of this chapter was supported by USPHS Grants MH30897 and HD05958.

trast to many "retarded" children, Kanner noted that autistic children sat up, stood, and walked at a normal age, often appeared graceful and agile in their movements, and displayed only relatively minor abnormalities in fine motor development. Based in part on the "intelligent physiognomies" he observed in some autistic children, and their unusual rote memory, Kanner believed that autistic children were "unquestionably" endowed with normal intelligence.

Few modern articles in the field of mental health have had the continuing impact on research and speculation about abnormal child development as this one study by Kanner. For better or for worse, the "syndrome" had become a reality to be dealt with by future experts. To the psychoanalytically oriented in the 1940s and 1950s, early infantile autism seemed a prototypic model for understanding the effects of deviant mother-child relationships. However, such a view added a further burden of guilt to already overburdened parents and may have contributed to a substantial delay in developing more effective educational and behavioral approaches for dealing with autistic children. With the resurgent interest in psychobiological matters in the 1960s and 1970s, early infantile autism (like schizophrenia and manic-depressive psychosis in adults) was viewed as an exciting challenge by research psychologists and psychiatrists interested in studying the neuropsychological aspects of deviant emotional, social, and cognitive development. Although the fruits of the latter studies have been relatively limited to date, the approach is certainly a step in the right direction. Such studies have already benefited autistic children in one important respect: by helping to convincingly establish that early infantile autism is primarily an organic condition, these studies made it possible for the parents of autistic children to lobby successfully for autistic children to receive governmental services and funds that have been earmarked for the developmentally disabled. Although it may be some time before our understanding of the pathophysiology of early infantile autism is adequate, it is certain that what we do learn about the condition will be of help in understanding the etiology, prevention, and treatment of the developmental disabilities and of mental retardation in general.

EARLY INFANTILE AUTISM AND MENTAL RETARDATION

Seventy-five percent of all autistic children function in the retarded range on psychometric testing. Numerous studies have shown that this observation is not solely a function of the social isolation of autistic children, but is a result of specific cognitive handicaps. Relatively few autistic children are untestable if the psychometric evaluation is in the hands of a psychologist expert in dealing with autistic children, but the outcome of such evaluation often indicates that the child is cognitively deficient. Even autistic children who have a fullscale IQ test score in the normal range will invariably be found to have achieved this score because of relatively high scores on block design and rote memory subtests, while their scores on language comprehension and abstract reasoning subtests will be in the retarded range. Such a finding can only serve to emphasize that there is a considerable overlap between the symptoms of children diagnosed as suffering from either early infantile autism or mental retardation.

What is even more striking is that both mental retardation and early infantile autism may be "caused" by similar conditions. The etiology of most cases of autism remains unknown, but the autistic syndrome has been noted to follow congenital rubella (Chess, 1971), tuberous sclerosis (Lotter, 1974), phenylketonuria (PKU) (Knobloch and Pasamanick, 1975), and encephalitis in infancy (Rutter and Lockyer, 1967). All of these conditions may also lead to nonautistic forms of mental retardation.

There are, of course, clinical differences between autistic and nonautistic retarded children. By definition, autistic children must exhibit severe abnormalities in relating to people and objects, above and beyond what might be predicted by their IQ scores. Mentally retarded children do not necessarily exhibit such abnormalities. Autistic children often reach their motor milestones at a normal age, and some may even begin to use words at the usual time, although all show severe delays in language and social skill acquisition by their second birthday. Most moderately or severely retarded children (apart from those whose intellectual impairment is secondary to brain injury, infection, or other pathology some time after birth) are delayed in their motor development from the first months of life. Autistic children may possess certain splinter skills to an unusual extent: good rote memory, extreme echolalia, excellent fine motor skills, or the capacity to quickly put together jigsaw puzzles and block designs. Such skills may be seen less frequently among nonautistic retarded children. Despite such differences between young autistic and retarded children, however, it has been noted (Rutter, 1968) that as they grow older, autistic children may begin to relate better to others and may lose or suppress their more bizarre motoric and perceptual behaviors, at which time the main diagnostic picture may be one of retardation rather than early infantile autism.

What then are we to make of the relationship between early infantile autism and mental retardation? The answer may lie in the fact that both are behavioral syndromes. Early infantile autism is diagnosed not by the results of a laboratory test, a neurophysiological investigation, or by finding a specific chromosomal abnormality. It is diagnosed when one observes a specific and striking concatenation of certain symptoms. These symptoms need not always appear simultaneously; for example, severe developmental language impairments may occur in non-autistic children in the absence of relationship abnormalities or a need for sameness. Twin studies (Folstein and Rutter, 1977) indicate that there appears to be a genetic determination of early infantile autism, and what is inherited is a form of cognitive abnormality that includes, but is not restricted to, autism. In a similar view, mental retardation is a behavioral syndrome defined solely by the age of onset, the person's psychometric scores, and ability to adapt to the demands of everyday life. To better understand the etiological relationship between early infantile autism and mental retardation, it may be helpful to recall the field theory model described in Chapter 4. This model holds that the symptoms and handicaps of any specific developmental disability are determined by the severity, time of operation, and interaction of many different psychobiological and environmental factors. Factors that might produce little psychopathological effect in a fully developed organism could have a severely disruptive effect at an earlier time of life.

Comparing autistic and retarded persons in this regard, it is useful to keep the person's full scale psychometric scores in mind. When the retardation is mild, the differences, both etiologically and symptomatically, are great. As noted in previous chapters, sociocultural factors play a major role in mild mental retardation and lead to a relatively uniform depression in subtest scores. Previous studies (see Cantwell, Baker, and Rutter, 1978) indicate, however, that sociocultural factors play a much less important role in infantile autism, while the as yet undefined organic abnormalities lead to inconsistent test scores.

When the degree of retardation is severe, it may be much more difficult to unequivocally state that one individual is autistic and another is simply retarded. Organic factors are likely to play a role in the handicaps of both individuals, and when a person has developed neither speech nor many social responses as a result of the degree of cognitive impairment, it may be incorrect to label such behaviors autistic.

Although it is clinically reasonable to diagnose early infantile autism in persons having an IQ score in the moderately retarded range, there may be less clear etiological differences between autistic and nonautistic individuals who are moderately retarded. In some instances, as noted earlier, similar factors (PKU, encephalitis, brain degenerative diseases) may lead to either type of developmental disability. Based upon a field theory model, one must presume that the specific outcome depends on differences in the severity of the factor in question, the time at which it affects the developing nervous system, and the manner in which other factors add to or subtract from its effect. A speculative model stressing the second of these possibilities is presented next.

THE DEVELOPMENT OF EARLY
INFANTILE AUTISM: A HYPOTHESIS

The hypothesis presented in this section is based upon a neuropsychological model of brain development described by Luria (1973). The model is more fully described in Chapter 7. For present purposes only one tenet of the model need be considered: those cortical areas (the tertiary analyzer and organizer systems) that play a decisive role in higher cognitive functions, including language, continue their development well into the first two years of life and may even develop, at a less accelerated pace, after that time (Luria, 1973, p. 87). The clinical characteristics of higher functioning "classically" autistic children reveal a pattern of strengths and handicaps that is of interest in regard to the latter model of development. Such classically autistic children reach their motor milestones at a normal age, and are said to be agile and alert. Their alertness, their agility, their ability to perceive, store, and repeat language in an echolalic fashion, and their skills in solving jigsaw and block design puzzles point to intact primary and secondary analyzer and organizer brain systems. In the auditory system, for instance, an intact secondary analyzer system is deduced from the echolalic child's ability to perceive and store phonemic sounds, while his ability to mechanically reproduce such material suggests an intact secondary organizer system in the frontal lobes. Conversely, their rigid and stereotyped behaviors and their inability to decode and encode language point to an abnormality in tertiary cortical systems, and in particular to the left hemisphere tertiary analyzer and organizer systems. In the first year of life, when the latter systems are far from fully developed, these children may often appear fairly normal, reaching their motor milestones at a normal age and even showing good rudimentary social relationships. Between 10 and 15 months of age, their parents report that they appear to suffer an arrest and even a regression in development, at which time the symptoms of a severe psychotic disorder become obvious. Ornitz, Guthrie, and Farley (1977) reported that, retrospectively, 60% of parents of autistic children reported having no concerns that their child was abnormal until after 12 months of age.

Three lines of argument can be invoked to support the hypothesis: experimental-psychological, neurodevelopmental, and electrophysiological.

Experimental-Psychological

Autistic children have been shown to be deficient (in contrast to mental age-matched normal controls) in the ability to encode or spontaneously generate patterns (Frith, 1970) and they demonstrate poorly organized eye movement search patterns when scanning a scene (Hermelin and O'Connor, 1970). Both of the latter phenomena are known to depend on an intact tertiary organizer system (Luria, 1973). Autistic children have also been noted to be seriously deficient in nonverbal communication (gestural communication, facial expression) and in the prosodic aspects of speech (DeMeyer et al., 1972). While little is known about the neural substrate of prosodic skills, it is tempting to speculate that they may involve secondary and tertiary analyzer-organizer systems of the holistic right hemisphere. Studies by Frith and Hermelin (1969), Bryson (1970), and Lovaas et al. (1971) have indicated that autistic children may also be deficient in dealing with cross-modal (visual-tactile, auditory-visual) associations. Again, cross-modal associations have been considered to be particularly dependent on an intact tertiary analyzer system in the brain (Luria, 1973).

Neurodevelopmental

If the hypothesis is true, one would expect that neuropathological conditions that have their onset when the tertiary organizer and analyzer systems are undergoing a major period of development would be most likely to produce a high-functioning autistic child. Those conditions affecting development in utero might produce more severe disturbances of secondary and tertiary system development and, if they occurred early enough, of primary systems as well. The available evidence is at least partly supportive of this hypothesis. As mentioned previously, the syndrome of early infantile autism has been noted to occur following PKU (Knobloch and Pasamanick, 1975), tuberous sclerosis with onset in early childhood (Lotter, 1974), congenital rubella (Chess, 1971), and viral encephalitis in the first years of life (Rutter and Lockyer, 1967). With the exception of congenital rubella, in all of these instances the onset of the condition was during the first year or two of life and had been preceded in cases of PKU and viral encephalitis by a period of normal brain development. With rubella, it is possible that the autistic symptomatology was less a result of the specific brain pathology per se and was more related to the severe hearing losses that accompanied the brain pathology.

Since many children with PKU, tuberous sclerosis, or viral encephalitis in early life do not develop autistic characteristics, but simply appear retarded, individual variations in the degree to which development had progressed, as well as individual differences in the severity of the pathological process, might explain why only some children become autistic.

Electrophysiological

Lelord et al. (1973) reported that in contrast to normal age-matched controls, autistic children do not show enhancement of their occipitally recorded auditory-evoked responses when the auditory stimulus was paired with a visual stimulus occurring 300 msec after onset of the auditory stimulus. Such a lack of cross-modal influence could be interpreted as supportive of an abnormality in the tertiary analyzer cortex. These results contrast with studies that have shown relatively few waveform differences in the P_2N_2 components of the auditory-evoked response in autistic versus normal children (Ornitz et al., 1968). Both Vaughan and Ritter (1970) and Peronnet et al. (1974) have argued that these components are produced in the primary auditory cortex. A final study that bears upon the question is that of Tanguay (1976), in which autistic children did not show the decrease in auditory-evoked responses amplitude over the right as compared to the left hemisphere in rapid eye movement (REM) sleep as did normal age-matched controls. The latter finding has been interpreted as suggesting that autistic children may fail to develop left hemisphere specialization as do normal children.

EARLY INFANTILE AUTISM AND
OTHER FORMS OF CHILDHOOD PSYCHOSIS

Although a child may be both autistic and retarded, there are a number of other syndromes and neuropathological conditions that may need to be differentiated from early infantile autism for diagnostic purposes. Most important among these, since they entail a radically different treatment approach, are impairments of vision and hearing. It is not unheard of for children to be referred to a mental health clinic with a diagnosis of possible early infantile autism, only to be found to have a serious hearing problem. In such instances, the provision of a hearing aid and an educational program designed for deaf individuals may result in a dramatic decrease of autistic symptomatology and an increase in the child's ability to communicate.

Other diagnostic terms have been used to label severely disturbed young children in the past, including *symbiotic psychosis, childhood schizophrenia, schizotypal childhood psychosis,* and *atypical childhood psychosis.* Often the terms have meant different things to different clinicians, which has led to considerable difficulty in comparing the results of different studies and reports. The most recent edition of the *Diagnostic and Statistical Manual (DSM III,* 1980) has attempted to reverse this situation by defining a small number of psychotic conditions in childhood, chief among which are *early infantile autism* and *atypical childhood psychosis.* The former condition can only be diagnosed if fairly well specified criteria of impaired interpersonal relationships, deviant or absent language development, and disturbed relationship to objects in the environment are met. The second category, atypical childhood psychosis, is somewhat less restrictive and is designed to include children who may have some of the features of early infantile autism but are not diagnosable as autistic under the strict criteria above. The category may also include somewhat older children whose behavior may be quite bizarre but who do not show overt signs of a thought disorder. *Thought disorder* (the term is defined in some detail in *DSM III),* delusions, and hallucinations are the necessary criteria for the diagnosis of schizophrenia in *DSM III.* Given these latter criteria, the *DSM III* diagnosis of schizophrenia can rarely be made in children who are less than 8 years of age. Such a diagnostic scheme implies that schizophrenia (as defined using the criteria usually applied to adolescents and adults) is diagnostically different from early infantile autism, a belief that is still far from resolved in the minds of some experts (Fish and Ritvo, 1979).

Could a psychosis arising between the ages of 5 and 12 lead to such a depression in mental capacity that, psychometrically, the child would be labeled retarded? A study by Russell and Tanguay (in preparation) suggests that although this may occur, the depression in IQ is not necessarily a result of the thought disorder per se, but occurs as a result of the long-term adverse effects of the child's bizarre behaviors on his school work and social relationships. Psychotic children are often excluded from school completely, or shunted to class for the educationally handicapped.

CONCLUSIONS

Like mental retardation, early infantile autism is a behaviorally defined syndrome. Its antecedent factors and symptoms may overlap with those of retardation or other developmental disabilities. The specific antecedent factors, their intensity, and the time at which they affect the developing organism are likely to affect which specific diagnostic syndrome will result. Although diagnostic labeling may be useful as a shorthand method of describing a child's clinical picture, and may be necessary for research, it has less use in determining choice of treatment. Treatment of all seriously handicapped young children must be based upon the specific profile of abilities and handicaps that the child exhibits. Treatment considerations that are outlined in subsequent chapters of this book apply equally to autistic and to nonautistic retarded persons.

REFERENCES

Bryson, C. Q. 1970. Systematic identification of perceptual disabilities in autistic children. Percept. Mot. Skills 31:239–246.

Cantwell, D., Baker, L., and Rutter, M. 1978. Family factors. In: M. Rutter and E. Schopler (eds.), Autism: A Reappraisal of Concepts and Treatment, pp. 269–296. Plenum Press, New York.

Chess, S. 1971. Autism in children with congenital rubella. J. Autism Child. Schizophr. 1:33–47.

DeMyer, M. K., Alpern, G. D., Barton, S., DeMyer, W. E., Churchill, D. W., Hintgen, J. N., Bryson, C. Q., Pontius, W., and Kimberlin, C. 1972. Imitation in autistic, early schizophrenic and non-psychotic subnormal children. J. Autism Child. Schizophr. 2:264–287.

Diagnostic and Statistical Manual (DSM III). 1980. American Psychiatric Association, Washington, D.C.

Fish, B., and Ritvo, E. 1979. Psychoses of childhood. In: I. Berlin and J. Noshpitz (eds.), Basic Handbook of Child Psychiatry. Basic Books, New York.

Folstein, S., and Rutter, M. 1977. Genetic influences and infantile autism. Nature 265:726–728.

Frith, U. 1970. Studies in pattern detection in normal and autistic children. II. Reproduction and production of color sequences. J. Exp. Child. Psychol. 10: 120–135.

Frith, U., and Hermelin, B. 1969. The role of visual and motor cues for normal, subnormal and autistic children. J. Child. Psychol. Psychiatry 10:153–163.

Hermelin, B., and O'Connor, N. 1970. Psychological Experiments with Autistic Children. Pergamon Press, New York.

Kanner, L. 1943. Autistic disturbances of affective contact. Nerv. Child. 2: 217–250.

Knobloch, H., and Pasamanick, B. 1975. Some etiologic and prognostic factors in early infantile autism and psychosis. Pediatrics 55:182–191.

Lelord, G., Laffont, F., Jusseaume, P., and Stephant, J. L. 1973. Comparative study of conditioning of averaged evoked responses by coupling sound and light in normal and autistic children. Psychophysiology 10(4):415–425.

Lotter, V. 1974. Factors related to outcome in autistic children. J. Autism Child. Schizophr. 4:263–277.

Lovaas, O. I., Schreibman, L., Koegel, R., and Rehm, R. 1971. Selective responding by autistic children to multiple sensory input. J. Abnorm. Psychol. 77: 211–222.

Luria, A. R. 1973. The Working Brain. Basic Books, New York.

Ornitz, E. M., Guthrie, D., and Farley, A. J. 1977. The early development of autistic children. J. Autism Child. Schizophr. 7:207–229.

Ornitz, E. M., Ritvo, E. R., Panman, L. M., Lee, Y. H., Carr, E. M., and Walter, R. D. 1968. The auditory responses in normal and autistic children during sleep. Electroencephalogr. Clin. Neurophysiol. 25:221–230.

Peronnet, F., Michel, F., Echallier, J. F., and Girod, J. 1974. Coronal topography of human auditory evoked responses. Electroencephalogr. Clin. Neurophysiol. 37:225–230.

Russell, A., and Tanguay, P. E. Mental illness and mental retardation: Cause or coincidence. In preparation.

Rutter, M. 1968. Concepts of autism: A review of research. J. Child. Psychol. Psychiatry 9:1–25.

Rutter, M., and Lockyer, L. 1967. A five to fifteen year follow-up study of infantile psychosis. I. Description of sample. Br. J. Psychiatry 113:1169–1182.

Tanguay, P. 1976. Early infantile autism: Clinical and electrophysiological research. In: E. Ritvo, P. E. Tanguay, B. J. Freeman, and E. M. Ornitz (eds.), Autism: Diagnosis, Current Research and Management, pp. 75–84. Spectrum Publications, New York.

Vaughan, H. G., and Ritter, W. 1970. The sources of auditory evoked responses recorded from the human scalp. Electroencephalogr. Clin. Neurophysiol. 28: 360–367.

ASSESSMENT OF SEXUALITY AND SEXUAL VULNERABILITY OF RETARDED PERSONS

Ludwik S. Szymanski and Paul E. Jansen

Chapter 9

Sexuality of mentally retarded persons is an issue of major confusion, anxiety, and importance. The myth of the "moral moron," the legacy of years past, still underlies many societal attitudes. Retarded adolescents or adults mainstreamed in the community may become overwhelmed by sexual stimulation inherent in our culture for which they are ill prepared. Their parents, often justifiably, are concerned about them being sexually exploited, but are not sure how it could be prevented. When establishment of a community residence in a residential neighborhood is proposed, fear of sexually uninhibited behavior of its retarded inhabitants often underlies the zoning battles waged by the community.

Mental health professionals are often consulted on these issues, but frequently only after a crisis has developed. If called in earlier, their understanding of both the conscious and unconscious factors involved in the situation could be helpful in bringing about compromise and resolution.

SEXUAL DEVELOPMENT

A belief in the myth that retardation is associated with lack of sexual inhibition may sometimes bring parents to seek professional advice, even for their preschool children. Occasionally, overt friendliness to strangers may in the parents' minds be invested with sexual connotations, or young, retarded children may be severely admonished if they masturbate, whereas such activity by a nonretarded child would be considered normal. More usually, however, it is only at the approach of adolescence, when the discrepancy between physical and emotional growth is evident, that parents' concerns and fears become especially strong. Mildly/moderately retarded adolescents or young adults functioning intellectually and socially on a much more immature level still usually have normal bodies. They experience sexual excitement, which is often puzzling to them, since many do not understand their sexuality, never having received sex education. They are under considerable internal and external pressure to "shape up" and be like their nonretarded peers. Their families are often ambivalent in their expectations. They wish for their retarded children to have friends of the opposite sex, but they also dread that they will get involved in sexual activity. As a result, they may closely supervise the youngsters, isolate them at home, and avoid talking with them about sex-related matters. It is not unusual that parents would ask for help in obtaining sterilization for a retarded child or adolescent.

Thus, retarded adolescents have little opportunity to satisfy their sexual curiosity and urges, which otherwise may be normal. As a result, they may become easy victims of sexual exploitation and abuse. Often they may actively or passively cooperate, out of fear, or wish to please the abuser (usually a nonretarded peer or an adult) and to secure his attention. They tend to deny the fact that they are exploited and make up fantasy stories about an allegedly close relationship they have established.

In their quest for social acceptance, retarded adolescents or young adults may go far beyond emulating their peers' dress and mannerisms or participating in sexual play. Pregnancy for a retarded female may become a status symbol. It offers the benefits of primary gratification in improving her self-esteem. The retarded mother expects a normal child with whom she can identify and thus partially deny her own retardation. The pregnancy also serves as proof that in some areas she can function just like anyone else. For instance, in one large state institution, young females would regularly escape and, after a varying period of time, return pregnant. Their institutionalized peers envied them because they had proved that they were wanted by normal men in the outside world.

This, and similar behavior of retarded persons, has been construed for years as evidence of their low moral standards. Actually, it should be seen as indirect sexual abuse of these unfortunate members of our society. This abuse is perpetrated by society not providing them with adequate education, vocational and social opportunities, sex education, and protection in normalized environments rather than in dehumanizing institutions. Inappropriate sexual activity may be the only available defense against depression and anxiety. Secondary gratification, such as increased welfare support for a retarded mother of several children, provides an additional incentive.

SEXUAL ABUSE OF RETARDED PERSONS BY
DENIAL OF THE RIGHT TO SEXUAL EXPRESSION

Sexual abuse or misuse is usually understood as a sin of commission of a sexually oriented action upon the victim. In the mentally retarded population sexual abuse is most commonly perpetrated not by delinquent individuals, but by society and its laws. This takes the form of the denial of the right of sexual expression, which includes denying heterosexual relationships, companionship, and the right to marry; forced sterilization; and withholding sex education. Even the laws that ostensibly protect retarded people from exploitation actually violate their rights. For instance, Massachusetts chapter 272, section 5 effectively forbids all unmarried retarded females to engage in sexual activity as long as they are classified "retarded," regardless of their abilities, although such laws pertaining to nonretarded persons are not enforced nor enforceable.

From a legal point of view, a child is a person under a certain arbitrarily chosen age. Sexual activity with children, even if they willingly participate, is forbidden by law. For instance, Massachusetts Statute 265, section 23, states: "Whoever unlawfully has sexual intercourse or unnatural sexual intercourse, and abuses a child under sixteen years of age shall, for the first offense, be punished..."

It is commonly believed that the person who attains this arbitrarily chosen age has sufficient psychological maturity to give free and meaningful consent to participate in the sexual act. In light of modern knowledge of child development, this is a fallacy, because it does not take into consideration individual differences in psychosocial development, which are not correlated with age.

With mentally retarded people, it is even more obvious that there is no correlation between chronological age and attainment of various skills—in particular, skills necessary for social adaptation. This would include judgment necessary for giving meaningful consent for sexual activity. In this respect, a mentally retarded adult (by chronological age) can be compared with a child below the age of majority.

At the beginning of this century, following the introduction of psychological testing and "discovery" of mildly retarded "morons," pseudoscientific studies such as The Hill Folk (Danielson and Davenport, 1912) "documented" high incidence of various forms of social maladaptation, such as alcoholism and prostitution, in offspring of families with allegedly low intellectual level. It was only a short step to the belief that mentally retarded people were oversexed and unable to inhibit sexual impulses. Enforced institutionalization and sterilization laws adopted in years that followed were seen as means to control the sexuality and procreation of retarded persons in order to protect the society.

Paradoxically, another set of myths maintains that mental retardation is associated with reduced or nonexistent sexual drive, and thus restrictions on mentally retarded persons' sexual opportunities do not take anything away from them, but are necessary to protect them against exploitation.

Morgenstern (1973) studied the community attitudes toward sexuality of the retarded and divided them into three categories: 1) *The subhuman:* "Nevertheless, there are individuals in our society who look upon the mentally retarded as subhuman anomalies...Should the question of their sexuality be raised at all, the attitudes it evokes may be the same as those evolved by the observance of two dogs copulating. In some instances, particularly after a sex crime has been committed, members of the community may immediately regard all the mentally retarded with suspicion." 2) *The child/innocent view:* "If the retarded's sexuality comes to the attention of persons with these attitudes, its expression is diverted into expression of other feelings. Innocence is expected to prevail; therefore, sexuality must be negated." 3) *The developing person:* "They take an optimistic view of the retarded as 'developing persons' with good potential for growth and inclusion within the mainstream of the community. In line with their beliefs, they advocate full rights for the retarded in all areas of living, including sex." However, advocates of these views do not necessarily put them into practice.

One might be tempted to speculate, from the psychodynamic point of view, that denial of sexual rights to mentally retarded persons is an extension of the attitude that they are eternal children. Sex is forbidden to children; it is the privilege of adults (parents). The notion of a child engaging in sexual activity may stimulate adults' anxiety, perhaps because their sexuality was suppressed in childhood. Any form of sexual expression may be suppressed; these are reviewed in brief.

Masturbation

Old myths about the danger of masturbation are disappearing and many, if not most, parents of normal children know that this is a normal developmental activity. Normal young children usually quickly perceive parental reactions to their masturbation and learn to conduct it in socially acceptable ways in privacy. A retarded child may not be as quick to grasp this point without specific teaching, and unless this is provided, may continue to masturbate in the open. Many, if not most, caregivers who accept masturbation by a nonretarded child may be threatened by masturbation by a retarded child and respond with punitive action. In some institutions, control of masturbation becomes a major problem and preoccupation of the staff. In some cases recently encountered by the authors, a modern version of the chastity belt was used—tight underpants taped to the delinquent's (or rather victim's) body.

Heterosexual Relationships

It is accepted that children in all developmental stages need exposure to people of both sexes and all ages in order to develop their identity and the repertoire of social interaction skills and socially acceptable behaviors (including the control of one's own sexual drive). Strangely, the opportunities for such exposure are often denied to mentally retarded people. (Paradoxically, they are under increased pressure to learn such skills and controls.) Retarded adolescents and adults in institutions (as described in more detail later in this chapter) are often routinely segregated by sex. Even for those living in the community, interaction with peers (of both sexes) may be difficult because of rejection by nonretarded persons or the unavailability of other retarded persons. Retarded adults and adolescents who do have an opportunity to meet or even date peers of the opposite sex do it often under strict supervision in "socials," chaperoned by caregivers anxiously watching for and stopping any physical closeness. However, any professional in the field of retardation is aware of the (particularly mildly) retarded person's need for, and ability to enjoy, companionship and sexuality.

Sexual Activity

Clearly, opportunities for sexual activity between mutually consenting adults who happen to be retarded may be few, if not nonexistent. Their actual intellectual abilities or adjustment do not matter; what matters is whether they are classified "retarded" or whether they live in a residential care program. Even modern community residences are not free of such biased policies: they emphasize suppression of sexuality rather than teaching socially acceptable expression. Carruth (1973) described a halfway house for high borderline retarded young adults. All were employed, paid at least part of the rent for their rooms, and were called tenants. Attempts at sex education were made, consisting of "showing old anatomy films and the use of a few outdated books." They were permitted to visit one another in their rooms during specified hours, but only after informing their counselors and leaving their doors open. When two tenants engaged in some homosexual activity in these conditions, they were admonished for behaving so in public. Obviously, such a setup was both illogical and in violation of one's right to privacy.

Sex Education

Although many educational programs for retarded persons include sex education, they are exceptions. On the other hand, as pointed out by

Johnson (1973), mentally retarded persons are in even more need of sex education than nonretarded ones. This is understandable in light of their lack of social skills and need for affection, which may make them vulnerable to (and unaware of) sexual misuse and abuse. Backer (1973) studied sexual knowledge of retarded adolescents living at home. Only slightly more than half gave correct answers to questions testing their concrete knowledge. However, even fewer scored correctly on questions relating to conception, contraception, and venereal disease.

The usual explanation for exclusion of mentally retarded persons from sex education has been that because of their poor judgment, if they know "how to do it," they will do it indiscriminately. However, there is no evidence to support this. Another argument sometimes advanced by educators is that sex education for retarded people is too emotionally charged for the parents who will oppose it. Again, our clinical experience has been to the contrary. Parents of adolescents seen in our clinic infrequently bring up this subject. However, when asked about it, they generally express great interest in having their children have sex education, but are usually at a loss about where to find such a program. Sometimes the parents are justifiably opposed to these programs if they are inappropriate in form or content, and conducted without parental knowledge. Similar observation of parental interest in this matter was made by Fischer and Krajicek (1974).

Right to Obtain Birth Control Assistance

Violation of the right to obtain birth control advice and materials is usually related to withholding sex education. There is no law that prevents providing such materials solely on the basis of mental capacity, or marital status, since the Supreme Court ruled in 1972 (*Eisenstadt* v. *Baird,* 40 U.S. 432) that unmarried persons had the right to obtain contraceptive devices. The common justification of withholding them from retarded persons is that they have insufficient mental capacity to cooperate and use contraceptive devices appropriately. Yet most can be trained to use these devices. Besides, measures such as intrauterine devices and long-acting hormonal injections may be used.

The Right to Have Children

The right to bear children involves several aspects, including engaging in sex, right to marriage, involuntary sterilization, and right to care for one's own children. The advent of eugenics at the beginning of this century led to introduction of laws on involuntary sterilization in the majority of states. They pertained to various "misfits" and epileptics, but the chief target was mentally retarded people. They were based on the ideas evolved by Goddard (1912), who felt that the morons were a menace to the society and responsible for most of the social problems. The forced sterilization of retarded people was supposed to protect society from this menace, as stated by U.S. Supreme Court Justice Holmes in his famous opinion in *Buck* v. *Bell,* 374 U.S. 200 (1927): "It is better for all the world if, instead of waiting to execute degenerate offspring for crime or to let them starve for their imbecility, society can prevent those who are manifestly unfit from continuing their kind...Three generations of imbeciles are enough." However, even in the last decade, involuntary sterilization laws remained on the books in about half of the states (Krishef, 1972), although they are rarely, if ever, used. Nevertheless, as recently as 1976, the Federal Court upheld in North Carolina a position of such law (that it is a duty of an institution's director to commence sterilization proceedings) if certain strict conditions and safeguards on behalf of the retarded subjects are met.

The current tendency is to replace involuntary sterilization of mentally retarded persons with voluntary sterilization. This approach, however, still presents the danger of abuse of their sexual rights, since "voluntary" is most difficult to define. For instance, voluntary agreement to sterilization may actually be a result of subtle coercion or a desire to please and obtain attention from caregivers who want them sterilized. Subjects are rarely well informed about the procedure, its irreversibility, and alternative methods of contraception that are available. For persons deemed too retarded to give consent, a fiction of voluntary consent through substitute consent of guardians has been invented. Recently, however, the courts have been recognizing that parental and children's interests differ and that parents, because of conflict of interest, may not give permission for sterilization.

Various measures have been proposed, such as appointing a guardian ad litem, or even an impartial committee to determine the necessity for sterilization, but these are still hotly debated. Contrary to general beliefs, retarded young adults who are sterilized "voluntarily" may perceive and distort what is happening to them and react emotionally to it.

Bass (1978) gives an excellent review of the literature on and current status of sterilization of retarded persons. A long proponent of voluntary sterilization, she pointed out recent legal developments that may lead to denial of voluntary sterilization to persons considered incompetent, even if they could give informed consent for this procedure and even if their fertility would be against their best interests. Vitello (1978) discussed this issue further and cited a recent case in which three families sued a hospital for refusal to sterilize their three blind, deaf, and severely retarded daughters. Clearly, much more discussion and research are necessary on the following problems (Bass, 1978): "measuring and predicting competency for parenthood; the childbearing practices of the mentally retarded; the impact of sterilization on the adjustment of mentally retarded people; the ability of mentally retarded people to give an informed consent."

The right of retarded persons to marry has been limited by law in some states on the ground of incompetence to understand marital commitments or enter into any contractual agreement (Friedman, 1976). The rights of mentally retarded parents to keep their children are also restricted by laws in many states, and in some the fact that a parent had been committed to a mental institution may be sufficient evidence for a child's removal from home (Friedman, 1976).

SEXUALITY OF RETARDED PERSONS AS A GENETIC THREAT TO SOCIETY

The restrictions on the sexuality and procreation of retarded persons had been based on the belief that mental retardation was caused solely by genetic factors. Therefore, such measures were expected to eliminate mental retardation and the burden retarded people imposed on the population at large. However, in light of modern knowledge of mental retardation, it is clear that many other etiological factors are involved. For instance, in the population seen at the Developmental Evaluation Clinic (Children's Hospital, Boston) mental retardation could be attributed to inheritance in only 4% of the cases. Currently, factors such as poverty, with associated malnutrition, poor perinatal care, and lack of early stimulation are considered to be important causes of retardation. Even if permitted to reproduce, mentally retarded people do not have larger families than those in the general population (Higgins, Reed, and Reed, 1962). The effect of procreation of mentally retarded people on prevalence of mental retardation has been studied by Reed and Anderson (1973). They found that retarded parents produced about 17% of all retarded children. If they were not permitted to have any children, the population of mentally retarded persons would decline only by that number. If, on the other hand, they were to procreate at the rate of their normal siblings, the proportion of retarded children in the population produced by retarded parents would rise from 17% to 26%, increasing the total percentage of retarded children in the population from 2.0% to 2.2%. This is unlikely to occur, however, because many retarded persons are sterile or do not survive to reproductive age.

Another argument against suppressing procreation of retarded persons on genetic grounds is that many genetically defective births can be prevented if prenatal diagnosis were made through amniocentesis. Furthermore no state forbids procreation on the ground that the parent(s) is a carrier of a genetic disease.

The second and more recently evolved argument for suppressing sexuality of retarded persons is sociological. It holds that they cannot be effective parents or maintain a self-supporting family. Few controlled studies exist to support this claim. Mattinson (1973) in England followed

36 retarded married couples with histories of institutionalization. Four couples separated or divorced. Of the 32 marriages that were maintained, one-third were "movers and shifters." There were only 40 children born to these 32 marriages. Two of the children died, and neglect was suspected in one case. Six were taken from their parents. No data were provided on the development of the children living with their parents. Floor et al. (1975) surveyed marriages of previously institutionalized retarded persons and concluded that 50% were capable of sustaining marriage for at least several years. The studies of Reed and Anderson (1973) provide evidence of increased risk or retardation in the offspring of retarded parents, although it is still debatable to what degree heredity and environment are responsible. Any clinician working in this field is aware that retarded parents as a group have difficulties in providing for the emotional and developmental needs of their children. For instance, Garber (1975) found that intelligence level of the mother was significant in predicting retardation of her children. However, similar or more severe problems are presented by many nonretarded parents as well.

SEXUALITY OF INSTITUTIONALIZED RETARDED PERSONS

Very little has been written about the sexuality of institutionalized retarded persons in the United States. In a chapter entitled "Sexual Behavior of Retarded in Institutions," Deisher (1973) commented that no factual information existed at that time regarding "attitudes on the part of staff members, and actual practices in institutions, in regard to sexual behavior."

Before one can reasonably discuss sexual abuse or exploitation of the institutionalized mentally retarded, some consideration should be given to the typical course of development of sexual behavior and sexual identity within the institutions themselves. State institutions ("schools") for the retarded in Massachusetts can serve as an example. Children are raised in a unisex fashion until secondary sexual characteristics become prominent (puberty). They eat, sleep, bathe, and go to the toilet in mixed sex groups until adolescence can no longer be denied. Then they are split up and grouped by sex and, in most cases, spend the rest of their institutionalized years in same-sex living environments. Thus, because of unofficial policies of expedience, most retarded, institutionalized teenage males may become involved in active or passive homosexual behavior, a situation that "solves" the problem of unwanted pregnancies.

Mulhern (1975) surveyed sexuality-oriented policies in 82 residential institutions. Only 23 had clear sexuality guidelines. There was considerable discrepancy between what the respondents felt the policies should be and what they actually were. More than half felt that private masturbation, brief kissing, and petting should be permitted, and 41 agreed in theory to permitting heterosexual intercourse (actually permitted in 8 facilities). Mitchell, Doctor, and Butler (1978) surveyed attitudes of 117 staff members in three residential institutions. A mean of 72% of the respondents agreed in theory to permitting limited heterosexual contact between the residents. Need for better sex education for the residents was stressed.

Fears expressed about institutionalized retarded children and adults being sexually exploited by direct-care staff are largely groundless today. Although an occasional incident is detected and reported, the problem is minimal in a reasonably well-supervised environment. Of course, in isolated situations where critical staff shortages make supervision difficult, more incidents are likely to occur. However, most direct-care staff members working with the institutionalized retarded would not be likely to make direct sexual overtures to a retarded individual. The reasons for this appears to be: 1) the self-concept of the staff persons themselves, which would be undercut if they attempted direct sexual contact with severely retarded residents, and 2) most staff would simply not tolerate direct sexual abuse of residents by other staff members.

It is less recognized, however, that the caregivers in residential facilities may unconsciously sexually exploit the residents while consciously rationalizing their activity.

A young female child care worker in an institution for the multiply handicapped developed a close but possessive relationship with an adolescent blind, epileptic, and retarded resident. She encouraged him to show her physical affection, including sitting on her lap and hugging her in a manner similar to "petting," which visibly excited both. The boy, however, was not able to handle this sensory stimulation, which led to temper tantrums or triggered his seizures. Attempts to interpret this behavior to the worker failed. She stubbornly maintained that the boy was too retarded to have sexual feelings and that he needed such physical closeness as evidence of love. She was unable to recognize her own sexual gratification from this relationship.

A male attendant in a residential facility decided that a profoundly retarded young adult resident should enjoy sexual gratification and started to teach him explicitly how to masturbate. There was no evidence that the resident had shown any spontaneous interest in sexuality. The staff member, however, enjoyed these lessons greatly.

If direct sexual abuse of the institutionalized retarded persons by the staff does not occur often, then does that mean there is no sexual exploitation at all within the institutions? Certainly not. However, in order to comprehend what kinds of sexual abuse do occur, one must first look at how sexuality fits into the day-to-day lives of institutionalized retarded persons.

To begin with, there is a caste system among staff and residents of large institutions that in some ways parallels the caste or class system of society at large. The major discernible castes are: 1) indirect-care (professional) staff, 2) direct-care staff, 3) higher functioning (mildly or moderately retarded) residents, and 4) lower functioning (severely or profoundly retarded) residents.

Over many years, as a microsociety forms within a closed institutional population, direct-care staff, in their appearance and behavior, typically serve as models for high-functioning residents to emulate in their dealings with lower functioning residents. Since a major characteristic of direct-care staff for high-functioning residents is social power over, and control of, institutional residents, these same high-functioning residents tend to try to exert corresponding and analogous control over low-functioning residents. In this context, sexual control and exploitation of lower functioning residents by higher functioning residents is only one of many elements of interresident exploitation of the less bright by the brighter. Economic exploitation is probably more common in institutionalized populations than sexual exploitation. Thus sexual behavior in institutions should perhaps be viewed in an *Adlerian* (power) rather than a *Freudian* (sexual) framework. It is not uncommon to find socially aggressive and dominant high-functioning males who have gathered together "harems" of institutional women. These women are, in turn, "loaned" or "rented" to friends of the dominant male resident in question; this is part of a much larger pattern of economic and personal exploitation.

Sexual abuse through denying sexual rights is even more prevalent with institutionalized than with noninstitutionalized retarded persons. However, it presents some special assessment and management problems.

Although the outer limits of the sexual rights and responsibilities of institutionalized retarded persons have never been clearly defined, a few trends seem evident today. First, there is a growing belief that, as citizens of a democracy, institutionalized retarded individuals should have the same sexual rights and privileges ascribed to members of American society at large. Second, institutional staff members have the right to impose some limits or restrictions on the moment-to-moment expression of retarded persons' sexual rights. Basically, direct-care staffs are given the task of managing the sexual behavior of the institutionalized retarded persons so that it is not socially disruptive.

An interesting method of managing sexual behavior devised within an institutional setting occurred in a long-term token-economy ward for severely and profoundly retarded males. When the token economy began, all the boys involved in it were young. However, as the program continued over several years, many of the boys reached puberty and began to masturbate openly and often. Masturbation during the workday was disrupting the work environment, and the direct-care staff decided that although masturbation obviously cannot be suppressed completely, it can be redistributed over the day so that it occurs at more appropriate times. To do this, the opportunity to masturbate became one of the items in the token economy, with the "price" varying depending on the time of day. For example, if resident x began to masturbate during a midday work or study session, he would be led to his bed and charged a number of tokens for the privilege. By making masturbation relatively expensive during the day, and leaving it freely available during evenings or other nonprogram times, the masturbatory behavior soon ceased to be a socially disruptive event. This solution to a common institutional problem was devised and run completely by ward-level staff members. They reported that the institutional administration would never have allowed this treatment to occur, because it would have forced them to publicly admit that masturbation was an ongoing problem with programming severely retarded teenagers.

The following is another example of sexuality-related problems in an institutional setting. In a large institution, sexual integration of a residential building for physically handicapped, retarded adults was carried out experimentally. As a result, two residents who became friends announced that they wanted to marry. Both residents were moderately retarded and severely handicapped; the woman, who was 31 years old, had cerebral palsy and spastic quadriplegia; the man, who was 41, had spastic paralysis. They approached the institution's Catholic chaplain, who refused to marry them unless the man "could maintain an erection for three minutes and ejaculate," i.e., perform his marital duties. Since sexual relations between them were impossible because of physical limitations, the couple next turned to the Protestant chaplain. He also did not want to marry the couple because he felt that they did not understand the total meaning and personal commitment that marriage implies. For now, the couple remains unmarried, although still close companions.

UNCONSTITUTIONALITY OF LAWS
RESTRICTING SEXUALITY OF RETARDED PERSONS

There are at least two basic flaws that render laws pertaining to various aspects of sexual behavior of retarded individuals unconstitutional:

1. These laws are aimed toward arbitrarily selected groups of individuals labeled retarded. They do not take into account individual differences and abilities that may be pertinent. For instance, two residents of a state institution, labeled retarded, may have sufficient judgment and understanding to use contraceptives and have sexual, mutually consented upon relations, although they may be incompetent to maintain jobs and be self-supporting.
2. These laws do not apply equally to all individuals in the population who exhibit the incompetence in question, but only to those labeled retarded. For example, a retarded individual may be denied the right

to marry if he is judged unable to support his family and provide proper care for his children. Yet people not labeled retarded are not required, as a condition for marriage, to prove that they are competent in these respects (Morgenstern, 1973).

PREVENTION AND MANAGEMENT OF SEXUAL ABUSE OF RETARDED PERSONS—QUALIFICATION OF THE PROFESSIONAL

The most important obstacle to normalized attitudes toward sexuality of mentally retarded persons is probably the misconception that they are basically different people who do not have normal needs, normal experience, or normal human emotions. These beliefs have distorted the understanding of their emotional and sexual development, feelings, and needs.

A professional called upon to counsel in cases involving sexuality and sexual abuse of retarded persons should be aware of, and able to overcome, these misconceptions, as well as his own conscious and unconscious bias (Szymanski, 1977). This might be based on feelings of guilt for not being able to cure the retardation, and may include overidentification, overprotection, or rejection and hostility, and a tendency to institutionalize the patient.

First of all, the professional should be trained and experienced in the field of mental retardation (as well as sexual abuse), whether physician, nurse, or mental health worker, although a well-trained child psychiatrist, because of a background in biological and behavioral sciences, may be the most helpful. Obviously, the professional should have been able to overcome his own biases about sexuality in general, and sexuality of retarded persons in particular. He should be warm and empathetic, eclectic in his approach, and able to evaluate the situation from different perspectives (e.g., sociological, behavioral, psychodynamic, educational).

The professional may play multiple roles in management of these cases. He may be called to examine the retarded victim of sexual abuse, assess and/or predict its psychological impact, and provide treatment if necessary. He may be asked to assess retarded persons' competence for legal or administrative purposes in cases involving marriage, contraception, sterilization, child custody, and abuse. He may be expected to consult other professionals, laymen, and establish sex education programs.

ASSESSMENT OF THE SEXUALLY ABUSED RETARDED PERSON

Professionals should assess the sexual development and the causes and effects of sexual abuse of a retarded individual within the context of the total development, adjustment, and abilities of that individual. Evaluation of the family is of paramount importance. Professionals have to understand the family's attitude toward mental retardation in general and toward their child in particular and the parents' ability and motivation to foster his independence and to see him as a human being with universal needs, including sexual ones. The family's strengths and weaknesses, the parents' marital stability, and the retarded child's role within the family have to be assessed. The sexual abuse may be (and usually is) only a symptom of disorder in any of these areas.

The retarded person's knowledge of sexuality should be assessed in light of his general developmental level and life experiences and not his intelligence. As pointed out by Johnson (1973), there is little correlation between sex IQ and general IQ.

A retarded child, or even adult, may need considerable emotional support during the evaluation. He may have been conditioned to see himself as a failure and a bad person and probably feels guilty for provoking sexual abuse. The mental health professional who interviews him may be seen as giving another "test" that will surely be failed. On the other hand, a friendly, warm, empathetic, but not degradingly paternalistic, interviewer may be rewarded with the patient's cooperation.

TREATMENT OF SEXUAL ABUSE

The needs of retarded, sexually abused/misused persons for treatment do not basically differ from those of nonretarded persons. Emergency supportive counseling and anxiety-reducing measures, including psychotropic agents, may be necessary. The main message of support to victims should be that the abuse is not their fault and that it will not make them bad persons. Similar emergency support may be necessary for the family as well. In cases where abuse by a family member is suspected, temporary removal of the victim from the home and reporting to the authorities will have to be considered.

The focus of long-term management should be on the total needs of the patient, not only on sexual behavior and development. This may include attendance at an appropriate educational or work program, and provision of appropriate living conditions and opportunities to socialize. All of these should reduce the need to achieve gratification and attention through inappropriate sexual behavior. Counseling the family and/or other caregivers, including the institutional staff, is obligatory. Counselors should help them, if necessary, to admit and conquer their prejudices about retardation and sexuality and eliminate guilt over their own ambivalent feelings toward the handicapped person and the resulting inappropriate reactions, such as overprotection or rejection. Long-term individual psychotherapy may be indicated, providing that the therapist is experienced in techniques of therapy with retarded persons. Such treatment may be very helpful, contrary to the misconception that retarded people are not bright enough to cooperate and benefit from it.

PREVENTION OF SEXUAL ABUSE

The most important area in effective prevention of sexual abuse of the retarded population is sex education. This subject has been reviewed in recent years by a number of authors, and good guides for professionals and parents are available (Bass, 1972; Fischer, Krajicek, and Borthick, 1973; Kempton, 1973, 1975). The National Association for Retarded Citizens also has a number of excellent pamphlets for retarded youngsters, their parents, and professionals. An effective sex education program has to be conducted in a directive fashion. Professionals have to anticipate the retarded person's questions and interests, often verbalize them for him, and lead him to answer in a clear, concrete, and unequivocal way. As pointed out by Gordon (1973), often a relatively small amount of information is sufficient, if it is given repeatedly. Concrete models, films, and simple drawings are useful. Last, but not least, professionals have to focus on much more than anatomy and physiology or reproduction. The youngsters must be taught in which situations a particular behavior is socially appropriate, principles of contraception; and so on. Most important, they have to be taught the responsibilities connected with sexual behavior, marriage, and parenthood. Retarded young adults may have strong wishes to be parents, even if they are not capable of fulfilling such responsibilities. Having a child has for them similar meanings as for nonretarded persons. In addition, having a child may be seen as something that they can do in spite of retardation, or perhaps in order to deny it. Obviously, such individuals will be poor risks in a contraception program (except sterilization) unless they are taught in a concrete form that certain responsibilities, e.g., supporting a family or caring for a child, are too difficult. If they are taught about and if they accept their limitations and strengths, they may be able, without loss of self-esteem, to relinquish their self-images as future parents and substitute them with images of successful, albeit in another area, productive persons.

Thus, in order to prevent sexual abuse of retarded persons, society must recognize that retarded persons at all levels of functioning have a right to sexual expression, just like any other citizens. This implies that the corresponding responsibilities should also be imposed on them, insofar as they are able to act in accordance with externally imposed societal rules. The role of professionals working with retarded children and adults (and their families) will be crucial in interpreting for each individual the appropriate balance between totally free expression and externally imposed inhibition or redistribution of sexual activity.

REFERENCES

Backer, H. 1973. Sexual knowledge and attitudes of mentally retarded adolescents. Am. J. Ment. Defic. 77:706–709.

126   Szymanski

Bass, M. 1972. Developing community acceptance of sex education for the mentally retarded. Siecus, New York.

Bass, M. S. 1978. Surgical contraception: A key to normalization and prevention. Ment. Retard. 16(6):399–404.

Carruth, D. G. 1973. Human sexuality in a halfway house. In: F. F. de la Cruz and G. D. LaVeck (eds.), Human Sexuality and the Mentally Retarded. Brunner/Mazel, New York.

Danielson, F. H., and Davenport, C. B. 1912. The Hill Folk. Cold Spring Harbor, Eugenics Record Office, Long Island, N.Y.

Deisher, R. W. 1973. Sexual behavior of retarded in institutions. In: F. F. de la Cruz and G. D. LaVeck (eds.), Human Sexuality and the Mentally Retarded. Brunner/Mazel, New York.

Fischer, H. L., and Krajicek, M. J. 1974. Sexual development of the moderately retarded child: How can the pediatrician be helpful? Clin. Pediatr. 13:79–83.

Fischer, H. L., Krajicek, M. J., and Borthick, W. A. 1973. Teaching Concepts of Sexual Development to the Developmentally Disabled. Development Unlimited, Denver.

Floor, L., Baxter, D., Rosen, M., and Zisfein, L. 1975. A survey of marriages among previously institutionalized retardates. Ment. Retard. 13(2):33–37.

Friedman, P. R. 1976. The Rights of Mentally Retarded Persons. Avon Books, New York.

Garber, H. 1975. The Milwaukee Project: An experiment in the prevention of cultural-familial mental retardation-intervention at birth. In: M. S. Bass and M. Gelof (eds.), Sexual Rights and Responsibilities of the Mentally Retarded. Bass, 1387 E. Valley Road, Santa Barbara, Cal. 93108.

Goddard, H. H. 1912. The Kallikak Family. Macmillan Publishing Co., New York.

Gordon, S. 1973. A response to Warren Johnson. In: F. F. de la Cruz and G. D. LaVeck (eds.), Human Sexuality and the Mentally Retarded. Brunner/Mazel, New York.

Higgins, J. V., Reed, E. W., and Reed, S. C. 1962. Intelligence and family size: A paradox resolved. Eugen. Q. 9:84–90.

Johnson, W. R. 1973. Sex education of the mentally retarded. In: F. F. de la Cruz and G. D. LaVeck (eds.), Human Sexuality and the Mentally Retarded. Brunner/Mazel, New York.

Kempton, W. 1973. Guidelines for Planning a Training Course on Human Sexuality and the Retarded. Planned Parenthood Association of Southeastern Pennsylvania, Philadelphia.

Kempton, W. 1975. A Teacher's Guide to Sex Education for Persons with Learning Disabilities. Wadsworth Publishing Co., Belmont, Cal.

Krishef, C. H. 1972. State law on marriage and sterilization of the mentally retarded. Ment. Retard. 10:36–38.

Mattinson, J. 1973. Marriage and mental handicap. In: F. F. de la Cruz and G. D. LaVeck (eds.), Human Sexuality and the Mentally Retarded. Brunner/Mazel, New York.

Mitchell, L., Doctor, R. M., and Butler, D. C. 1978. Attitudes of caretakers toward the sexual behavior of mentally retarded persons. Am. J. Ment. Defic. 83:289–296.

Morgenstern, M. 1973. Community attitudes toward sexuality of the retarded. In: F. F. de la Cruz and G. D. LaVeck (eds.), Human Sexuality and the Mentally Retarded. Brunner/Mazel, New York.

Mulhern, T. J. 1975. Survey of reported sexual behavior and policies characterizing residential facilities for retarded citizens. Am. J. Ment. Defic. 79:670–673.

Reed, S. C., and Anderson, V. E. 1973. Effects of changing sexuality on the gene pool. In: F. F. de la Cruz and G. D. LaVeck (eds.), Human Sexuality and the Mentally Retarded. Brunner/Mazel, New York.

Szymanski, L. S. 1977. Psychiatric diagnostic evaluation of mentally retarded individuals. J. Am. Acad. Child Psychiatry 16:67-87.

Vitello, S. J. 1978. Involuntary sterilization: Recent developments. Ment. Retard. 16(6):405-409.

TREATMENT

Just as previous studies have indicated that mentally retarded persons may suffer from any of the known forms of mental illness or personality disturbance, the chapters in this section emphasize that they may benefit from all of the usual methods of treatment. The focus is upon five popular methods of mental health treatment: individual, family, group, behavioral, and pharmacological therapy. Treatment must, of course, be chosen in accordance with the needs and capacities of the individual and his family. In some instances, more than one approach may be needed for effective intervention. Although administration of various treatment modalities may be delegated to specific members of the interdisciplinary team, all team members must be at least generally familiar with the indications, potential benefits, and shortcomings or side effects of the methods in question. Only if this latter requirement is met will retarded persons be assured of receiving appropriate, effective, and efficient mental health treatment.

Professionals experienced in working with younger persons

should find themselves on familiar ground in the four chapters that follow. They will be aware that psychotherapy must be tailored to fit the language capacity of the person being treated, and that play therapy may be useful in some instances. Group therapy may mean family therapy, involving the person's parents and/or other care-givers. Behavioral approaches, designed not solely to decrease maladaptive behaviors but to aid in the development of self-help and interpersonal skills, are a particu-larly popular treatment modality. Finally, medication, although not capable of directly improving cognitive capacity or correcting deviations of development, may be a very useful adjunctive treatment for mentally retarded or develop-mentally disabled persons who are hyperactive, depressed, or suffer from a late-onset form of schizophrenia.

INDIVIDUAL PSYCHOTHERAPY WITH RETARDED PERSONS

Chapter 10

Ludwik S. Szymanski

Psychotherapy of retarded and nonretarded persons is essentially similar, but therapeutic goals and techniques are adapted to retarded persons' unique life circumstances and developmental level (particularly in the communicative and cognitive spheres). This has been pointed out by Yepsen (1952) and is still relevant:

> In the application of the principles of counseling to the influence and control of the mentally retarded, it is not necessary to abandon the basic techniques which are effective with any other group of individuals. However, there is likely to be a different emphasis upon the basic techniques because of the type of person whose behavior and attitudes it is desirable to change.

There is no generally accepted, unequivocal definition of psychotherapy. Eysenck (1966) described it as a prolonged interpersonal relationship, into which one participant (the patient) enters because of an emotional/interpersonal maladjustment, and the other one (the therapist) because he is specially trained to help, utilizing psychological methods based on some formal theory. Bialer (1967) similarly emphasized "psychological procedures," as did Hinsie and Campbell (1970).

Various terms to describe this process are used interchangeably; psychiatrists frequently prefer *psychotherapy* and nonmedically trained professionals prefer *guidance* or *counseling*. Others differentiate between these terms. Hinsie and Campbell (1970) defined *counseling,* or *guidance,* as a "type of psychotherapy of the supportive or re-educative variety; often the term is applied to behavioral problems not strictly classifiable as mental illness, such as vocational or school or marriage problems."

In this chapter, psychotherapy is discussed as a treatment procedure performed by a trained mental health professional, through application of psychologically based verbal and nonverbal means, within the context of relationship with the patient or "client" and with definite goal(s) of improving the patient's coping abilities and/or ameliorating psychopathological symptoms.

HISTORICAL CONSIDERATIONS

Paradoxically, there seem to have been more studies on psychotherapy with retarded persons published in earlier years than in recent ones. Many of the early papers edited by Stacey, DeMartino, and Sarason (1957) are still relevant. More recent studies have been reviewed by Albini and Dinitz (1965), Sternlicht (1965), Jakab (1970), and particularly extensively by Loft (1970). Chidester (1934) published an early report on the feasibility of psychotherapy with a retarded child. Thorne (1948) stressed the importance of having clear objectives of therapy, and reported that in an uncontrolled study of institutionalized individuals, "systematic counseling and psychotherapy has been an unqualified success." Glassman (1943), comparing outcome of psychotherapy between matched groups of children, found that dull normal ones did at least as well as, if not better than, the bright ones. Chess (1962) reported on successful outcome of psychotherapy of 29 retarded children. Selan (1976) reported on successful outpatient mental health programs for retarded adolescents and adults living in a community (but no specific data were given). In spite of an early positive report (Chidester and Menninger, 1936), there have been very few reports in the psychoanalytic literature on treatment of retarded individuals, and only two in the history of the *Psychoanalytic Study of the Child* (Ack, 1966; Smith, McKinnon, and Kessler, 1976), both anecdotal, on children with low-normal intelligence. Healy and Bronner (1939; see also discussion by Sarason, 1953) reported that outcome in patients at a child guidance clinic was associated with IQ scores, but they did not feel that there may be direct causal relationship.

All of these studies suffer from the same methodological problems as studies of outcome of psychotherapy in general, such as lack of matched controls, lack of uniform diagnostic definitions, and lack of concrete criteria of improvement (Meltzoff and Kornreich, 1970). However, as pointed out by Frank (1975), clinical estimates of overall improvement must also be accepted as a valid measure.

Opposition to psychotherapy of retarded persons has come from diverse camps. Psychoanalytically oriented therapists consider lack of abstract-conceptual skills and language deficiency to be insuperable obstacles to development of "insight," and the tendency to dependency an obstacle to resolution of transference, both seen as prerequisites to the success of therapy. The client-centered approach (Rogers and Dymond, 1954) shares the view that normal cognitive skills are required for developing "insight." Behaviorally oriented therapists often see disturbed behavior as a reaction to external reality only (thus indirectly denying retarded persons' capacity to experience inner feelings that might also contribute to such behavior).

These views have been discussed and opposed by Thorne (1948), Abel (1953), and more recently Loft (1970). In the author's experience, the opposition to psychotherapy of retarded persons is most often based on ignorance. Many child psychiatrists who were initially skeptical become enthusiastic about working with retarded patients after they start seeing their first case.

Some state that for economic reasons it is more important to provide psychotherapy to bright "neurotics" rather than retarded people, who would remain retarded anyway. This view ignores the facts that: a) curing retardation is not the goal, b) amelioration of mental disturbance may permit retarded individuals to live almost normal lives in the community rather than in an institution, c) bright neurotic patients often function well anyway, and d) we do not have the right to measure human worth by intelligence.

THE CONTEXT OF PSYCHOTHERAPY

To be effective, psychotherapy cannot be an isolated procedure, but should be part of a comprehensive process with therapeutic, educational, and habilitative goals. Various professionals, the family, and the patient should interact in this process almost as members of an interdisciplinary team. This is necessary considering a retarded person's dependency on multiple services, the effect of which is synergistic rather than additive. For instance, psychotherapy, in conjunction with casework with the family and behavior management at school, may ameliorate separation anxiety. This permits the patient to cooperate in training programs and gain skills that, in turn, improve his self-esteem and general coping abilities. Accurate and comprehensive diagnostic assessment (as described in Chapter 6) is a prerequisite for psychotherapy. The indications for individual psychotherapy are essentially the same as for nonretarded patients: presence of mental disturbance in which psychological factors play an etiological and/or aggravating role; patient's potential to form a sufficient relationship with the therapist and to communicate to some degree, verbally or nonverbally; and expectations that amelioration of psychological symptoms will improve a patient's ability to utilize his cognitive potential.

Level of intelligence per se does not determine suitability for psychotherapy, but it may influence the choice of techniques and goals. Thus, therapy with individuals functioning at a lower intellectual level will focus more on behavioral techniques and teaching concrete coping skills. Patients functioning on a higher intellectual level may also learn to recognize and communicate verbally their feelings (rather than to act them out) and to utilize the therapist as a model for identification and as a source of corrective emotional experience; for even higher functioning individuals, therapy will be primarily verbal and its goals may include insight development and conflict resolution. Of course, one cannot guide therapy solely by the patient's intelligence level; in most cases, elements of all the therapeutic processes mentioned here will be utilized.

GOALS OF PSYCHOTHERAPY

To be effective, psychotherapy for a retarded person (or anyone, for that matter) should be goal oriented (Thorne, 1948; Jakab, 1970). Defining the goals is not always easy. Retarded persons (as are children) are usually brought in by parents or other caregivers. Various professionals, such as teachers and counselors, are often instrumental in the referral. These professionals voice complaints about the patient's behavior and have expectations of what the therapy can achieve. These complaints may reflect the caregivers' discomfort rather than the patient's maladjustment. Thus, an active and curious resident in an institution can be seen as disruptive and aggressive rather than bored and seeking a measure of independence. As opposed to these verbalized, manifest complaints, there are latent complaints and expectations ("hidden agenda"), not verbalized, sometimes unconscious, but often emotionally charged: e.g., an expectation that psychotherapy will cure the patient's retardation. Some expectations may reflect the family's cultural values and should be respected unless they are detrimental to the patient. A compromise is necessary, then. Sex education is a good example. In order to avoid confusion, disappointment, and acting against the patient's interests, the therapist must: a) understand all these complaints and expectations, b) establish priorities for realistic goals and intermediate objectives, c) secure understanding of and agreement on these goals by all involved parties, and d) review and readjust the goals, as necessary, in the course of therapy.

Reconciling these often contradictory expectations requires the therapist to establish good rapport with the patient, the family, and the involved professionals; being open; and not hiding behind professional jargon and generalities, but communicating clearly and concretely.

Some of the commonly encountered goals of psychotherapy include helping the patient in understanding his handicap and feelings associated with it, recognizing strengths, setting realistic expectations of self, improving frustration tolerance and impulse control, learning social coping skills and socially acceptable behavior to the maximally possible degree, overcoming egocentricity (as much as is developmentally possible), recognizing and learning to express emotions appropriately, and solving conflicts of dependency and guilt.

Psychotherapy is expected to result in an increase of the patient's drive toward independence and improvement in self-image. Some patients may have been ignored for years unless they acted out, and the therapy may provide them with an opportunity to be listened to. Patients should be encouraged and taught to express (appropriately) opinions, ideas, feelings, and wishes. One of the important goals is for patients to learn, within their limitations, to rely on themselves in making realistic decisions, and not to expect the therapist to be an overcontrolling parental figure. This intermediate objective of decision making (and confidently admitting their own mistakes) leads to larger goals of improving self-esteem. The therapeutic contract should be seen as a relationship into which the patient enters with the maximum possible degree of choice and with the responsibility to cooperate. Even having retarded patients (if capable) call by themselves for an appointment is an important step toward these goals. One of the therapist's goals is to steer between the Scylla of overprotecting, overcontrolling, and otherwise exploiting the patient and the Charybdis of overwhelming the patient with exaggerated respect and inappropriate responsibilities and expectations that he cannot handle.

TECHNIQUES OF PSYCHOTHERAPY WITH RETARDED PERSONS

Directiveness

It is generally accepted that therapy with retarded persons should be directive. Controversy often exists about the optimal degree of directiveness in psychotherapy of nonretarded patients, particularly children. Most child therapists are still influenced by Axline (1947), who stated, "The child leads the way, the therapist follows." Client-centered therapy and classical psychoanalysis are also nondirective. Brief psychotherapy and behavior therapy would be examples of more directive approaches.

Retarded persons are frequently brought into therapy because they are distractible, dependent, and tolerate frustration poorly. They might therefore be fearful and expect criticism and may see a passive therapist as being dissatisfied with them. In order to function effectively, they need direction in a therapeutic situation. Directiveness in this context means setting structure and limits as necessary and maintaining focus of the therapeutic interaction on relevant issues. However, the therapist has to be sure to give the patient an opportunity and encouragement for spontaneous productions and expression of feelings; he should not force an issue or give leading questions but should lead the patient in the desired direction.

> An 11-year-old, mildly retarded girl with Down's syndrome was referred because of unruly, demanding, immature behavior, reinforced by her over-protective and inconsistent parents. If permitted, she spent entire sessions engaging in repetitive play without any pattern, giving orders to the therapist, or dozing off. Interpretations of this behavior were useless. Firmer limits and structure were set. She was told that even if some issues, such as her separa-tion anxiety, were hard to talk about, they were important. Direct question-ing, empathizing statements, simple interpretation of her feelings, and con-crete suggestions resulted in her cooperation and behavioral improvement, on which she reported with pride.

Thus, to paraphrase Axline, one may state that if the child leads the way, the therapist follows—but first he has to show the child where he should lead him.

Verbal Techniques

Language used with retarded patients should be brief, concrete, clear, and adapted to their level of understanding. The therapist should be sure of the patient's comprehension, since in order to please the therapist (and deny their own inadequacy) these patients tend to state that they under-stand even if they do not. Much verbal therapy has a "here-and-now" focus. Concrete examples relevant to the patient's problems are most useful. Lacking conceptual skills, the patient may be unable to project himself into the past and report, e.g., on his inability to tolerate losing a game, which led to his exclusion from his peer group. The therapist may ask him to play some game during the session, make him lose, and talk immediately about his feelings at that moment. However, higher func-tioning persons may be very able to talk meaningfully about past experi-ences relevant to current issues under discussion, much in the same way nonretarded patients participate in dynamically oriented psychotherapy. DeMartino (1954) reported on the revealing nature of the dream content of retarded persons. Perhaps the most common mistake of inexperienced therapists is not talking with verbal retarded patients about their feelings and problems, under the false assumption that they are incapable of dis-cussing them. On the other hand, a not uncommon mistake is leading the patient into dwelling on "interesting" fantasy material, which may be threatening to a person with poor ego functions and may weaken his reality testing. The therapeutic process is essentially a reality-oriented, teaching-learning experience. A retarded person's acting out of an emo-tion may be, to a substantial degree, because of ignorance that other ways of handling the emotion are more socially acceptable. He may have to be taught that the emotion he experiences is appropriate, but its expression is not. He could have learned, through past experience, that a temper tantrum gets him attention from his caregiver (even if negative). Appropriate ways of handling emotions may have to be taught to him concretely through verbal explanations, play-acting, doll or puppet play, or identification with the therapist, all supported by empathy and reinforcement appropriate to his level of functioning. As in any learning, repetition is important.

Improving the patient's tolerance of frustration (or in psychoanalytic terms, transition from pleasure principle to reality principle) is often one of the initial steps. An eclectic approach is necessary, such as verbal explanations, desensitization through milieu manipulation (to create increasing degrees of frustrating situations), and positive reinforcement of successes. However, because of retarded persons' sensitivity to criticism and expectation of failure, therapists should always focus first on the patients' strengths and provide an opportunity for success (e.g., through talking about their achievements or engaging during the therapy sessions in tasks in which the patients are proficient).

Longer periods of silence, if unaccompanied by some appropriate activity, must be avoided. Usually a patient lapses into silence not because of resistance but because he does not know what to say, and based on past experiences of ridicule he does not want to say something wrong. Retarded people learn fast that (unless they have obvious phenotypical abnormalities) silence serves as a "cloak of competence" (to use the words of Edgerton, 1967). Of course, at times silence may reflect anxiety about a particular issue. Empathetic and warm support by the therapist is usually sufficient to overcome it. A silent, staring, and waiting therapist is seen as rejecting and critical.

Nonverbal Techniques

Nonverbal techniques, such as play or other concrete activities, and nonverbal communication are important in psychotherapy of retarded people of all ages because of the patients' deficiencies in verbal communication skills and better response to concrete as opposed to conceptual activities.

Play in Psychotherapy   Ericson (1950) pointed out that play has an important role in a child's development in achieving new stages of mastery and that it is not a mere recreation, as adult play might be. In the years that followed, "play therapy" became an important approach, pioneered by researchers such as Axline (1947), a proponent of nondirective play therapy, and Klein (1955). A valuable review of early contributions can be found in Haworth (1964) and of more recent ones in Schaefer (1976).

It is difficult to consider play therapy as a specific technique. As pointed out by Harrison (1975), play is an integral aspect of most psychotherapy with children and it makes little sense to refer to it specifically as "play therapy." Obviously, not every play session with a child is therapy; yet, perhaps because of lack of trained personnel, any play session is frequently called "play therapy." In this chapter the focus is on utilization of play within the context of comprehensive psychotherapy, with clear therapeutic goals by a trained professional who understands the dynamics and meaning of child's play and uses this knowledge in order to achieve these goals.

Leland and Smith (1965) wrote extensively on the use of play in therapy of retarded children and saw it as a technique for teaching communicative, motor, and social skills. Similar approaches were taken by Morrison and Newcomer (1975), who saw an increase in such skills in a small group of treated institutionalized children. These authors, however, used play essentially as a teaching-stimulation tool and not as part of a psychotherapeutic process.

There are several uses of play as a psychotherapeutic tool. It is a means of communication for both verbal and nonverbal patients, although capacity for internal symbolic language may be a prerequisite for symbolic use of play. Play provides practice of mastery over life events through reenacting them (as pointed out first by Freud (1955) on the example of a child who "practiced" the experience of disappearance and return of his mother). Ericson (1950) called play a child's "microsphere," a safe harbor, a world of manageable toys. In psychotherapy of a retarded child, who needs concrete substrate for verbal discussion, play serves as a microcosm, a sort of "model psychodrama." Relevant issues may be first enacted in play and then may be discussed either directly (as the child's own concerns) if the child can tolerate it without play interruption (Ericson, 1950) or indirectly within the context of the make-believe world of play. A dollhouse with a doll family is particularly well suited for this purpose. Play also serves as a neutral "icebreaker" in the initial stages of therapy and as a bridge to establishing patient-therapist rapport; later it can be a safe shelter if the therapy becomes too anxiety provoking.

Directiveness is useful in play if balanced with initial nondirectiveness, permitting free expression. This structuring will help to channel the play activity into what is most relevant to therapeutic goals, particularly if the patient is distractible. The therapist may also purposely set up specific play situations focusing on the child's relevant conflicts, and may then manipulate the play toward a constructive resolution.

> An 11-year-old, mildly retarded girl with Down's syndrome was referred because of uncontrollable, demanding, manipulative behavior, separation anxiety, and negativism. In nondirective play she endlessly manipulated toys

without any predominant theme. Interpretations, support, limits were to no avail. Dollhouse play was suggested. In its course, scenes of Oedipal attachment and separation anxiety were played out with active direction of the therapist, as well as verbally interpreted. When this was well tolerated, direct discussion of the girl's home behavior ensued with subsequent improvement reported by the parents.

Play may be very effective in therapy of older retarded individuals. Its use should not be guided solely by the patient's mental age (MA) but also by his social maturity, chronological age, and self-awareness. A retarded adult, even with an MA of 7 years, is still an adult, aware of it, and insulted if told to engage in "child's" play. However, he may benefit from reality-oriented activities within the context of therapy sessions, if properly chosen and directed; for example, a brief trip to a store may test a patient's self-control and social skills. His maladaptive behavior can be concretely and immediately pointed out and alternative behavioral patterns may be suggested and modeled by the therapist.

Other Nonverbal Techniques Nonverbal communication (term coined by Ruesch and Kees, 1956), including body language, gross motility, and vocal intonation, is an important means of communication, particularly with individuals with verbal language deficiencies. Many nonverbal expressions are universal; others may be idiosyncratic. Therapists should become familiar with such behaviors of their patients during therapy, both by direct observation and by history obtained from caregivers. For instance, in one patient seen in our clinic, sudden overactivity and whining signaled anger, which would rapidly erupt into either running away or physical aggression. If recognized early, it could be prevented by setting limits and giving liberal verbal reassurance.

If feasible, videotaping the session may help patient and therapist to recognize such communications. An early classical and still relevant study of nonverbal communications was written by Darwin (1873) and a more modern one by Feldman (1959).

Setting the Limits

Appropriate limits are necessary in psychotherapy. Some therapists, especially those who are psychoanalytically or client-centered oriented, feel that any limits stifle the patient's spontaneity and put the therapist in the position of a rejecting parent. Others (Bixler, 1949) feel that limits are therapy. It is doubtful that any therapist does not set limits for his patients, particularly children, at least by implication if not expressly. Limits are necessary and therapeutic with retarded patients, although not because they are more aggressive. These patients may have low frustration tolerance, may be overactive, or simply may not know how to act in a given situation. A variety of behaviors may require limits: excessive noise, destructiveness, direct aggression, and accosting others during trips outside. Unless prevented, these behaviors might escalate to the point that limits with punitive connotations must be set. Generally, such limits are set on person-directed aggression, very disruptive behavior, and property destruction (except for toys specified for this purpose).

Limits should be set in clear, brief, concrete form, without criticism; for example, it is better to say "We must behave quietly in order not to disturb others in the clinic" rather than "Do not make so much noise." If inappropriate behaviors are the result of excessive stimulation, e.g., during a visit to a coffee shop, desensitization may be used: first, talking about it, then role playing, and later taking increasingly longer trips (within the patient's tolerance) to the shop.

PHASES OF THE PSYCHOTHERAPEUTIC PROCESS

The process of psychotherapy is commonly divided into three stages: initial, "working through" (or middle), and termination. They are not sharply delineated, however. Certain themes may be typical for certain stages, but because of the retarded patient's tendency to regression and need for repetition, they may recur in any stage.

Initial Phase

Therapy goals, ground rules, and rapport are established in the initial phase. The patient's language and cognitive skills permitting, the problems that brought him into therapy are discussed. If possible, he is led to recognize them by himself; otherwise, the concerns of his caregivers are presented to him. This is done in clear and concrete terms, avoiding what could be construed as criticism. For example, a statement like "Your parents would like you to be happier" may be better accepted than "They don't like that you yell at your mother and hit her." The patient's tendency to projection should not be confronted directly: an answer to "It's my mother's fault" may be "Let's find out what you and I can do to make things better," adding "Your mother tries too—that's why she also comes for talks here." This gives the patient some chance to exercise mastery over his life without having to admit to being at fault. Some concrete externalization of the patient's problems may provide an ego syntonic avenue to their acceptance: "Your problem is that you get angry and say things too fast; many people have the same trouble. You and I are going to learn to fight this problem." In this stage, as well as in later stages, empathy and support are given liberally.

Middle Stage

The bulk of the psychotherapeutic work is usually done in the middle stage. Rapport and therapeutic alliance have already been established.

The patient sees the therapist as a concerned and trustworthy, but firm, person. The therapist should empathize with, but not overprotect, the patient and should understand him and communicate effectively with him. As a result of this rapport, the therapist can use himself as a powerful therapeutic tool (Tisza, 1975). He serves as a model for identification through talking about and demonstrating directly how he would behave in situations similar to those under discussion. He can be said to serve as the patient's supportive, external ego, but he encourages internalization and avoids increasing the patient's dependency. He organizes his observations of the patient's behaviors in a clear and concrete form and presents it to the patient, thus giving him self-understanding as a first step to mastery. This is very necessary in light of the retarded person's egocentricity and difficulties in concept formation and self-observation. One can draw here a parallel with Keith's (1968) concept of the therapist having synthesizing and observing functions as a sort of auxiliary ego.

Issues relating to the patient's developmental difficulties, even if not presenting problems on referral, have to be discussed; unfortunately, many therapists, perhaps because of their own anxiety, maintain a conspiracy of silence about it. Confrontations are to be avoided ("Tell me how you feel about being retarded"). Instead, with empathy, the patient is led to bring it up on his own: "You told me you have been called names by other people. It's unfair and must be difficult on you. What names did they call you?" Definitions are not taken for granted, and if the patient mentions that he is retarded, the therapist should explore what he means by it. If necessary, clear and appropriate explanations are given. The therapist can use descriptive and nonderogatory terms, such as *troubles in learning.* Support and empathy are helpful: "I also have troubles in learning music—it's a sort of retardation in music." One should also focus on the patient's strengths: "What things can you learn easily and are you good at?"

It is expected that during this stage of therapy the ego is strengthened and forces used for inefficient defenses are released and sublimated into constructive behaviors in areas of competence.

Termination Stage

Termination of psychotherapy may be threatening to mentally retarded patients. They are frequently dependent and sensitive to rejection. Their therapist could well have been one of the few supportive and empathetic persons in their lives, and losing him may evoke regression, depression, and acting out. Preparation for termination should be gradual and is done throughout the therapy, through developing the patient's ego strengths and sense of mastery. Vacations and other absences of the therapist are very useful as concrete starting points for analyzing the patient's reactions to past losses and for preparing him for loss of the therapist at the termination of therapy. Timing of announcement of termination date will vary with a patient's ability to perceive time framework. Optimally, he should be led to "discover" it as a sort of vote of confidence in his abilities, that he will not need therapy anymore. Follow-up visits may be scheduled. Well-functioning support systems, both outside of and within the family, will help to maintain the gains acquired during the therapy. Issues such as the patient's perception of the termination and associated feelings (such as anger) should be explored just as with nonretarded patients, either verbally or through play.

CONTACTS WITH THE FAMILY

If the patient lives with his parents (or other family members), casework with his family is an essential part of his psychotherapy because of his dependency on family members. This casework may range from intensive psychotherapy to occasional advice on resource findings.

The cardinal rule is to remember that the parents are not a priori patients and they should not be treated as such (unless they explicitly need and request psychotherapy for themselves). Because they are prone to feelings of guilt (for the patient's retardation and/or maladjustment), caution should be exercised in order not to aggravate these feelings. May (1958), himself a physician, wrote a pathetic account of how he and his wife were subjected to psychoanalytic treatment in order to "cure" their autistic and retarded twins. When recommending casework, the therapist should explicitly explain its goals and relevance to the child's problems; for example, goals of teaching the parents behavior management techniques and alleviating their tendency to overprotect the child are more acceptable than vague "helping with the feelings about your child." It is important not to assume automatically that inappropriate handling of the child and/or feelings like "chronic sorrow" (Olshansky, 1962), guilt, and anxiety are caused by a neurotic conflict concerning the child's retardation. In fact, reasons like ignorance and lack of services are most often responsible.

As in any casework or psychotherapy, a variety of issues may be relevant, depending on the individual case. The following outline is an attempt to simplify classification of issues often encountered:

A. Parent education
   1. Behavior management techniques
   2. Specific developmental delays, abilities, and needs of the child
   3. Techniques of helping the child to achieve the maximum level of independence possible
   4. Long-range planning for normalized living
   5. Sex education
   6. Resource finding

B. Emotional adjustment
1. Adaptation to child's retardation and dealing with associated feelings: guilt, depression, anger, death wish, and resulting defenses, such as overprotection
2. Provision for own needs for emotional fulfillment, privacy
3. Learning to achieve gratification from the child
C. Family adjustment
1. Marital conflicts, particularly regarding the retarded child
2. Needs of siblings
3. Retarded child's role in family dynamics

The therapist should be flexible, eclectic, and familiar with various techniques of psychotherapy. Usually, the parents are seen jointly (although individual meetings may sometimes be indicated or requested). Optimally, their (retarded) child should participate at least part-time in some of the meetings. This enables the therapist to observe parent-child interaction and behaviors, which contributes to the therapist's understanding and permits immediate and concrete interpretations. Also, the parents may utilize the therapist as an identification model in learning to communicate appropriately and respectfully with the child, setting limits for him, having appropriate expectations of him, and giving him support. With younger children, the parents may also be encouraged to play during such sessions. With verbal adolescents and young adults the interaction will be similar to one in "regular" family therapy. Siblings and other significant family members may be included if their contribution to the family's pathological dynamics concerning its retarded member is considerable. In some cases only family sessions may be held, but usually the retarded person requires the support of an individual relationship with the therapist.

TRANSFERENCE AND RESISTANCE

Retarded people respond to the therapist and the therapeutic situation, including manifesting resistance and transference, just as nonretarded ones do. The forms in which these reactions are displayed are different, however; retarded patients' reactions are usually more regressive and primitive and correspond to the patients' developmental-social level. On the other hand, if approached properly, retarded patients have been observed consistently to be much less resistant to psychotherapy than nonretarded peers, perhaps because of higher dependency needs and lack of sophisticated, intellectual defenses.

The patient may fear the therapist's criticism, his finding out about the patient's shortcomings, of behaving inappropriately, and of subsequent rejection by the therapist. These fears are usually based on traumatic past experiences. Dependency on the therapist and need for his approval are universal. This corresponds to the "outer directedness" of retarded persons described by Zigler and Balla (1977). These patients learn quickly that the therapist's attention can be more readily secured by appropriate behavior, however. Conversely, regression may be a form of expressing anger. Love and anger may also be expressed more directly than by a nonretarded patient of the same chronological age:

> A 17-year-old, mildly retarded boy, after his therapist returned from vacation, reported with anxiety about dreaming that the therapist died in a plane crash while away. Subsequently, he was able to discuss his feelings about the therapist's absence when the latter assumed an empathetic and noncritical stance.

> An 11-year-old, mildly retarded girl started to invite her therapist to visit her at home. She wasn't able to discuss her attachment to him directly, but did it through puppet play, following which the invitations ceased and her attachment to the therapist became more constructive.

THE THERAPIST AS A "REAL PERSON"

Retarded patients, as do younger children, may have difficulties in differentiating help and support on an ideational level from help and support on a concrete level. They also have multiple handicaps, needs, and service providers with whom the therapist must collaborate. Thus, the therapist has to enter the patient's life to an appropriate degree as resource finder, advocate, and consultant to teachers. School and home visits may be necessary. During the therapy sessions he must often provide direct role modeling and advice. Thus, the therapist must be (and feel comfortable in this role) a "real person" and not only a neutral "therapeutic mirror."

PROBLEMS OF COUNTERTRANSFERENCE

The usual problems of the therapist's countertransference are complicated by his reactions to the patient's retardation. Jakab (1970) has pointed out that the therapist starts with a handicap since after the treatment is completed the subject of his endeavors will still be defective (retarded). The therapist's guilt (usually unconscious) for not being able to cure the patient may lead to defensive maneuvers, such as overprotection, lack of limits, and inappropriate expectations. Some therapists harbor unconscious omnipotent wishes to cure these patients (Jakab, 1970), with resulting unrealistic expectations and superficial behavior changes, and suppression of symptoms. Therapists with rescue wishes will identify with, and overprotect, the patient, thus encouraging his acting out. Often the therapist may see these patients as children whom he should "parent," thus leading to competition with the parents:

The mother of an 11-year-old, very anxious, mildly retarded girl was hostile and defensive toward the child's therapist and complained bitterly about the child's terrible behavior at home. The beleaguered therapist defensively, and with unconscious but obvious glee, reported to the mother how well the child behaved during therapy sessions. Soon the child became resistant to coming to therapy, which was later traced to the mother openly expressing to the child her anger at the therapist.

The sexuality of older patients, particularly its inappropriate expression, may be a threat to the therapist. He may deny it altogether, or "push" this issue as vicarious discharge of his own conflicts. Some therapists see their patients as unable to experience emotions, too fragile to discuss them, and hardly talk with them, concentrating instead on activities, whereas others press analytic interpretations beyond the patients' understanding. In some cases, therapists may act out against such "uninteresting" patients assigned to them against their wish.

These unconstructive reactions can be prevented and modified through the therapist's training and supervision. In most cases, as their therapeutic skills increase, therapists will learn to derive considerable professional gratification from treating retarded and otherwise developmentally disabled patients.

Last, but not least, the problems of confidentiality must be mentioned. The need for confidentiality in psychotherapy, even of children, is well accepted and has been pointed out by Ross (1966). However, even experienced therapists tend to see retarded patients of any age as different and incompetent children and violate rules of confidentiality they would otherwise observe if the patient were a "normal" child. Respect for the patient as a human being should not be dependent on his IQ. If anything, retarded patients are more in need of protection of confidentiality. Their multiple caregivers and service providers usually request, and need, communication from one another, and the therapist's reports may be widely distributed. Cursory parental permission for such communications may be sufficient legally, but not ethically. Whenever feasible, the patient's permission should be secured. What will be communicated and why should be carefully explained to him. Besides being ethical, such an approach has therapeutic value because it demonstrates concretely to the patient that he is treated with respect.

REFERENCES

Abel, T. M. 1953. Resistances and difficulties in psychotherapy of mental retardates. J. Clin. Psychol. 9:107–109.

Ack, M. 1966. Julie: The treatment of a case of developmental retardation. Psychoanal. Stud. Child 21:127–149.

Albini, J. L., and Dinitz, S. 1965. Psychotherapy with disturbed and defective children: An evaluation of changes in behavior and attitudes. Am. J. Ment. Defic. 69:560–567.

Axline, V. M. 1947. Play Therapy. Houghton Mifflin Co., Boston.

Bialer, I. 1967. Psychotherapy and other adjustment techniques with the mentally retarded. In: A. A. Baumeister (ed.), Mental Retardation. Aldine Publishing Co., Chicago.

Bixler, R. H. 1949. Limits are therapy. J. Consult. Psychol. 13:1–11.

Chess, S. 1962. Psychiatric treatment of the mentally retarded child with behavior problems. Am. J. Orthopsychiatry 32:863–869.

Chidester, L. 1934. Therapeutic results with mentally retarded children. Am. J. Orthopsychiatry 4:464–472.

Chidester, L., and Menninger, K. A. 1936. The application of psychoanalytic methods to the study of mental retardation. Am. J. Orthopsychiatry 6:616–625.

Darwin, L. 1873. The Expression of the Emotion in Man and in Animals. John Murray Publishers, London.

DeMartino, M. F. 1954. Some characteristics of the manifest dream content of mental defectives. J. Clin. Psychol. 10:175–178.

Edgerton, R. B. 1967. The Cloak of Competence: Stigma in the Lives of the Mentally Retarded. University of California Press, Berkeley.

Ericson, E. H. 1950. Childhood and Society. W. W. Norton & Co., New York.

Eysenck, H. J. 1966. The Effects of Psychotherapy. International Science Press, New York.

Feldman, S. S. 1959. Mannerisms of Speech and Gestures in Everyday Life. International Universities Press, New York.

Frank, J. D. 1975. Evaluation of psychiatric treatment. In: A. M. Freedman, H. I. Kaplan, and B. J. Sadock (eds.), Comprehensive Textbook of Psychiatry. 3rd ed. Williams & Wilkins Co., Baltimore.

Freud, S. 1955. Beyond the Pleasure Principle. The Standard Edition of the Complete Psychological Works, Vol. 18. The Hogarth Press, London.

Glassman, L. A. 1943. Is dull normal intelligence a contraindication for psychotherapy? Smith College Stud. Social Work 13:275–298.

Harrison, S. I. 1975. Individual psychotherapy. In: A. M. Freedman and H. I. Kaplan (eds.), Comprehensive Textbook of Psychiatry. Williams & Wilkins Co., Baltimore.

Haworth, M. R. (ed.). 1964. Child Psychotherapy. Basic Books, New York.

Healy, W., and Bronner, A. F. 1939. Treatment and What Happened Afterwards. Judge Baker Guidance Center, Boston.

Hinsie, L. E., and Campbell, R. J. 1970. Psychiatric Dictionary. Oxford University Press, New York.

Jakab, I. 1970. Psychotherapy of the mentally retarded child. In: N. R. Bernstein (ed.), Diminished People. Little, Brown & Co., Boston.

Keith, C. R. 1968. The therapeutic alliance in child psychotherapy. J. Am. Child Psychiatry 7:31–43.

Klein, M. 1955. The psychoanalytic play technique. Am. J. Orthopsychiatry 25:223–237.

Leland, H., and Smith, D. E. 1965. Play therapy with mentally subnormal children. Grune & Stratton, New York.

Loft, G. 1970. Psychotherapy of the mentally retarded: Values and cautions. In: F. J. Menolascino (ed.), Psychiatric Approaches to Mental Retardation. Basic Books, New York.

May, J. 1958. A Physician Looks at Psychiatry. John Day Co., New York.

Meltzoff, J., and Kornreich, M. 1970. Research in Psychotherapy. Atherton Press, New York.

Morrison, T. L., and Newcomer, B. L. 1975. Effects of directive vs. nondirective play therapy with institutionalized mentally retarded children. Am. J. Ment. Defic. 79:666–669.

Olshansky, S. 1962. Chronic sorrow: A response to having a mentally defective child. Social Casework 43:191–193.

Rogers, C. R., and Dymond, R. F. 1954. Psychotherapy and Personality Change. University of Chicago Press, Chicago.

Ross, A. O. 1966. Confidentiality in child therapy. Ment. Hygiene 50:360–366.

Ruesch, J., and Kees, W. 1956. Nonverbal Communication. University of California Press, Berkeley.

Sarason, S. B. 1953. Psychological Problems in Mental Deficiency. Harper & Bros., New York.

Schaefer, C. E. (ed.). 1976. Therapeutic Use of Child's Play. Jason Aronson, New York.

Selan, B. H. 1976. Psychotherapy with the developmentally disabled. Health Social Work 1:74–84.

Smith, E., McKinnon, R., and Kessler, J. W. 1976. Psychotherapy with mentally retarded children. Psychoanal. Stud. Child 31:493–514.

Stacey, C. L., DeMartino, M. F., and Sarason, S. B. (eds.). 1957. Counseling and Psychotherapy with the Mentally Retarded: A Book of Readings. The Free Press, Glencoe, Ill.

Sternlicht, M. 1965. Psychotherapy techniques useful with mentally retarded: A review and critique. Psychiatr. Q. 39:84–90.

Thorne, F. C. 1948. Counseling and psychotherapy with mental defectives. Am. J. Ment. Defic. 52:263–271.

Tisza, V. B. 1975. Training the child psychiatrist. J. Am. Acad. Child Psychiatry 14:204–209.

Yepsen, L. N. 1952. Counseling the mentally retarded. Am. J. Ment. Defic. 57:205–213.

Zigler, E., and Balla, D. 1977. Personality factors in the performance of the retarded: Implications for clinical assessment. J. Am. Acad. Child Psychiatry 16:19–37.

FAMILY ADAPTATION TO THE DIAGNOSIS OF MENTAL RETARDATION IN A CHILD AND STRATEGIES OF INTERVENTION

Chapter 11

Mary B. Hagamen

During the past 15 years there has developed an extensive literature dedicated to helping parents adapt to the diagnosis of mental retardation in their child (Koch and Dobson, 1971; Klaus and Kennel, 1976; Ferholt and Solnit, 1978). Much has been written about parental attitudes and defenses, particularly as they relate to the autistic child (Goldfarb et al., 1970; Matheny and Vernick, 1970). Other writings pertain to training parents to work with their own children in such a way as to foster cognitive and social development (Becker, 1971; Patterson and Guillion, 1971; Barnard and Powell, 1972; Hunter, 1972; Schopler and Reichler, 1972; Wing, 1972; Watson, 1973; Kozloff, 1974). Still other publications relate to the public health aspect of support systems designed to maintain retarded youngsters in the community (Schopler and Reichler, 1976; Hagamen, 1977). It is well established by many authors that emotional disturbances are three to five times as common in the retarded population as in the population at large, or up to 50% of the mentally retarded have some kind of emotional disturbance (Chess, 1977). This chapter concerns parental reaction to mental retardation in general, the variables that affect parents' capacity to adapt positively, and some accentuated patterns of care.

Solnit and Stark (1961) wrote that parents of newborns need to mourn the anticipated normal baby before they can attach to the baby who is defective. But how does one mourn while caring for a cuddly baby, or how does one care for a baby when one is in mourning? The studies on maternal-infant bonding by Klaus and Kennel (1976) and more recently by Emde and Brown (1978) have begun to expand our understanding of the attachment process that occurs when a baby is born with a recognizable mental retardation syndrome.

The popular book *On Death and Dying* by Kübler-Ross (1969) challenged mental health professionals to better understand the emotions that are precipitated by loss. She described the feelings common to people who know that they have life-threatening illness, such as cancer, and described people's reactions to their impending deaths as occurring in stages. Klaus and Kennel (1976) have also used stages to describe the reaction of parents to the birth of a defective baby. This is a helpful concept to bear in mind in reviewing parental reactions to the parents' loss of their expectation for a healthy, normal child and their caregiving patterns in providing for a retarded youngster.

No matter what a parent's level of adaptation, socioeconomic status, educational level, general health, marital status, or geographical location, having a mentally retarded child is associated with a stress of considerable proportions. Although every child born makes a lifelong impact on the family, changing the family profile, aspirations, and expectations, the change of image to the individual members and to the family as a whole is more profound when it is learned that the child will be retarded. Even strong, healthy, well-educated parents with comfortable emotional and fiscal resources can be devastated when they find out that the much-anticipated baby will be limited in competence. However, in the long run, caring for a retarded child can be a positive experience as well.

VARIABLES AFFECTING ADAPTATION

We cannot address the spectrum of parental reaction to retardation without recognizing the many critical variables that affect parental reactions; perhaps most significant is the range of limitations involved in mental retardation, which extends from profound, to mild, to borderline. Next in significance are the age at which retardation is recognized and by whom it is recognized, the sophistication of the service providers in both health and educational settings, the resources available to meet the specific needs of the child and his family, and the broad cultural variation among parents, which is affected by socioeconomic class, geographical region, and ethnic heritage. Finally, the personalities of the parents and the size and structure of the family greatly affect parental reaction to a handicapped child.

One of the most important factors in parental reaction to a defective baby is that the parents' prenatal fantasies of what the child might become are shattered. When the retarded child is the firstborn it is difficult for two reasons. First, many cultures have endowed the firstborn son with special privileges, and families develop specific expectations for that heir. When these cannot be fulfilled, there may be a more difficult adjustment for the parents and grandparents. Second, if there are older children in a family, they can frequently share in the caregiving activities, thus easing the strain on the parents. The impact of an affected only girl, or only boy, as well as one member of a twin or triplet set, compounds reactions and creates difficulty in adaptation. In a study of several hundred handicapped children, Barsch (1968) found that the decision to have no more children depended on the interaction of two variables: the age of the mother and the severity of the child's handicap. Other factors that pertain to the family's capacity to cope with the birth of a retarded baby are the educational levels of the parents, social and marital interaction patterns, parental religious beliefs and practices, and the parents' communication patterns and value systems. Although a higher level of intelligence is no guarantee that parents will be more capable of coping, it is generally felt that if parents have the capacity to understand clearly what is wrong with their child and what can be done about it, they are in a much better position to play an effective role in treatment planning.

Although ability to incorporate a disturbed retarded child into a family has been demonstrated at all socioeconomic levels, people in the more affluent levels are less apt to comfortably maintain a child in the home after the preschool years. This is particularly true if the mother is career oriented, because she is likely to depend on household help, have a crowded schedule, and have less flexibility and time available for her retarded child's special needs. Now that mothers as well as fathers are likely to be away from home frequently, it is often harder to assimilate a retarded youngster into the family. The presence of a retarded, disturbed older child in such a fast-paced home can create a climate of tension that is destructive to every family member. In earlier times, when mothers were more apt to be full-time homemakers and use domestic help to provide relief, it was easier to manage a limited youngster in the home after the preschool years. In rural settings, acceptance is apt to be less stressful because mentally retarded persons can frequently be useful. On a farm there are multiple routine chores, such as milking cows, gathering eggs, and picking garden produce, that can be done by a retarded family member when there is someone near to supervise. This gives the affected child and his parents a sense of worth.

Anything that dilutes the intensity of the interaction between the primary caregiver and the limited child will increase the possibility of a positive adjustment, such as other people in the household to whom the caregiver and child can relate and daily activities outside of the house, to provide social contacts, education, and recreation for the child. Outside contacts for the mother are also important and seem particularly helpful when they are with other mothers of handicapped children. Large families tend to manage the mentally retarded child with greater ease than do small families, although this is not invariably true. The more compatible, congenial people there are in the environment of the retarded child, the more supportive interaction there will be for the child and the family. There is thus established a shared support system that decreases the stress on the parents. A nuclear family that is characterized by strong religious beliefs, a definite value system, and an open pattern of community communication can provide for a retarded child with considerably less strain than can a nuclear family without community ties and with a life-style that is largely self-sufficient (e.g., families in which members do not share responsibilities of child care).

How professional services are administered closely affects a family's reaction to a mentally retarded member. Szymanski (1977) reported that he continuously encountered families who had been severely traumatized by the manner in which they were informed of the diagnosis. Such families report that physicians have diagnosed retardation simply by informal impression (e.g., "He looks retarded"); these impressions frequently were recorded in the hospital charts and were subsequently perpetuated in stereotyped phrases, such as "This well-known retarded child is being admitted..." The retarded child with an emotional disturbance is frequently seen by a large number of professionals from various disciplines. Unless these professionals are used to working together and have a common philosphy, it is easy for the parents of the affected child to become confused as they try to comprehend the total picture. Their reaction may even appear pathological as they struggle to synthesize the diverse information they have received. The attitudes of the professionals are critical to the parents' awareness, understanding, and acceptance of their child's condition. The level of sophistication of the health and educational service system available to meet the needs of the retarded child can have a tremendous effect on the way the parents of the child react. If the system is able to provide the family with a clear understanding of the child's condition, its cause, treatment goals, and the prognosis, the family will be much better able to comply with professional recommendations on how to handle the child and will experience a far greater level of satisfaction with their ability to cope with the situation. It should be understood that the parents' comprehension of the child's situation is a process that takes place over time.

SPECTRUM OF REACTION IN PARENTS OF RETARDED CHILDREN

Bearing in mind the many variables described previously, a few generalizations can be made about the reaction patterns of mature parents when they become aware that their child will be mentally retarded.

Even when a child is diagnosed as mentally retarded at birth, the reality of the situation does not register during the first informing interview. Understanding the child's condition and what it means to his future is only initiated by the professional who first reveals this information. Parents' understanding and awareness develop over the coming weeks and years. Because of multiple variables, the significance of the handicap can change as resources necessary to meet the needs of the family wax and wane. When told of the child's deficit, most families are shocked and automatically deny the diagnosis. They go on to feel confused, saddened, and guilty. A potpourri of emotions develops. Some parents become anxious and fearful, others are angry. Figure 1 portrays the emotional response of these parents in a helpful way. Initially, since the parents have had little experience with mental retardation, the true significance of what it will mean for them does not sink in. Reorganization may take weeks, months, even years, and some parents never reorganize to a constructive stage. Emde and Brown (1978) reported on the initial family crisis created by the birth of a Down's syndrome baby and further elaborated on the process of adaptation by describing six cases taken from a prospective, longitudinal study of social affective development in infants. This valuable report, done in the context of investigation of normal attachment behavior, etches in bold relief the complications of attachment that occur with the mother-Down's baby dyad. The expectations of the parents for a normal baby are shattered. They demonstrate shock, which is frequently followed by denial and the need to work through their emotions so that they have energy available for attachment

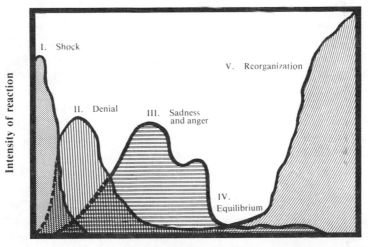

Figure 1.   Hypothetical model of the sequence of normal parental reactions to the birth of a child with congenital malformations. (Reprinted with permission from Drotar, D., Baskiewicz, A., Irvin, N., Kennell, J. H., and Klaus, M. H., The adaptation of parents to the birth of an infant with a congenital malformation: A hypothetical model. *Pediatrics,* 1975, *56,* 710–717. Copyright American Academy of Pediatrics 1975.)

to their special child and the multiple accommodations necessary. Parents of a Down's baby, although intellectually aware of their child's handicap, may have great difficulty realizing the extent of its limitations. Ferholt and Solnit (1978) have pointed out that if the handicap is only intellectual, it is especially hard to deal with because it is invisible, ambiguous, and, in early years, unpredictable. With intellectually handicapped children, longer periods of denial may result and parents often experience repeated episodes of loss and grief each time the defect becomes more apparent.

Emde and Brown's (1978) description of mother-Down's infant attachment opened a new area of investigation: maternal-infant attachment in instances where the baby is handicapped. When parents learn at birth that their child will be different, there is a good opportunity to study the entire bonding process. For mixed conditions, such as autism associated with mental retardation and other types of pervasive developmental disorders resulting in severe mental handicaps, the recognition of the deficit is prolonged for varying lengths of time, thus creating an atmosphere for further distortion of attachment. This delayed recognition also potentiates confusion, entanglement of emotions, and an enlarged cast of characters as parents survey health and educational services to find resources, which are frequently lacking. This prolonged period of stress makes both the parent and the child high risk candidates for emotional reactive disorders. Studies documenting the early attachment process in children whose mental retardation is not detectable in infancy have yet to be published, but will inevitably come along as more comprehensive, prospective, longitudinal investigations on parent-child interactions are done. No matter what the parents' underlying mental status, the late-to-be-diagnosed child can be a source of conflicting opinions among family members, who all may have individual perceptions and opinions, and local providers of health and educational services, who frequently contest diagnoses involving poorly understood and newly described syndromes of children with developmental disabilities (if these require expensive services). There is less conflict when there is an early, definitive diagnosis, as in Down's syndrome.

Because of the better-understood longitudinal patterns of development in Down's children, their parents are spared much of the conflict that besets parents of late-to-be-diagnosed youngsters. The more normal a child appears and the older he is before developmental disability is suspected, the greater tendency there will be for family members to deny the existence of the problem. The general range of situations in the diagnosis of mental retardation extends from a Down's baby, diagnosed at birth, to a borderline youngster whose learning disabilities may not be appropriately recognized until the later (usually school) years. Sometimes these children initially seem to have such fine social graces that no one can believe they are so limited. As a result, they may suffer from a variety of pressures before their true situation is recognized, which places the child at high risk for a reactive emotional problem. As the family realizes that a member is retarded, the next move is usually to collect facts about the child's condition. The sophistication with which this information gathering takes place is frequently, but not always, related to the family's educational level and socioeconomic status. Information gathering can range from conferences with friends and relatives to library searches, to contact with local service centers, to direct phone calls to child development specialists at prestigious universities. During this time, some families go through a series of consultations for other opinions.

GROWING UP WITH RETARDATION

Regardless of the information gathered, most parents come to intellectualize and deny the severity of the handicap. This is particularly true if the youngster is without physical stigmata. As noted earlier, initial denial is a common, almost reflex, action. Parents need to have a breathing spell and a chance for optimism. The handsome appearance or winsome behavior of a retarded youngster, if present, provides that chance. As parents come to focus on the positive attributes of the child rather than hope for rapid mental development, they gradually begin to lower their expectation for academic achievement and begin thinking of more realistic life goals for their retarded child. Some parents are able to adjust their routines and life-styles to accommodate the needs of their children, and provide routines that focus on the development of language, social behavior, and the sharing of responsibility in the activities of daily living. Parents realize that pity is unacceptable and they cultivate respect for the child as an individual. Such parents have a capacity to conquer the difficult tendency to overprotect and are remarkable in their ability to guide their child toward his potential for self-sufficiency. That is not to say that mature parents do not get carried away, from time to time, as advocates for their youngster. Whereas some might call this overprotection, in the case of the mature parent it is more often than not an attempt to get those who are in contact with the youngster to better understand his needs. This is particularly important if the child has mixed handicaps. For instance, parents of children with severe communication disorders, such as autism, frequently have great difficulty helping teachers understand the relationship between receptive aphasia and disturbed behavior. These children, who cannot understand their environment because of a communication problem, are apt to overreact in a bizarre way that is confusing to educational personnel if they have not had much experience with this type of condition.

With the realization that their child is retarded, will attend special educational programs, and will be a lifelong responsibility, many parents become involved in parent organizations (see list at the end of this chapter). Their roles in these groups are determined by their own personality preferences and assets. Some parents focus on fund raising; others develop expertise in advocacy, public relations, legislation, or research. Perhaps one of the more important aspects of these organizations is the informal parent-to-parent counseling that takes place unofficially. This reinforces physician counseling and helps parents of newly diagnosed children to better understand the youngsters' condition. Parents report consistently that parent-to-parent contacts are the most valuable support available when they learn that their child is retarded.

LIFE PLANS

By the time their child is a young teenager, most parents are aware of the degree of the handicap and have begun to study the options available to them for long-range alternatives to the home care of their child. A life plan must be made for adulthood. Whatever the plan, its goal is to help the young retarded adult gain some degree of autonomy, whether it be the ability to separate and survive in an institutional environment or to live in a community setting. Efforts are being made to keep retarded adults in the least restrictive possible and the most normal milieu. This normalization philosophy is the primary theme of public programs for retarded persons and has resulted in the closing of institutional admissions for all but the most severely handicapped retarded persons.

Young adulthood can be a stormy time for retarded persons, comparable to the early teenage years of average children. Many parents elect to keep mildly retarded young adults at home, making special efforts to help them gain an individual identity through mastery of employment in a sheltered workshop, the use of public transportation, and involvement in local recreation programs. All parents of retarded persons worry about what will happen after they are gone. A few parents will provide endowments to private institutions that will ensure lifelong care of their retarded child. In most cases, however, placement in a community setting in early adult life is the most appropriate plan. Separation from home is a normal event. As we strive to normalize the lives of retarded persons, efforts are made to provide them with a separate and individual life outside the family. Both parents and retarded young adults frequently welcome this stage; however, it requires a period of special adaptation for retarded persons and their parents, since interdependence is more intense. Community placement during young adulthood is liberating for all involved. Efforts should be made to do this at an elected time rather than wait until the parents die or are too debilitated to care for the retarded individual, creating a physical and emotional crisis.

Once the retarded adult is living away from home in a community residence or other facility, most parents try to withdraw and allow their child to develop his maximum degree of independence. This is not an easy thing to do; it follows years of focusing almost entirely on their retarded child. Some parents have been able to avoid the trap of social isolation and to maintain outside interests despite their dedication to the care of their family member. The lives of others revolve primarily around their retarded older child and they require considerable adjustment following the separation of that young person from their home.

DEFENSES USED BY PARENTS OF RETARDED CHILDREN

The defenses used to provide relief from the emotional conflict and anxiety created by the birth and responsibility of a retarded child are relatively uniform. Initially, there is denial, a defense mechanism that operates unconsciously and is used to resolve emotional conflict and allay anxiety by disavowing thoughts, feelings, wishes, needs, or external factors that are consciously intolerable. For parents informed that their child will be mentally retarded, there is disbelief and almost instinctual denial. With information gathering, meeting other parents of retarded children, introduction to resource people in the field, and concurrence of the diagnosis from other professionals, anxiety tends to dissipate and denial gradually fades to realization that the child is different and has special needs. As time passes, the parents frequently feel rejecting and hostile toward their handicapped child. This is particularly true when the child is emotionally disturbed. Anger is common and is at times projected outside the home, but is sometimes directed toward the affected youngster, which may cause, in turn, the parents to feel very guilty. Parents search for reasons why their child is singled out and review events in their life history looking for the cause. Old wives tales surface. Genealogies are produced and blame is passed around. The faith of religious parents is often shaken; others with strong religious beliefs see the child as punishment for past sins. A study by Kramm (1963) found that 12% of parents with Down's syndrome children believed that a direct act of God caused the children's condition. Parents' guilt is usually unwarranted and seems to be a normal response for dealing with the unanswerable question of the cause of their child's problem. Olshansky (1962) wrote sensitively of the state of chronic sorrow seen in many parents of retarded children. As with any loss, there is apt to remain some scar. This sorrow is justifiable and in itself is not an indication for psychotherapy.

Compensation is a defense mechanism that operates both consciously and unconsciously, which parents often use to make up for the

deficiency of their child, ergo the family and themselves. Parents participate in a variety of compensatory activities to collect as much information as possible, becoming active in parent-child training programs and
engaging in child-focused activities. Instinctual drives that might put the
mother at risk for child abuse are frequently diverted into constructive
energies. Infant stimulation programs supervised by developmental
specialists increase the chances of transforming a mother's negative feelings into positive ones as she watches her baby develop, with others able
to point out the subtleties of the baby's accomplishments. Stone and
Chesney (1978) reported on an infant program for handicapped babies in
which they were able to enhance social development by facilitating
mother-child interaction. This kind of a program helps overcome the distortion of mother-infant bonding that occurs as a result of the limited
feedback some retarded babies provide for their mothers.

   Substitution, in which an unobtainable goal is replaced by one that
is obtainable, gradually evolves as denial continues to recede, anger
abates, and the family becomes more reality oriented. Although some
chronic sorrow is apt to remain, the parents begin to accept the child and
enjoy his presence. Over time, they lower their expectations and aspirations for their child's future life, accepting special schools, the need for
help from the community, and long-range plans in accord with the
child's abilities. Sublimation continues to play a role in the way the
mature parent adapts, and is most likely responsible for the founding of
many service organizations, the promotion of school programs, and the
writing of legislation for the benefit of retarded children.

ACCENTUATED PATTERNS OF PARENTING

The ambivalence generated by the retarded child in the family seems to
cause accentuated patterns of child-rearing. The most frequently seen
pattern is one of overprotection. Levy (1970) has written extensively on
child-rearing and has described the excessive maternal care involved in
raising a retarded child under four headings: excessive contact, infan-
tilization, prevention or lack of independent behavior, and excess of
maternal control. With the developmentally delayed child, it is natural
and frequently essential for the mother to extend her care beyond that
necessary for the average child. Although many families handle this, it
can create a strain on the marriage that fosters resentment in both
parents and causes a series of reaction patterns that provide feedback for
reinforcing overprotection. Withdrawal of the father, with increased
overattachment by the mother to the affected youngster, happens with
greatest frequency. The stress placed on the mother may generate feelings of anger toward the child and a reaction formation that accentuates
the overprotection. Overprotective mothers of retarded children are frequently victims of their own strong superegos. Had their children not

been retarded, they most likely would not have displayed intense, obsessive, compulsive, pathological child-rearing. Overprotection is frequently inversely proportional to the strength of the marriage. It is hard to say what comes first—incompatibility leading to overprotection, or vice versa. However, it is a vicious cycle that is hard to interrupt. Levy (1970) stated that when the husband and wife are sexually compatible and have social interests in common, they thereby set up a number of conditions that operate against the mother-child monopoly.

The institutionalization of the retarded child may be seen as rejection. Until roughly the mid-1960s, parents were often advised not to become attached to their handicapped youngsters and to institutionalize them as soon as possible. Many parents rejected this advice and maintained the youngster at home, where they worked hard to provide an appropriate atmosphere during the early years of life. In cases (fortunately increasingly rarer now) when parents of profoundly retarded children are advised to consider institutions, they often develop a sense of failure and might make a conscious but painful decision to institutionalize their child. Once this has occurred, many parents find continued contact with the child in the institution so distressing that they avoid him and, in a sense, behave as if the child were dead. Visits to the facility are minimal and, when they do occur, are brief and sad, resembling the kind of annual pilgrimage made to the cemetery on Memorial Day. Such parents adapt relatively well to a life that is devoid of stress inherent in caring for the child at home but cannot tolerate the pain created by regular visits. They are supportive and grateful to institutional staff, are anxious to make sure material needs are met, and are frequently overwhelmed by sorrow during their visits. Rejection seems to be a harsh way to describe their reaction; in fact, parents who avoid contact after placement of their retarded youngster seem to do so in an ego-syntonic way. They know that they are unable to handle the pain evoked by frequent visits to offspring who are unresponsive without becoming overwhelmed by depression; thus they frequently avoid all contact.

True rejection may be seen in parents who have been inadequately nurtured in their own early lives and who are limited by intelligence, experience, and/or education. The stresses of caring for the child are less tempered by the welfare emotions of joy and pride. Preoccupation with their own needs may result in neglect of the needs of the retarded child. Such immature parents are apt to be erratic in their behavior. On occasion, they willfully neglect the retarded baby while showering attention and material goods on unaffected children.

FAMILY DYNAMICS

The retarded child has a profound impact on family dynamics. This can be positive or negative. In general, the impact on the family reflects the parents' level of adaptation. When they have a sound relationship, communicate openly in the family, and can arrange their lives so that no one family member is deprived of his own chance to develop as a result of having to care for the retarded member, the family may be strengthened by the presence of a handicapped child. Holt (1958) called attention to a study of British families with retarded children from which he concluded that they often gained better spiritual and ethical values; however, families with retarded children do tend to have more problems in individual and marital adjustment as well as in child-rearing and sibling relationships. Children tend to respond to a retarded sibling as their parents do; so parents who are ashamed of their handicapped offspring and try to hide the condition will transfer that attitude to their other children, who may grow up feeling stigmatized. In many families the presence of a retarded child may initiate a series of unhealthy responses; for instance, the emotional withdrawal of either spouse, with overattention given by one to either the retarded child or another child in the family. Social isolation is prominent with parents of severely retarded children because they are often unable to find babysitters who are willing and able to care for a handicapped youngster. This happens also with mildly retarded children if they are emotionally disturbed.

The decreasing availability of residential placements, because of the recent trend away from institutional care, has placed an enormous strain on some families. Even families who have adapted well to the diagnosis of retardation and have been able to keep their handicapped youngster at home during the formative years may become vulnerable to crisis later on. Particularly difficult to care for at home are multiply handicapped children, e.g., a deaf/mute/retarded/blind child with congenital rubella, who is also aggressive and self-abusive. It is not uncommon to see a family decompensate as they are pushed to exhaustion in caring for such a child. This kind of tension often leads to a reactive mental disorder among one or more family members.

SIBLINGS

Normal siblings of retarded children may feel unusual pressure to achieve in order to make up for their parents' disappointment over having a retarded baby. With a time-consuming retarded youngster in the family, it is often hard for normal siblings to have their needs met appropriately. This can lead to resentment, anger, guilt, and decreased self-worth. Resentment is generated when siblings feel that the handicapped child is more loved, given more attention, or given more material things. Frequently, siblings see the retarded child getting away with behavior that would be unacceptable for other family members, and most siblings are quick to point out that the affected child has better control than the parents realize and is really masterful at "putting them on." Like other family members, siblings are ambivalent; a positive attitude toward the retarded or handicapped youngster is often coupled with resentment. All siblings must make some kind of adjustment. Barsch (1968) surveyed 260 parents of retarded children on their impression of sibling reaction. He concluded that parents felt that the everyday living between their normal and handicapped children was a pleasant one. "Only a small percentage of parents...could be considered as confronted with a great deal of negativism and resentment by siblings which posed a serious family problem."

STRATEGIES FOR INTERVENTION

Because of rapidly changing attitudes toward handicapped people—recognition of their rights and the trend away from institutionalization and toward normalization—intervention strategies today are different than they would have been a few decades ago. Changes in medical technology have had only a small effect on intervention strategies. Whereas in the first half of this century, pioneering professionals in the field of mental retardation worked to develop the best institutional care, today's workers have the far more complicated task of integrating the handicapped child into an accepting environment within the family and the community.

The responsibility has shifted from one that is centralized (institutions) to one that is shared by many people (family and community). The family doctor is no longer the sole authority but also (if trained and willing) the coordinator, facilitator, communicator, or interpreter who aids families in their new role of maintaining their affected member comfortably and productively as a member of society. Thus, the focus of the physician (or other core professional) has shifted from the child alone to the child, the family, and the community. Whereas earlier professional responsibility appeared to be set up so that one professional (for instance, the family physician) assumed full responsibility for the retarded individual until he was passed to the institution administrator, there are now many people playing a role in the diagnosis and disposition of the affected child. The earlier pattern of care was static and finite; the current pattern of care is characterized by constant change. Mainstreaming involves interfacing with more and different professionals, paraprofessionals, and peers, often for shorter periods of time.

Because of the diversity of special resources available in this country to aid mentally retarded children and their families, it is hard to propose a model for intervention that is universally applicable. However, there will usually be a central authority, often a primary care physician or a developmental pediatric specialist, to whom the parents look for guidance in decision making and for help with crisis intervention. When this authority is located in a distant university center, it is useful to have a local, specially trained person whom the family trusts. This might be a nurse, social worker, psychologist, or other person qualified to implement the treatment plan recommended. Private professional advocate groups can offer information on available resources, such as schools and camps, and can be most helpful to families who need guidance in developing community treatment plans. No matter what the resources and what professionals are available to guide the way, it is important that efforts be made to fulfill certain goals in working with the family of a mentally retarded child:

1. *To provide anticipatory guidance in such a way that family members understand the child's condition in the context of their family situation.* The parents must have knowledge of the disorder, its cause, its treatment, and its prognosis. They should then be helped to gather information to expand their basic understanding of what is happening.
2. *To educate the family to work with professionals in a partnership in order to provide for optimal development of all family members.* Parents should be helped to recognize their needs and their normal children's needs in addition to those of the retarded child. The physician who conducts the informing conference and his designated team members usually help with this. Although a plan for care of the child and family education are initiated at this conference, they are actually ongoing processes, which continue for months, years, and even decades.
3. *To guide the family in life planning for their retarded member, taking into consideration their individual concerns, trends away from institutional care, and the resources available to them in government support services.*

THE FAMILY CONFERENCE

The family conference, frequently called the informing interview, is a critical milestone in the development of the parent-professional partnership. It should involve both parents simultaneously, no matter what the couple's relationship, because there is always a potential for distortion and misunderstanding when parents are first informed of their youngster's condition, and such misunderstanding can cloud the important issues when one parent must tell the other.

The style of the conference will vary with the style and availability of professional staff. It has become routine in many developmental centers to have a social worker, or other professional who will be working with the family on a continuing basis, attend the conference in order to be sure of the information transmitted; the social worker would then be available to help clarify any misunderstandings of the child's condition that may arise later.

Parents are often unable to grasp what is said to them about their child in the initial interview. Usually there is denial, but occasionally a parent may magnify the problem and then reject the youngster, and even the family. Hagamen (1976) reported on a survey of parents of children with autistic features and suggested that a second family conference be scheduled 2 to 4 weeks after the initial meeting, thus providing parents with a chance to ask questions and consolidate their knowledge.

Professionals, particularly those who are providing primary care, may be inclined to minimize a child's deficit for a number of reasons. Physicians may have guilt feelings because they cannot propose a cure. They are human beings, and it is difficult under these circumstances to relay bad news, because of compassion for the family (and fear of their reaction). Some physicians will minimize or deny the child's early developmental delay. Some will feel that the diagnosis and prognosis are best absorbed in small doses. Others will abruptly confront the parents with the diagnosis of the child's retardation and will give a pessimistic prediction of the child's future abilities (which is often unwarranted at this early stage). This last point is important; when dealing with very young children for whom the outcome is uncertain, there is always the danger of setting up a negative self-fulfilling prophecy. Experience has shown that understanding what the diagnosis of mental retardation means personally to a family is a process that can take months or years. During that process, it is essential that parents have professional guidance in finding the best and most recent information available about their child's condition. Without this, they are vulnerable candidates for the unproved treatments and miracle cures that abound. Parents also need a chance to understand and resolve their feelings of guilt, denial, sadness, and anger. This is never easy; however, with the better-understood syndromes it proceeds more smoothly in the early stages than in conditions like autism, where the child's general appearance is normal and developmental deficits may be associated with confusing "islands of intellect" (high concrete skills in certain limited areas, such as mathematical calculations).

Szymanski (1977) pointed out the need for professionals at the family conference to discuss the strengths of the child as well as the weaknesses in a "balance sheet outline." This approach can also be used to describe the child's progress in each of several areas of development: physical, emotional, language, intellectual, and social. Parents are encouraged to review their own observations of the child along these lines. Many parents are apt to have reinforced their denial of the child's problem by viewing a singular area of high performance as being indicative of superior ability. A careful review across all developmental lines not only can give them a more realistic awareness of the child's current status but also can be the foundation for a more comprehensive perspective as they watch their child grow. Knobloch and Pasamanick (1974) have advised physicians on how to conduct the past evaluation interview. They encourage questioning the parents to ascertain how well they understand their child's conditions and advise the physician to try to answer four questions: What is wrong? Why? What can we do about it? What can we expect in the future? This is a practical, effective way to approach the task of communicating to parents the information needed. For some disorders, relatively specific answers are available to all four questions, but in many other conditions, particularly with very young children, such information is not yet clear, making acceptance and adaptation difficult for all involved.

When parents can review each stage of development separately and can understand how slow development in one stage (e.g., language) can affect development in another (e.g., social skills), they can begin to view the development process objectively, understand their role in intervention, and control negative reactions (e.g., overprotection). The informing conference lays the groundwork for this realization.

PARENT-PROFESSIONAL PARTNERSHIP

Without the trust of the parent, an intervention program will fail. However, it is difficult to elicit trust from confused parents who have been told different things by different people. Trust is fostered by the professional's demonstration of his understanding of the child's behavior and is reinforced by other parents who have trusting relationships with professionals. Often there is someone in the family's community with whom they have had a long-standing relationship they can trust—the primary care physician, an understanding teacher, a neighbor, or a friend. Open minds are essential to a good working relationship between parents and professionals. Both the parents and the professional must be tolerant of each other's opinion and be able to explore disagreement. More often than not, agreement between parents and professionals is obscured by poorly expressed ideas. Professionals should given parents the chance to describe nontraditional methods of intervention they may have heard of, and parents should give professionals the chance to explain why they do or do not recognize their value. (Information collected in this way from parents can frequently be the foundation for later investigation of empirical findings.) Through honest dialogue and by keeping open minds, parents gradually will acknowledge their denials and begin to understand their child.

Common Goals

Parents and professionals should agree on some short-range goals regarding their expectations. Long-range prognosticating is almost impossible and dangerous, but setting short-range, time-limited, attainable goals can do much to foster a good working relationship. The goals should be reasonable in order to provide for some measure of success. Gradually, as trust builds and those involved gain an idea of the progress to be expected, more longitudinal planning can be attempted.

Continuous Communication

Arrangements should be made at the outset for continuous communication, both structured and unstructured. Parents need to have the responsibility of observing and reporting progress at regular intervals and should be given a number to call (preferably a developmental center) in times of crisis, because so many primary care physicians are not trained in mental retardation and are unfamiliar with the vicissitudes of rearing a developmentally disabled youngster. Crises can frequently be handled by telephone if the local helping professional is present with the family. The records from a developmental center can be helpful if a new primary care physician is called upon to care for a family with a mentally retarded member. Continuous communication helps the professional who is interested in longitudinal studies because it results in a richer awareness of a child's development, which enhances standardized observations.

PARENTAL REQUIREMENTS FOR EFFECTIVE INTERVENTION

Parents must be able to realize that their child has a problem and the degree of the problem. Some families tend to deny that anything is wrong with the affected child; other families tend to maximize the child's problem, focusing on the weaknesses rather than the strengths. Whatever the initial attitude of the parents, they must be willing to view the child's strengths and weaknesses in an appropriate context. For an effective parent-professional partnership, the parent needs a solid understanding of current information available on the child's condition.

   Parents of children with developmental lags must be willing to work regularly with their child during infancy and the preschool years in order to provide adequate stimulation for developing skills. This requires guidance and training, which are most effectively accomplished through the use of teachers who come to the home several days a week in order to guide the mother in the stimulation of her baby. Infant curricula are comprehensive and geared to help lags in physical, cognitive, emotional, and social development. Such programs focus on improving the quality of the mother-infant interaction as well. This kind of parent tutoring should not be confused with such undesirable situations as parents who drill their mildly retarded older child on academic subjects in a frustrating, unrealistic way. There are many infant programs throughout the country for handicapped children that are of great value in training parents as development specialists. In the preschool years at home, parents are in a position to provide continuous stimulation for communication and social interaction, which professionals are not able to do.

There is much to be gained by parents sharing their observations with the specialist. Frequently, the parents' originality and creativity in striving to help their disabled youngsters overcome deficits can provide observations that lead to far-reaching insights on the part of professionals. For best results in intervention, parents need to be able to share their anxieties about their child, the future, and their own feelings with professionals or other informed people, such as other parents. It is essential to keep things in perspective. In training programs, particularly for preschool children, a spiral of optimism that grows to unrealistic heights frequently develops. This creates magical expectations for progress, which, when unfulfilled, lead to exhaustion of energy. Hopes cannot be raised repeatedly without some outward show of progress.

FAMILY SUPPORT SYSTEMS

Family support systems have become an integral part of community care of mentally retarded persons. In order to support a mainstreamed retarded person in the community, provisions must be made for an educational program, a recreational program, and medical care; but the components needed to support the family of the retarded child are less well defined. Hagamen (1977) reported that low-functioning children were admitted to psychiatric hospitals not because of change in the child's behavior but because of particular stress on the family. It follows that intervention techniques might better be directed toward helping maintain family homeostasis.

As discussed earlier, parents who are able to mourn the loss of the anticipated normal child are better able to attach to their handicapped child. Solnit and Stark (1961) pointed out that it is a mistake to "cure grief quickly." Mourning is always individualized and is related to the rate at which denial abates. It is essential to respect individual differences in mourning because counselors can increase anxiety and depression when they are not sensitive to the parents' tolerance of lost hope.

Support for the family includes a review of the emotional needs of the parents, the siblings, and other related family members and, when indicated, a referral for supportive counseling for specific reactions. Most parents gain the greatest emotional support from talk with other parents. Professionals should have a working relationship with parents in a variety of organizations for the handicapped in order to facilitate this parent-to-parent communication. In order to keep a retarded child at home, it is essential for the parents to be in control. Because retarded children are special children, they are often overindulged and become management problems. Thus it is important to provide parents with training programs in behavioral management in order to sharpen their child-rearing skills. This is most effectively done through 6- to 10-week courses for groups of 10 to 15 parents. Courses are run by well-trained behavioralists and train parents in the use of operant conditioning techniques, which are very useful in dealing with disturbed, low-functioning children. Kozloff (1974) wrote a detailed book to help parents understand the principles of behavior management and how to write programs for their own children. In addition to handling their own emotions and developing skills for raising disturbed, retarded children, family support systems also require some degree of home support. All home support systems are geared to relieving the family of the 24-hour care of a disturbed, retarded child. If this care is draining to the mother and other caregivers, it is important that they be relieved before there is any evidence of emotional disturbance in the retarded child. Home support has been described by Kaufman and Bordin-Sandler (1974) in the form of a family aid program. These two psychologists set up classes to familiarize high school and college students interested in psychology with the behavior and management of retarded children. In cooperation with the local chapter of the National Society for Autistic Children, graduates from these classes were matched with families who had requested help in the home caring of their disturbed, retarded children. These family aides provided individual attention to the child and were used in a variety of ways, from babysitters to communication tutors. In this way, families were able to get out and avoid social isolation. Homemakers can be a useful form of family support. Increasingly, government agencies are sponsoring short-term homemaker service for health-related family crises. If this kind of support does not alleviate the stress of the family, perhaps the disturbed child should be put in respite care from the home for a short time. Special camps provide a 2-month respite for many parents of retarded children. Visits to relatives and temporary foster placement are other possibilities. The final form of family support is to prepare the parents for stressful stages and for decision making. The family is supported by providing anticipatory guidance in a very gentle way, individualized to suit the personality of the parents and the resources available at the time.

SUMMARY

The following outline summarizes the process of family adaptation to an emotionally disturbed, mentally retarded child:

1. Parents of such children adapt in accordance with variables related to emotional stability, educational level, socioeconomic status, family size and structure, and culture.
2. The stress of having a disturbed, retarded child in the family may create a severe hardship for parents and siblings.
    a. Some strong families are able to overcome their feelings about the handicapped child by mourning the loss of the idealized, anticipated baby and developing a realistic approach that enables the affected youngster to separate and develop his own skills in order to spend his adult life away from the family in a hostel, group home, or institution.
    b. Less well adapted families may tend to deny the handicap or its severity, or overprotect or reject the child, setting the stage for emotional disturbances.
3. The mentally retarded youngster is at high risk for emotional problems.
    a. In retardation, there are frequently irregular lags in various aspects of neurological development that result in uneven maturation in physical, cognitive, emotional, and social growth. This creates a counter-productive crossover effect that is frequently manifested in disturbed behavior.
    b. Parental reaction in retardation is often of a type that either fosters emotional disturbance or exacerbates a behavior problem that originates from the child's neuropathology.
4. The trend away from institutional care has resulted in the home care of most retarded children. The role of the professional in the field of retardation has shifted from centralized responsibility for the child in the institution to a decentralized community approach.
5. Management now concentrates on the entire family and is shared by a multitude of professionals, necessitating coordination and communication among many people.
6. Family support systems that provide for the development of all family members as well as for the retarded individual are necessary.
7. Family support systems involve a comprehensive program for the affected person and attention to the emotional needs of other family members, training and behavior management for parents, and respite from continuous 24-hour care of the retarded child through family aid, homemakers, or temporary foster care.
8. When resources for placement are not available, the stability of the family is threatened and emotional disturbance in the affected member is apt to occur.
9. All parents cannot maintain their retarded child at home without jeopardizing their own health or that of other family members; this

must be recognized and accepted as a challenge for planners in preventive psychiatry.

10. Strategy for intervention involves early intensive family support with opportunity for frequent respite and emergency placement of the retarded child when necessary to maintain the opportunity for growth of other family members.

PARENT ORGANIZATIONS

National Society for Autistic Children
1234 Massachusetts Avenue, N.W.
Suite 1017
Washington, D.C. 20005
Phone: 202-783-0125

Epilepsy Foundation of America
225 Park Avenue South
New York, NY 10002
Phone: 212-677-8550
        and
1828 L Street, N.W.
Washington, D.C. 20036
Phone: 202-293-2930

Association for Children with Learning Disabilities
4156 Library Road
Pittsburg, PA 15234
Phone: 412-341-1515

National Association for Retarded Citizens
2709 Avenue E., East
Arlington, TX 76011
Phone: 817-261-4961

REFERENCES

Barnard, K. E., and Powell, M. L. 1972. Teaching the Mentally Retarded Child: A Family Care Approach. C. V. Mosby Co., St. Louis.

Barsch, R. H. 1968. The Parent of the Handicapped Child. Charles C Thomas Publisher, Springfield, Ill.

Becker, W. 1971. Parents Are Teachers: A Child Management Program. Research Press, Champaign, Ill.

Chess, S. 1977. Evolution of behavior disorder in a group of mentally retarded children. J. Am. Acad. Child Psychiatry 16(1):4–18.

Drotar, D., Baskiewicz, A., Irvin, N., Kennell, J. H., and Klaus, M. H. 1975. The adaptation of parents to the birth of an infant with a congenital malformation: A hypothetical model. Pediatrics 56:710–717.

Emde, R. N., and Brown, C. 1978. Adaptation to the birth of a Down's syndrome infant: Grieving and maternal attachment. J. Am. Acad. Child Psychiatry 17(2):299–323.

Ferholt, J. B., and Solnit, A. J. 1978. Counseling parents of mentally retarded and learning disordered children. In: L. E. Arnold (ed.), Helping Parents Help Their Children. Brunner/Mazel, New York.

Goldfarb, W., Sibulkin, L., Behrens, M., and Jahoda, H. 1970. The concept of maternal perplexity. In: J. Anthony and T. Benedek (eds.), Parenthood. Little, Brown & Co., Boston.

Hagamen, M. B. 1976. Autism—Can we do a better informing interview? Paper presented at the American Academy of Child Psychiatry annual meeting, October, San Francisco.

Hagamen, M. B. 1977. Family support systems: Their effect on long-term psychiatric hospitalization in children. J. Am. Acad. Child. Psychiatry 16(1):53–66.

Holt, K. S. 1958. Home care of severely retarded children. Pediatr. J. 22:744.

Hunter, M. H. 1972. The Retarded Child from Birth to Five: A Multidisciplinary Approach for Parent and Child. John Day Co., New York.

Kaufman, K. A., and Bordin-Sandler, S. 1974. Behavioral approaches to autism. Paper presented at the American Psychiatric Association annual convention, May, Detroit, Mich.

Kaufman, K. A., and Bordin-Sandler, S. 1975. The family aide program: A baby-sitting and relief service for families of autistic children. Paper presented at the National Society for Autistic Children annual meeting, San Diego, Cal.

Klaus, M. H., and Kennell, J. H. 1976. Maternal-Infant Bonding. C. V. Mosby Co., St. Louis.

Knobloch, H., and Pasamanick, B. 1974. Gesell and Amatruda's Developmental Diagnosis: The Evaluation and Management of Normal and Abnormal Neuropsychologic Development in Infancy and Early Childhood. Harper & Row Publishers, New York. pp. 360–361.

Koch, R., and Dobson, J. C. (eds.). 1971. The Mentally Retarded Child and His Family. Brunner/Mazel, New York.

Kozloff, M. 1974. Educating Children with Learning and Behavior Problems. Wiley-Interscience, New York.

Kramm, E. R. 1963. Families of Mongoloid Children. Government Printing Office, Washington, D.C.

Kübler-Ross, E. 1969. On Death and Dying. Macmillan Publishing Co., New York.

Levy, D. 1970. Maternal overprotection. In: E. J. Anthony and T. Benedek (eds.), Parenthood, pp. 387–409. Little, Brown & Co., Boston.

McCollum, A. 1975. Coping with Prolonged Health Impairment in Your Child. Little, Brown & Co., Boston.

Matheny, A. P., and Vernick, J. 1970. Parents of the mentally retarded child: Emotionally overwhelmed or informationally deprived. In: S. Chess and A. Thomas (eds.), Annual Progress in Child Psychiatry and Child Development, Vol. 3. Brunner/Mazel, New York.

Olshansky, S. 1962. Chronic sorrow: A response to having a mentally defective child. Soc. Casework 43:190–193.

Patterson, G. R., and Guillion, M. E. 1971. Living with Children: New Methods for Parents and Teachers. Research Press, Champaign, Ill.

Schild, S. 1971. The family of the retarded child. In: R. Koch and J. C. Dobson (eds.), The Mentally Retarded Child and His Family, pp. 431–442. Brunner/Mazel, New York.

Schopler, E., and Reichler, R. J. 1972. How well do parents understand their own psychotic child? J. Autism Child. Schizophr. 2:387–400.

Schopler, E., and Reichler, R. J. 1976. Developmental therapy: A model for providing individual services in the community. In: E. Schopler and R. J. Reichler (eds.), Psychopathology and Child Development, pp. 347–373. Plenum Press, New York.

Solnit, A. J., and Stark, M. H. 1961. Mourning and the birth of a defective child. In: R. Eissler et al. (eds.), The Psychoanalytic Study of the Child, Vol. 16, pp. 523–537. International Universities Press, New York.

Stone, N. W., and Chesney, B. H. 1978. Attachment behaviors in handicapped infants. Ment. Retard. 16(1):8–12.

Szymanski, L. S. 1977. Psychiatric diagnostic evaluation of mentally retarded individuals. J. Am. Acad. Child Psychiatry 17:67-87.

Watson, L. S. 1973. Child Behavior Modification: A Manual for Teachers, Nurses and Parents. Pergamon Press, Elmsford, N.Y.

Wing, L. 1972. Autistic Children: A Guide for Parents and Professionals. Brunner/Mazel, New York.

GROUP PSYCHOTHERAPY WITH RETARDED PERSONS

Ludwik S. Szymanski and
Quinn B. Rosefsky

Chapter 12

REVIEW OF LITERATURE

Group therapy with retarded persons has been described in literature since Cotzin (1948) reported on behavioral improvement of retarded boys in an institution following 10 group therapy sessions. Most of the reports on this subject were published in the 1950s and 1960s; only two studies in the 1970s could be found (Baran, 1972; Richards and Lee, 1972).

Existing studies suffer from many of the methodological problems from which studies of psychotherapy in general suffer: varying diagnostic criteria of retardation, lack of controls, lack of standardized treatment techniques or of uniform criteria of patient selection, and inadequate measures of outcome.

With the exception of Michal-Smith, Gottsegen, and Gottsegen (1955), Rudolph (1955), and Richards and Lee (1972), most studies have been conducted in institutional settings. Five of the reviewed studies used both control groups and some form of rating scales to measure improvement of the experimental patients. Four reported that the experimental groups were improved (Yonge and O'Connor, 1954; O'Connor and Yonge, 1955; Wilcox and Guthrie, 1957; Snyder and Sechrest, 1959). In addition, many authors have stated that group therapy with retarded persons may be helpful: Cotzin (1948), Fisher and Wolfson (1953), Astrachan (1955), Michal-Smith et al. (1955), Rudolph (1955), Stubblebine (1957), Kaldeck (1958), Miezio (1967), Anderson (1968), Landau (1968), Slivkin and Bernstein (1968), and Baran (1972).

The techniques employed by most of these studies largely reflected the cognitive capacity and age of the patients who composed the groups. Gorlow et al. (1963) utilized role playing, films, parties, psychodrama, and much active structuring. Sternlicht (1964, 1966) used such unorthodox techniques as having the therapist demonstrate his physical force through Indian wrestling and play with balloons.

Some studies have used nondirective, permissive techniques (Fisher and Wolfson, 1953; Yonge and O'Connor, 1954). O'Connor and Yonge, using controls and rating scales, demonstrated improvement in workshop behavior of experimental subjects. Vail (1955), however, attributed failure of his group to the permissive techniques used without structure or limits.

The need for a directive approach was advocated by a number of authors (Snyder and Sechrest, 1959; Gorlow et al., 1963; Slivkin and Bernstein, 1968). Some authors who were initially relatively permissive noticed later the necessity to be more active and directive in leading their therapy groups (Cotzin, 1948; Astrachan, 1955; Wilcox and Guthrie, 1957; Landau, 1968).

In summary, keeping in mind their many shortcomings, the studies described in the literature indicate that group psychotherapy is a useful tool with retarded patients and that eclectic techniques and directive approaches should be utilized, depending on the group's composition.

TYPES OF THERAPY GROUPS

There are two basic types of therapy groups: traditional, composed of retarded persons identified as patients, and multiple family groups (MFGs), which include the retarded patients and their family members, particularly their parents or other caregivers. Each type has its advantages and disadvantages. There are also activity groups, particularly for younger persons, which are not oriented primarily toward verbal therapy.

The traditional groups offer a confidential setting, which is important to adolescents who attempt to individuate themselves from their families, identify with their peers, and discuss their private thoughts, including negative feelings toward their parents. These processes might be inhibited by the parents' presence. On the other hand, groups composed solely of retarded persons have a number of shortcomings. The leader may have to rely only on patients' stories, which sometimes distort reality. Retarded persons are usually more dependent on their families than their nonretarded age mates, and such dependency may be fostered by the parents; but the dependency will remain unaffected unless the families are involved in the therapeutic process. A traditional approach would utilize concurrent casework with the parents, individually or in a group.

The former requires considerable professional time. The latter is more economical, but must be based on discussion of reported, rather than directly observed, parent-child interactions. These problems are overcome to a considerable extent in family group therapy, in which several sets of parents and their retarded children participate. This technique was pioneered in 1950 by Laqueur (1976), who treated hospitalized schizophrenic patients. His chief goal was to improve communication between the patients and their families. Based on general systems theory, this approach was described as unique because it "allows the suprasystem, the outside world, society, to enter into the therapeutic relationship" (Laqueur, 1976). The outside world was represented by members of other families in the group. The mechanism of change was believed to include processes such as breaking the intrafamilial code, learning by analogy, identification with other group members, and use of other families as cotherapists. Multiple family therapy has also been described and discussed by other writers (Bowen, 1976; Reiss and Costell, 1977). It has not been explored, however, with developmentally disabled persons and their families.

The choice between these two modalities depends on several factors, such as the predominant concerns of the patients that must be addressed and their relationship with their families. Parents who tend to complain about their retarded children or embarrass them in public may need some preparatory work individually or in a parents' group. In some cases best results may be obtained by having some individuals participate in both these types of group therapy. Last, but not least, proficiency of the leader in conducting a particular type of group is important as well.

THE SETTING AND DURATION OF THE THERAPY GROUP

The therapy groups described in the literature have usually been conducted as a part of a program in a residential institution, training school for delinquents, or prevocational or vocational training. In these situations, the leader has an advantage of obtaining additional information on the group members (particularly if they are unable to provide it themselves), which helps him in establishing therapy goals for the group. He may also consult other workers in the program in setting up a supportive milieu for the patients. However, leaders have to be extremely cautious in order not to breach rules of confidentiality. Higher functioning group members may be particularly concerned about such contacts, and open discussion with them is necessary in order to decide to what degree, if at all, the leader can communicate with other workers in the program. With the current increase in direct services provided by community mental health facilities to retarded patients, such groups will be more frequently conducted as a clinical service, unassociated with any other program.

   The length of group attendance is defined by the needs of a particular individual, as well as by the group setting:

1. *Time-limited groups* are useful with more dependent individuals, because pressure to discuss specific topics can be exerted and the group can serve as a catalyst for action, rather than as a forum for indefinite complaining and sympathy-seeking. If the group is part of a time-limited educational or other program where clients enter and leave as a group, simultaneously, its duration will have to coincide with that of the program. These groups are usually closed (no new members join after the group begins).
2. *Indefinite-duration groups* can help personal development through members understanding and monitoring each other's daily actions and interactions on a long-term basis. They may be appropriate with groups who live together, e.g., in community residences. These groups may be closed or open to new members, depending on the nature of the setting.
3. *Mixed groups* are sometimes scheduled in conjunction with educational and other programs that have members entering and leaving at different times. The older members may help by sharing their insight and experience with the newcomers, but their domination of the group must be prevented.

   It may also be helpful to have past group members "visit" the group at times, to share their experiences after leaving the group (and the associated program). This may be particularly helpful in stimulating discussion of topics like independence.

COMPOSITION OF THERAPY GROUPS

Four to six families in MFG, or six to eight members in a traditional group, seems to be the most appropriate size; it is small enough to permit the participants to know each other and to be handled by group leaders, and yet big enough to avoid focusing too often on a particular family or individual. The clients in groups conducted in our clinic, as well as those reported in the literature, have been in adolescent-adult age groups. Younger ones would usually fit more into activity groups, although if their level of communication and cognition permits, they could participate in verbally oriented groups.

   Some heterogeneity in patient selection is useful, because it permits patients to complement each other; for instance, more active and verbal members may serve as identification models for quiet and passive ones. Some of our groups included patients with a variety of personality disorders, including manic-depressive illness and psychosis. In working with adolescents and young adults who usually have difficulties in peer and heterosexual interaction, it is useful to have a mixed group of males and females, to enable role-playing and discussion of these issues.

Group members do not necessarily have to be of the same intelligence. However, there should not be too wide a range in their abilities to communicate within the group. Retarded adolescents may be quite intolerant of lower functioning peers. They may consider it an insult to themselves to be put in a group with someone more "retarded" than themselves, and may laugh at that person or not participate actively in the group. In some MFGs in the Developmental Evaluation Clinic (DEC), the parents of higher functioning persons spent considerable time complaining that the topics of the discussion were irrelevant for their much brighter children. Inclusion of a person whose behavior disrupts the group may be inappropriate if he does not respond to peer pressure. For the same reasons there should not be too wide an age spread between the clients.

It is useful to do a diagnostic evaluation on each person before he joins the group in order to assess his ability to contribute to, and benefit from, the particular group.

Both parents should participate in the MFG (or other caregivers, if the client does not live with his parents). Siblings may also participate if they are willing, if they play a major role in caring for the client, and if their level of development permits meaningful participation. However, the leader should consider logistics—the group may become too large if siblings are included. In the following discussion, references to families include siblings. However, in groups conducted at the DEC, siblings participated infrequently—usually only if they performed a major caregiving role with the client.

THE REQUIREMENTS OF A GROUP LEADER

The attributes of a group leader can be divided arbitrarily into several categories:

1. Leaders should be knowledgeable of and experienced in the fields of developmental disabilities and mental retardation. Practical experience in working on an interdisciplinary developmental disabilities team is invaluable.
2. Leaders should be knowledgeable of and experienced in individual psychopathology, individual and group psychotherapy, and multiple family therapy. Relatively few therapists have had opportunity to treat retarded patients, individually or in groups, and still fewer have had experience leading multiple family groups. An otherwise experienced therapist may learn these skills through participating as co-therapist or "therapist trainee" with experienced therapists.

3. Therapists are not immune to misconceptions and emotional reactions to mental retardation. Such biases, unless recognized and dealt with, may greatly limit the therapist's effectiveness (Szymanski, 1977). These limiting factors include ignorance (of mental retardation), conscious and unconscious biases about mental retardation, and emotionally charged personal experiences with mentally retarded persons. Some therapists, perhaps because of unconscious guilt feelings (e.g., that they are unable to cure mental retardation), may tend to overprotect and paternalize. They may avoid discussing with the group more emotionally charged topics on the premise that the group members would not understand or could not tolerate such topics. They may instead encourage participants to dwell endlessly on "safe" topics. Some therapists without experience in mental retardation tend to see group participants as amusing and silly, and they may even encourage the participants to "clown" during group sessions.

4. Leaders should be flexible. They should be able to be direct without being overly controlling or intrusive. They should not overdo intellectualizing, nor should they resort to moralistic exhortations. They should be empathetic but not paternalistic. They should be patient and able to function as a "real" person who provides direct support, a model for identification, and a bridge to reality.

Two co-leaders of opposite sexes have an advantage of providing models for identification for co-ed groups.

GOALS OF THERAPY

With respect to therapy goals, therapy groups for retarded persons are more similar to groups for children than to groups for nonretarded persons of the same chronological age, in that referrals are initiated by caregivers and the goals, at first, are often established by caregivers and therapists. Later on, part of the group's task may be to have the members recognize their concerns and define their own goals (as their cognitive-conceptual abilities permit). Even then, their distractibility and immaturity may require the leader's active intervention in order to have the group's work proceed toward these goals. Thus, the goals should be well defined in the leader's mind, but broad and flexible enough to accommodate modifications as necessary. A "contract" is useful, especially with families of the patient, to clarify what the group is expected to achieve and what it is not and to avoid future misunderstandings. Caution should be exercised in order to have the treatment benefit the patients rather than offer convenience to the caregivers only. For instance, in institutions, a resident who seeks independence may be considered a troublemaker and sent for treatment, whereas a passive and dependent resident may be considered well adjusted. If the groups are time limited, the goals, by necessity, must also be limited to those that are most pressing and realistically attainable. In traditional groups of retarded patients, the most frequent goals are improvement in peer interaction and interpersonal communication; learning to recognize and to verbalize feelings (instead of suppressing or acting them out); learning to monitor their own and peer behavior; developing emotional acceptance of their handicaps; recognizing their own strengths; dealing with their sexuality; and recognizing the consequences of socially unacceptable behavior. The long-term goals include reducing depression and anxiety, increasing motivation to become more independent, and improving self-image.

Some groups are set up for special, limited purposes, such as preparation to leave an institution or home, or for sex education. Even in these groups, leaders need to be prepared for frequent necessary shifts toward more universal issues.

The goals of MFGs are to a large extent similar. However, the parents' presence creates, in a sense, a microcosm of society at large. Thus, MFGs offer to the retarded members and their families an opportunity to learn by analogy from other group members and to feel less isolated because of their own handicap (or having a handicapped child). Other goals include helping the families and their retarded members to improve their communication, learning to share feelings about one another, and focusing on strengths instead of dwelling on weaknesses. Further goals may include guiding the parents to encourage supportively and with empathy their retarded child in his quest for independence, and simply respecting him as an individual, rather than stereotyping him.

USEFUL TECHNIQUES IN LEADING
GROUP THERAPY FOR RETARDED PERSONS

Concreteness

Verbal communications to mentally retarded people must be concrete and clear. Simple illustrative examples, preferably based on events happening during the group meetings, are most helpful. When exploring a new topic, a step-like approach may be used. For instance, in one of our groups, the leader asked a question about school. It became obvious that the members were not sure what they were supposed to talk about, and only more structured questioning (what class did they attend, was it a special one or not, how many friends did they have) resulted in constructive discussion of their school problems. Leaders should still first try to give the group members an opportunity to answer unstructured questions, such as "Tell me about your school," because these can produce valuable material.

The degrees of concreteness and simplicity of verbal communication by the leader should be carefully adjusted to the receptive language abilities of group members; mentally retarded persons are very sensitive to being considered children and addressed as such.

The therapist has to be a concrete, "real" person to group members. He may bring up examples from his own life that are relevant to the discussion. Group members may ask concrete, even personal, questions of the leader that on the surface may be out of context; these may be motivated by their genuine wish to learn through direct identification and should not necessarily be interpreted as evidence of excessive dependency.

Managing Silence

As in any verbal therapy, there may be periods of silence. They do not necessarily reflect resistance (as one would interpret them with nonretarded patients). Rather, they may reflect not knowing what to say and fear of saying something foolish (often based on past bitter experience), and basic passivity and dependency. The leader should not permit the silence to continue too long, but should break it with communication of empathy—verbally or nonverbally, but noncritically. He may then guide the members to explore reasons for the silence and means of preventing it. With time, they will identify with him and the group will manage the silences by itself.

Directiveness

Groups composed of retarded individuals may find it difficult to stay with the topic of the discussion unless the leader structures the meeting.

Group members may suddenly "come out of the blue" with a seemingly irrelevant question or topic. For instance, in one of our groups, in the midst of a long discussion about independence, an adolescent boy suddenly asked the leader, "Have you ever been on a jet plane?" From his point of view that question was relevant. Independence meant for him travel, which was associated with flying on a plane, which he had never done. He was curious to hear more about air travel and he wanted to learn from the leader's experience. With the egocentricity of a young child, he disregarded the rules of socially appropriate behavior and changed the topic of discussion in order to gain information for himself.

Leaders are often in a dilemma about whether they should follow the new topic brought up by group members or whether they should direct them to continued discussion of the previous one, especially if the new one seems to be more important. Leaders should avoid, however, a "zig-zag" course in which topics are changed continuously. In any case, they should not assume automatically, as they would in leading groups of nonretarded individuals, that every change of topic must be based on resistance of group members to discussion of certain emotionally charged issues.

Skilled leaders may also direct the group through tangential associations into discussion of the topic that they consider important and that the group had not brought up. At times leaders may introduce the new issue openly.

UTILIZATION OF GROUP PROCESSES AS A THERAPEUTIC TOOL

Group leaders should be able to catalyze a feeling of solidarity and cohesiveness in a group of unrelated individuals. It is difficult to do with retarded persons, who are often deficient in peer-relating skills and experience and tend to relate to, and depend on, caregiving authority figures (in this case, the group leaders). Thus, at least at first, the group members tend to address the group leader, who they see as a protector and parent substitute, rather than talking to one another. The leader must then redirect their attention and encourage them to talk with one another. This should be done diplomatically, bearing in mind the considerable sensitivity of retarded people to criticism. For instance, instead of saying, "Jim, don't talk to me, but to your friends," the leader should say, "I think that Pat is interested in hearing what you have to say; could you explain it to her as well?" Later, when the leader has good rapport with the group, he may be more direct. Other group members may then be asked to comment on Jim's way of talking and may be led to "discover" that he was ignoring them. Then they may be asked how they feel about it and may be led to telling the "offender" to act differently in the future. This approach is most helpful in that it teaches group members to monitor one another's behavior. A similar approach is used in managing other behaviors, such as monopolizing the group's attention by talking constantly or maintaining constant silence.

Generalizing and learning by analogy are important and helpful group processes. Whenever there is an opportunity, the group members are asked whether they have problems similar to those being discussed and they are encouraged to talk about them. The leader often sets an example (e.g., stating that he could never learn music), indicating that a group member could have similar problems in other areas of learning. Retarded adolescents in particular have been very responsive to learning that others have similar problems to theirs. For instance, the leader may start by pointing out to group members that all of them have complained about problems in learning. He may say that in his experience, young people with such difficulties are often subjected to ridicule and teasing by their peers and may inquire whether they have had such experience as well. Often, upon hearing that they have not been the only ones to be teased about their retardation, group members may start verbalizing eagerly about what happened to them. Peer support and identification are very helpful in breaking the vicious cycle of dependency-helplessness-depression-withdrawal. The leader may encourage such support by asking the group to advise a member on how to handle a problem under discussion and to share their experience in this respect. A concrete plan of action may even be devised and followed up on during subsequent meetings. Positive reinforcement of successes by the group members is very important.

In summary, the leader encourages peer relationships and allows peer pressures to eliminate inappropriate, or build up appropriate, behaviors. The leader can be viewed as a "real" person, as a model for identification. The members provide one another with trust, encouragement, intimacy, sharing, and a support system.

PHASES OF GROUP DEVELOPMENT

Yalom (1970) pointed out that the phases of group development are rarely well demarcated and often overlap. This is even more true in groups composed of retarded persons, because of their tendency to regression and distractibility and their need for repetition. Yalom spoke of three stages: the initial stage of orientation, hesitant participation, and search for meaning; the second stage of conflict, dominance, and rebellion; and the third stages of cohesiveness. The following description includes modifications necessary when working with retarded patients. Of course, all groups are different, depending on the personalities and needs of the members and not merely their intelligence; thus these phases reflect common denominators and not obligatory developments.

Introductory Stage

The introductory phase (first one or two meetings) focuses on the members defining themselves. This is necessary because in most cases the members were brought to, or told to join, the group, rather than having requested it for treatment of consciously experienced symptoms. Thus the group must define its goals. This should not be accomplished through a lecture, with the leader telling the members what in his opinion is wrong with them. Rather, the leader should lead them to explore their fantasies about the group's purpose and then, through questions, lead them to the point that they will tell about their problems, difficulties, or unhappiness. Since even older retarded persons know little about verbal therapy, the leader will have to help them understand how this may help to express feelings and to develop better adjustment skills.

A useful technique is to go around the group and ask each member to identify himself and describe his problems, life, interests, or family. Group leaders are no exception in this process, and they should be the first to introduce themselves. For instance, the group leader telling about his interests and his strengths, as well as his weaknesses, may break the ice for the other group members and indirectly let them know that it is quite normal and human to have certain disabilities. At this early stage no pressure is applied to have them reveal their problems in detail.

Discussion of the ground rules of the group is necessary. This may include appropriate behavior (for the particular group). The members have to be reassured about the rules of confidentiality. They should learn that everyone in the group is expected to speak. This should be demonstrated concretely in the first meeting. These processes of the introductory stage may surface again and will have to be reinforced throughout the remainder of the group's duration, as necessary.

Initial Stage

The initial stage expands on the introductory phase. The members evaluate each other, and the leader. As in nonretarded groups, the leader is the source of attention, a healer and authority figure. The members bring up seemingly trivial issues, usually a story of a recent experience. These are similar to what Semrad called "goblet issues," described by Schutz (1966), and cited by Yalom (1970), used as a tool to assess the responses of other group members. They reappear in almost every meeting, but should be seen as reflecting primarily the retarded individual's lack of social skills, inability to distinguish important and unimportant topics, and distractibility. In the initial stage of the group they play a useful role in permitting the members and the leader to "size up" one another. Also, these superficially trivial topics may be used by the leader as a starting point for discussion of more general, conceptual, emotionally charged issues.

Second Stage

The second stage is characterized by members entering into in a power struggle with others and, in a sense, with oneself. Efforts to get attention from the leader continue. Preadolescent "joking" and making fun of others, or of the leader, may emerge. Direct challenging of the leader for group leadership is rare, unless working with borderline retarded or severely retarded/disturbed, aggressive persons. However, members may indirectly challenge the leader (e.g., laugh at the "shrink"), usually to reassure themselves that they are not "crazy." They also question the wisdom of being in the group. In this stage, the leader guides the group, with the necessary degree of directiveness, to mutual support and empathy (to replace dependency on him). This in turn leads to a restatement of their own problems and expectations, but in more detail and depth than before. Ambivalence develops: members look forward to the meetings as special, good times, but since the leader does not permit them to dwell only on "safe" issues, the group discussions are also anxiety provoking.

Third Stage

The third stage is marked by the group functioning predominantly as a cohesive unit. The members expect, give, enjoy, and compete for mutual attention and support. Their own problems and sad experiences are recounted, but with minimal resistance and with genuine affect. Sensitivity to being seen by others (and themselves) as defective is shared. Becoming more independent outside the group is attempted, described, and discussed. A similar process may happen within the group. The members may meet socially, or request to have the group meet without the leader. If they do have a basically trusting relationship with him, this may represent a constructive attempt at independence rather than destructive resistance. Regressions to earlier phases occur frequently, either by the group as a whole or by an individual member. If it happens, the leader has to find out the cause and discuss it with the group in as much detail as possible.

Termination Stage

Because of the retarded individual's dependency, low self-image, and experiences of rejection, temporary regressions usually occur in the termination stage. Depending on the setting, the group may be terminated as a whole, or each member may leave at different times. Under the leader's guidance, the members may share their apprehension at the loss of group support; they may "practice," in role playing, mastery of social situations they may encounter; they may make plans for continuing contact and friendship. If the group is open ended, the departing member may be invited to visit later, both to receive support and to stimulate further group development through sharing his own experiences.

ISSUES DISCUSSED IN GROUP PSYCHOTHERAPY
WITH MENTALLY RETARDED PERSONS

The issues that are discussed depend on the needs of the particular group. However, in our experience, there have been a number of topics common to all groups, some of which are reviewed briefly here.

Independence and Plans for the Future

When group members are asked in an unstructured way about their plans for the future, they tend to verbalize socially acceptable phrases, such as

"I want to get a job" or "I want to have a home." They may mention possible occupations without giving much thought to them or without questioning whether they are realistic goals. They may express ambivalence about becoming independent, for instance, by stating that they are afraid to live on their own. These feelings and fears should be explored and shared. "Having a family" and "being a housewife" are associated often by the retarded members only with concrete activities, such as washing dishes and doing laundry. The leader may then have to guide the group toward comprehending the responsibilities connected with being parents or housewives. In the next stage, connections are made between requirements for various jobs and group members' specific difficulties, which they have themselves described in previous meetings. Thus, slowly they start to realize that many of their plans for the future are unrealistic. Some sadness at this point will be evident. At that time the discussion should turn to group members' abilities and how they could be utilized in realistic planning for the future. The better-functioning group members may be "drafted" to tell their accomplishments, for instance, getting a job. The discussion of this topic should end on a constructive and helpful tone.

Discussion of Own Handicap

Discussing their handicaps is usually difficult for group members. It has to be led up to gradually and without excessive pressure. Considerable support may be necessary because this issue is emotionally charged. Group members may bring up various derogatory names they have heard others call them. The leader will have to empathize with them and with their feelings, which may have to be verbalized for them. A member's sharp confrontation with the need to identify his handicap, particularly when it is retardation, may be very traumatic.

Occasionally a group leader may discover—to his surprise—that group participants who mention that they were called "retarded" do not know what this means. They respond with visible relief to the explanation that retardation means delay or poor development in certain areas, but with the possibility of good abilities in different areas. They are also often greatly supported by the realization that other group members, particularly those who have shown better adjustment, have similar handicaps. Group members often prefer to be identified throughout the remainder of group therapy as having "problems in learning" or "being slow in learning," which is more descriptive of their problems and has no negative connotations. Developing a label that is descriptive, socially acceptable, and nonderogatory is helpful.

When discussing a particular handicap, it is important to refer to it in functional terms—the actual difficulties and limitations it imposes on the person's life. Thus, the goal is to teach group members to accept their own handicaps without excessive emotional reaction and to be able to establish an identification based on their abilities, not only on their disabilities. Acquiring verbal "insight" is not sufficient; more often than not, this would consist of group members' passive repetition of the leader's statements. Each discussion of a particular handicap should lead to talking about what can be done about it. Group members should be encouraged to offer their own compensatory solutions, perhaps based on their own experience. The leader may also bring up directly his own opinion, particularly if it is based on past experience, either his own or with his other patients. The remedial steps that are suggested should be concrete and simple to ensure that group members understand them. Whenever necessary, group members have to be helped to accept that a particular difficulty is here to stay and that they have to learn to live with it. They may need support (stress on their abilities) in order not to consider it a pronouncement of their failure or "badness."

Inappropriate Behavior

A variety of inappropriate, usually attention-seeking, behaviors may be exhibited by different group members, depending on the composition of the group. Sternlicht (1966) described ingenious techniques for handling such behaviors, including a show of physical strength in order to impress the group with the leader's abilities and to prevent aggressive acting out. In primarily verbal groups of less retarded persons (on which this chapter is focused), aggressive behavior is rarely a problem. Inappropriate social behavior may be the primary factor limiting the individual's adjustment. This may be reported by the individual himself, observed directly in the group, or described by caregivers. The leader should guide the group and the person involved in discussing such behaviors during the group meeting. The goal is to make the group members recognize these behaviors, the motivation behind them, and their negative consequences. Other group members are enlisted to monitor their peers' behaviors and to verbalize their observations. In the next stage, the group helps devise a set of more appropriate compensatory behaviors for the individual involved. This is illustrated by the following example:

A mildly retarded adolescent spent her time at work, as well as at home, talking incessantly and complaining about her fate and misfortunes. People who heard her for the first time usually expressed a great deal of pity and compassion for her, on which she thrived. In a short time, however, no one wanted to listen to her again, and people would actually avoid her. The group leader knew about this problem and permitted the girl to behave in a similar way during the first several group meetings. From then on, he let the group members verbalize their annoyance at her monopolizing of the group, and led the girl to understand that her behavior caused her to lose friends and have problems at work. Group members suggested to her that she should stop talking and volunteered to monitor her behavior, which they did quite well during subsequent sessions. As a result, the girl stopped monopolizing the group, although occasional reminders to her were necessary.

Technical refinements, such as watching videotapes or listening to audiotapes of past group meetings, may help the members realize the inappropriateness of their behavior.

Peer Relationships

The topic of making friends is a painful one for retarded persons. Most of them are rejected and ridiculed by nonretarded peers, who at best silently ignore them. If no transportation is available, it may be difficult for them to visit handicapped friends who live far away. Many retarded adolescents are also unwilling to "identify" themselves through attending social meetings of retarded persons, and they may prefer, often with encouragement from their parents, to stay at home. In many cases, inappropriate social behavior may be the main obstacle to making friends, particularly for mildly or borderline retarded people. The group may be helpful to such persons through discussion of feelings and/or inappropriate behaviors. The group may also become for them a kind of "learning ground" for making new friends, in this case, with other group members. Another technique may be leading the group members to accept that nonretarded peers may not have been interested in them not because they are "bad," but because of lack of common interests.

Sexual Issues

Adolescents and young adults with mild and moderate retardation have many concerns, questions, and doubts about their sexuality and opportunities for its expression. The group leader who encounters questions about sexuality can find very good guides in the existing literature. (This topic is discussed in more detail in Chapter 9.) Sometimes, what appears to be an interest in understanding sexuality is actually based upon concerns about one's own adequacy and independence in general rather than about genital-sexual functions. Thus, in some groups, members who start to talk about "sex" are actually concerned about making friends, being like their nonretarded peers, or leaving the safety of their homes and families. In some groups, concrete sex education may be necessary. The mental health professional as a leader has an advantage of having sufficient background and understanding of the member's psychosocial development, so he can merge sex education with discussion of other issues, such as independence, self-image, and peer relationships.

Expression of Feelings

Many retarded people who are otherwise verbal lack self-understanding and skills for expressing feelings, because of cognitive-conceptual and language deficits combined with environmental deprivation, lack of stimulation, or past negative responses of listeners to their concrete or "childish" statements. They learn (if they do not have phenotypical abnormalities) that silence is for them a sort of "cloak of competence" (Edgerton, 1967). Feelings like anger, anxiety, or sadness may be unrecognized, suppressed, or acted out. The group may serve as a forum to learn to understand one's own feelings and to communicate them constructively and in a socially acceptable way. Using concrete examples of behavior observed during the meetings, or experiences reported by the members, and using himself as a model for identification, the leader teaches how a member might feel in a certain situation, how these feelings are verbalized constructively, and how they could have motivated a member's inappropriate behavior. As usual, repetition is important, and throughout subsequent meetings, the members are encouraged to monitor one another's behavior and help the peer to verbalize instead of act out.

TECHNIQUES USEFUL IN LEADING MFGS

Techniques useful in leading MFGs are similar to those used in traditional groups. The leader frequently serves as a model for identification for the parents by addressing the children in a nonpaternalistic way, by giving them noncritical empathy and support, by showing respect for their opinions, by encouraging independence, and by simply listening to them. Often, especially at the beginning, he may have to protect the retarded child from traumatic criticism from his parents. It is useful to ask whether the parent has something positive to say and how he thinks his child feels about his statements, and to encourage the child to tell his parents how he feels. Similarly, intervention is needed when a parent presses a silent child to say something, not realizing that the silence may be a passive-aggressive attempt at independent decision making. A parent may embarrass an older retarded child by revealing to the group his private affairs. Limits may be set on this directly (e.g., by prohibiting it) or indirectly (e.g., by asking the child how he feels about it). Interpretation may be called for when the child verbalizes inappropriate demands on the parent or behaves provocatively. In all instances, stress is put on group interaction. Thus the leader had to address the whole group, not just the parents, the children, or one family only. Universality is encouraged by calling upon all members to bring out their own opinions or relevant experiences and to give advice.

STAGES OF MFG DEVELOPMENT

Laqueur (1976) described three phases of MFG: initial interest, resistance, and working through. These roughly parallel the phases of group therapy, discussed previously. Again, these phases are not sharply demarcated. The following phases may also be prominent in MFGs.

The Introductory Stage

The first one or two meetings comprise the introductory phase, which includes the group defining itself (introduction of members, setting goals, making ground rules). Typically, a father introduces himself, his wife, and his children. The leader may then state that each member is expected to speak for himself, thus setting the tone for the process of independence building and individuation of the retarded members, which will continue throughout the group's duration. In the first meetings the children tend to sit next to their parents, but as the group progresses, they separate and cluster together. Other processes in this phase are similar to those in the introductory stage of traditional group therapy.

Initial Stage

The initial phase is often characterized by the parents complaining about their children: their dependence, their lack of friends, their lack of work, their lack of social opportunities. This is usually underlined by anger at the child and by guilt about his retardation. A parent may jokingly wonder whether his child will complain that his home is bad and will reveal family secrets. He may pressure the child to talk about his problems and failures. If this happens, the leader must introduce and reinforce the basic ground rule: that the group's focus must be not solely on the children, but on both them and their parents, and especially on their interaction. A variety of processes are used to reinforce this. The leader encourages universality by asking frequently whether other members, including the parents, have had similar problems. As in therapy groups in general, "sizing up" of one another, and the leader, takes place in this stage.

Second Stage

In the second stage, some members (usually parents) attempt to compete with the leader and with one another. They may attempt to dominate the group by "interrogating" and "analyzing" others, often to avoid talking about themselves. Some retarded members will also try to dominate the group, by focusing the group's attention on themselves through inappropriate verbal and other behavior, or embarrassing their parents as a way of punishing them. These maneuvers usually reflect similar interactions at home and are brought into focus through the leader's intervention, such as asking other group members to comment on the interaction. This further encourages group cohesiveness as a therapeutic community. Independent and constructive comments from the children are particularly invited and encouraged; they are one step toward individuation. As in previous stages, the parents may directly or indirectly vent their anger (and project guilt) by embarrassing their retarded child in a variety of ways. The leader will have to intervene early or the children might become convinced that the group is a dangerous place for them. Turning the problem to the group's attention and utilizing group pressure for its solution is optimal.

Third Stage

By the third stage, the group should be functioning as a cohesive unit. Members of one family do not hesitate to comment on another one's problems or inappropriate interactions, thus acting as a microcosm of society at large. The children feel more confident and verbalize spontaneously or with little prompting. The parents listen to them and show respect for their feelings. The group focuses not only on members' (especially retarded children's) liabilities, but also on assets. Universality is utilized, and the parents identify and empathize with the children. Not infrequently, a parent will report that he also had a problem in the past similar to his child's. An important goal of therapy at this stage is teaching the families appropriate and constructive means of interaction and problem solving. Thus the members are encouraged not to dwell on problem description and seeking intellectual insight, but to focus on concrete plans for remedying the situation. Peer support and pressure (by other families) are encouraged, and specific plans and "contracts" are drawn up (verbally) and followed through in later meetings. Failures of these are analyzed, again with help of other families.

Termination Phase

The termination may be easier to accomplish in the MFGs than in the traditional therapy groups because the retarded person will have supportive and constructive intrafamily relationships, and will thus need less support from the leader and the group. Several of the families participating in the group may continue their relationship beyond the group's duration. The group may also elect to hold a reunion(s). This would permit renewing supportive relationships and "brushing up" on handling certain issues. It would also provide the leader with the opportunity for follow-up on members' progress.

EXAMPLES OF TOPICS DISCUSSED IN MULTIPLE FAMILY THERAPY

Independence

Their children's independence is usually of primary concern for parents, who may have ambivalent feelings about it. Parents may verbalize anger at the child's continuous dependence on them, but they also undermine his quest for independence for reasons such as fear that the child will fail, or wish to continue to care for him. The leader must distinguish between parents' realistic complaints and this ambivalence and guide the group in making this distinction. He may express his empathy but should avoid taking sides. He may help the children to recognize their fear of separation from their parents. This may be facilitated if the more successful retarded individuals share their own feelings, experiences, and ambivalence about independence with the less successful ones. The same applies to the parents sharing their experiences, ambivalence, and uncertainties about what expectations are appropriate. In some groups run in the DEC, some parents stated, "We do not expect enough of them." A mother who had agreed to stop overcontrolling her son stated, "I had to bite my tongue." In another group, several of the children complained that their parents ordered them around too much, making them feel angry and stubborn. They felt that if the parents would trust them, they would actually achieve more on their own. At the suggestion of the group leader, an agreement was made in which two pairs of parents agreed to stop "needling" their children about maintaining weight-reducing diets and the children agreed to watch the diet on their own. Two weeks later, one of the youngsters proudly reported losing 8 pounds; the other one lost fewer pounds, but her parents also admitted that they were not able to completely stop criticizing her. The families may also use the groups to exchange realistic and concrete information (for instance, about organizing community residences), but this should not lead to avoidance of emotionally charged concerns.

The Presence and Nature of the Handicap

Family groups usually handle discussion of handicaps in a way similar to that described for group therapy in general. The parents, surprisingly, often show little open denial of retardation, perhaps because, after facing their child's handicap for many years, they have finally come to terms with it. They may dwell on small differences between handicaps, such as stating that a borderline or mildly retarded child should not be put in a special class with more retarded persons. They may ask questions of the leader, e.g., to explain diagnostic labels. In some cases, an underlying "chronic sorrow" (Olshansky, 1962) reaction to a child's retardation is evident and has to be interpreted as essentially normal (unless it impairs parental functioning and relationship with the child). Mobilizing support of other group members may be very helpful.

Therapeutic Processes in the MFG

All of the processes described previously for "regular" therapy groups can be discerned here as well. In the MFG the presence of families other than one's own creates a "microcosm of society" and enables other therapeutic processes to exist (Laqueur, 1976). These may include breaking the intrafamilial code and use of other families as cotherapists.

The group participants learn much through analogy (listening to other group members who have had experience with similar difficulties and succeeded in resolving them). As an added benefit, support is derived from learning that other parents and/or children have similar troubles. The members also learn by identification with other group participants, including the leaders. Confrontation may be frequent. For instance, one parent may bring into focus an inappropriate interaction between another parent and his retarded child. As opposed to similar confrontations happening within a family, this is nonpunitive, because the observer is not emotionally involved in the issue. At the same time it serves as a model of the reaction of society at large to the behavior in question. Under the direction of the leaders, the thrust of such a confrontation is toward constructive resolution, utilizing personal strengths and experience learned from others.

A very important continual therapeutic process within these groups is learning to communicate. Laqueur (1976) called MFGs a "sheltered workshop in family communication." This is exemplified by the frequently observed relative silence of the children during the first phase of therapy and their eagerness to verbalize during the later meetings.

ASSESSMENT OF THE RESULTS

Difficulties in designing and conducting a reliable assessment of the results of psychotherapy are well known to a practicing clinician. As pointed out by Strupp and Bergin (1969), it would be necessary to define particular interventions that result under specific conditions in specific changes. This may be particularly difficult with retarded persons who depend to a great extent on a variety of environmental conditions. This is especially true if group therapy is part of a more comprehensive educational or other intervention. Under these conditions one cannot completely discount clinical (anecdotal) assessment of change in the course of this therapy, and this approach has been often used in the studies described previously. The group leader should follow-up on the progress of the group as a whole and the clients as individuals. For the former, variables such as group cohesiveness, group (versus individual) centeredness, and responsiveness are important. For the individual, improvement in his specific areas of difficulties should be monitored, as well as factors such as empathy, ability to verbalize constructively and responsively, improvement in self-image, spontaneity, and peer interest. Gislason et al. (1978) attempted to monitor adolescent group progress utilizing instruments like the California Personality Inventory and the Hill Interaction Matrix. Measurement of changes observed during the group meetings was possible, but it was unclear whether they generalized to the members' extra-group functioning. Observations of change in interaction in follow-up, or "reunion," group meetings may be helpful. Szymanski and Kiernan (in preparation), in such a follow-up of an MFG, noted improvement in child-parent interaction and communication patterns, mutual empathy, and understanding. They concluded that family group therapy with retarded persons was a useful and economical therapy tool for learning better coping strategies.

REFERENCES

Anderson, J. E. 1968. Group therapy with brain-damaged children. Hosp. Community Psychiatry 19:175–176.

Astrachan, M. 1955. Group psychotherapy with mentally retarded female adolescents and adults. Am. J. Ment. Defic. 60:152–156.

Baran, F. N. 1972. Group therapy improves mental retardate behavior. Hosp. Community Psychiatry 23:7–11.

Bowen, M. 1976. Principles and techniques of multiple family therapy. In: P. J. Guerin (ed.), Family Therapy, Theory and Practice. Gardner Press, New York.

Cotzin, M. 1948. Group psychotherapy with mentally defective problem boys. Am. J. Ment. Defic. 53:268–283.

Edgerton, R. B. 1967. The Cloak of Competence. University of California Press, Berkeley.

Fisher, L. A., and Wolfson, I. N. 1953. Group therapy of mental defectives. Am. J. Ment. Defic. 57:463–476.

Gislason, I. L., Redman, M., Bailey, L., and Pattison, E. M. 1978. Evaluation of adolescent group therapy. Presented at the annual meeting of the American Academy of Child Psychiatry, San Diego, Cal.

Gorlow, L., Butler, A., Einig, K. G., and Smith, J. A. 1963. An appraisal of self attitudes and behavior following group psychotherapy with retarded young adults. Am. J. Ment. Defic. 67:893–898.

Kaldeck, R. 1958. Group psychotherapy with mentally defective adolescents and adults. Int. J. Group Psychother. 8:185–192.

Landau, M. E. 1968. Group psychotherapy with deaf retardates. Int. J. Psychother. 18:345–351.

Laqueur, H. P. 1976. Multiple family therapy. In: P. J. Guerin (ed.), Family Therapy, Theory and Practice. Gardner Press, New York.

Michal-Smith, H., Gottsegen, M., and Gottsegen, G. 1955. A group technique for mental retardates. Int. J. Group Psychother. 5:84–90.

Miezio, S. 1967. Group therapy with mentally retarded adolescents in institutional settings. Int. J. Psychother. 17:321–327.

O'Connor, N., and Yonge, K. A. 1955. Methods of evaluating the group psychotherapy of unstable defective delinquents. J. Genet. Psychol. 87:89–101.

Olshansky, S. 1962. Chronic sorrow: A response to having a mentally defective child. Social Casework 43:191–193.

Reiss, D., and Costell, D. 1977. The multiple family group as a small society: Family regulation of interaction with nonmembers. Am. J. Psychiatry 134:21–24.

Richards, L. D., and Lee, K. A. 1972. Group process in social habilitation of the retarded. Social Casework 53:30–37.

Rudolph, G. DeM. 1955. An experiment in group therapy with mental defectives. Int. J. Soc. Psychiatry 1:49–53.

Schutz, W. C. 1966. The Interpersonal Underworld. Science and Behavior Books, Palo Alto, Cal.

Slivkin, S. E., and Bernstein, N. R. 1968. Goal directed group psychotherapy for retarded adolescents. Am. J. Psychother. 22:35–45.

Snyder, R., and Sechrest, L. 1959. An experimental study of directive group therapy with defective delinquents. Am. J. Ment. Defic. 64:117–123.

Sternlicht, M. 1964. Establishing an initial relationship in group psychotherapy with delinquent retarded male adolescents. Am. J. Ment. Defic. 69:39–41.

Sternlicht, M. 1966. Treatment approaches to delinquent retardates. Int. J. Group Psychother. 16:91–93.

Strupp, H. H., and Bergin, A. E. 1969. Some empirical and conceptual bases for coordinated research in psychotherapy: A critical review of issues, trends and evidence. Int. J. Psychiatry 7:18–90.

Stubblebine, J. M. 1957. Group psychotherapy with some epileptic mentally deficient adults. Am. J. Ment. Defic. 61:725–730.

Szymanski, L. S. 1977. Psychiatric diagnostic evaluation of mentally retarded individuals. J. Am. Acad. Child. Psychiatry 16:67–87.

Szymanski, L. S., and Kiernan, W. Multiple family group therapy with developmentally disabled adolescents and young adults. In preparation.

Vail, D. J. 1955. An unsuccessful experiment in group therapy. Am. J. Ment. Defic. 60:144–151.

Wilcox, G. T., and Guthrie, G. M. 1957. Changes in adjustment of institutionalized female defectives following group psychotherapy. J. Clin. Psychol. 13:9–13.

Yalom, I. D. 1970. The Theory and Practice of Group Psychotherapy. Basic Books, New York.

Yonge, K. A., and O'Connor, N. 1954. Measurable effects of group psychotherapy with defective delinquents. J. Ment. Sci. 100:944–952.

PSYCHO-PHARMACOLOGY AND THE MENTALLY RETARDED PATIENT

Chapter 13

Timothy M. Rivinus

Medical misuse has long been associated with psychotropic medication for the retarded patient. Yet the same rules that apply to the use of psychotropic medication in adults and children of normal intelligence apply to retarded patients. Psychotropic drugs should be used to treat specific diagnoses, syndromes, or symptoms for which specific drug efficacy has been scientifically established. The patient's, family's, staff's, and clinician's own fantasies of medication should be openly explored and put into realistic perspective before as well as during the administration of any psychotropic medication. Whether the retarded patient is at home or in a supervised or institutional setting, accurate assessment of the effectiveness of the drug must always be made. Safeguards against drug abuse must be built in to prevent abuse by the patient or his caregivers. Proper medical precautions, observations for side effects, and contraindications need to be observed. Last, psychotropic drugs should not be used in lieu of environmental improvement and interpersonal input. To be maximally effective, psychotropic medication should be used as part of a team approach to the patient. As such, medications are always an adjunct to other therapeutic and habilitative measures, including education, employment, self-help, and behavioral training.

This chapter reviews the pertinent literature relating to psychopharmacology in the retarded patient with reference to study design and incidence. The specific drugs, specific psychiatric syndromes, and specific behavioral symptoms in the retarded are reviewed with reference to the programmatic approach of the individual patient. Conclusions are drawn as a result of this review.

ROLE OF THE PSYCHIATRIST

As a member of an interdisciplinary team caring for the retarded patient, the psychiatrist is in a position of interpreter of psychopharmacology to other professionals. This role is similar to that of the direct psychiatric consultant to the patient and his family. The psychiatrist needs to interpret the little that is known and much that is unknown in the field and to help colleagues understand the adjunctive uses, risks, and shortcomings of psychotropic medication.

Psychotropic agents in institutionalized mentally retarded patients have been and continue to be widely abused (Lipman, 1971). Drugs are often used to remedy staff shortages, for staff convenience, to act out unconscious group or individual conflicts, or as punishment. Most misunderstandings in the use of drugs with retarded people seem to result from the inherent frustrations of working with this type of patient. Families, caregivers, and clinicians sometimes act out these frustrations by inappropriate demands and uses of drugs. The retarded patient is always the victim (Mosher, 1975), and it is the duty of the psychiatrist to prevent this process.

REVIEW OF LITERATURE

Review of Previous Review Studies

A number of authors (Rosenblum, 1962; Freeman, 1970; Sprague and Werry, 1971; Lipman et al., 1978) have emphasized the methodological limitations of the majority of psychopharmacological studies done with retarded subjects. Lack of: controls, double-blind design, and dosage information; inadequate measurement of change; and environmental influences were the most frequent criticisms.

Among the important conclusions drawn from previous reviews are:

1. Retarded patients who have reversible symptoms related to acute schizophrenic or affective disorder, hyperactive retarded children with attention and concentration problems, and epileptic patients whose uncontrolled seizures interfere with functioning can often be helped by psychoactive medication.
2. No psychoactive drug has yet been shown to directly increase mental capacity in retarded persons (Wolfensberger and Menolascino, 1968;

Freeman, 1970, 1971; Sprague and Werry, 1971; Conners, 1972, Lipman et al., 1978).

3. Neuroleptic drugs, although sometimes helpful in the thought- and behavior-disordered mentally retarded patient, can themselves decrease learning and cognitive performance (Freeman, 1970; Sprague and Werry, 1971).

Overview of Drug Studies with Mentally Retarded Persons

For the purposes of this chapter, previous reviews of drug studies with mentally retarded subjects (Freeman, 1970; Sprague and Werry, 1971; Lipman et al., 1978) were resurveyed and updated. A total of 166 publications were reviewed and are summarized according to study design and class of drug in Table 1.

Sixty percent of the drugs studied were neuroleptics. In recent years, studies using the antimanic agent lithium have been added and comprise 2% of the total number of studies reviewed. Forty-three percent of the studies (more in the newer literature on the subject) were performed with double-blind placebo-controlled design. Only 23% of the studies were performed on the noninstitutionalized retarded subjects. Of the 72 double-blind placebo-controlled trials, 33 (20%) used random assignment, 30 (18%) employed refined statistical analysis, and 29 (18%) used standardized symptom assessment scales. It is also clear from such a review that the state of drug assessment in the retarded patient is limited because of the many methodological difficulties of studying the effects of psychotropic drugs in such a heterogeneous group.

Review and Conclusions on the Incidence of
Drug Usage in Institutionalized Mentally Retarded Persons

In 1966, Lipman (1971) reviewed drug usage in 173 institutions for the retarded and found that 51% of institutionalized persons were administered

Table 1.   Classification of psychopharmacological studies with the mentally retarded by drug class and study design (excluding anticonvulsants)

Neuroleptic drugs	Double-blind placebo control	Other	Total	%
Phenothiazines	25	75	100	60
Other	6	10	16	10
Antianxiety	6	0	6	3
Stimulants	25	3	28	17
Antidepressants	4	2	6	4
Lithium	3	1	4	2
Combinations	3	3	6	4
Total	72	94	166	100
% of Total	43	57	100	100

psychotropic drugs. Chlorpromazine (Thorazine) and thioridazine (Mellaril) accounted for 58% of these. Twenty-five percent of these institutions had many patients who had been on psychotropic drugs for over 4 years without change or systematic review. Sprague (1975) reviewed 1,094 mentally retarded residents in a midwestern institution and found that 64% received psychotropic or anticonvulsant medication. Polypharmacy (the use of two or more neuroleptic drugs, antianxiety or antidepressant drugs combined) was frequent. In a survey of four state mental hospitals in the South, Marker (1975) reported that 60% of the institutionalized retarded persons received neuroleptic drugs, thioridazine (Mellaril) and chlorpromazine (Thorazine) being the most widely used. Seventy-five percent of these patients were on two or more psychotropic drugs at the same time. Some received as many as five to eight drugs at one time. DiMascio (1975) surveyed 2,000 residents of two institutions for the retarded in the northeastern United States. Fifty-three percent of the residents of one institution, as opposed to 25% of residents of the other (with no other major differences in level of care), received psychotropic drugs.

Cohen and Sprague (1977) compared two midwestern institutions for the retarded, one large and one small, and found psychotropic drug use to be about 50% in both. Massive doses of various drugs were employed in 20% to 35% of both populations, with no difference between the large and small institutions.

A survey (Rivinus, 1978) of an institution of 1,500 mentally retarded individuals showed the incidence of neuroleptics as of 1973 (before regular psychiatric consultation was available) to be 57%, with polypharmacy used in 27%. After 4 years of regular psychiatric consultation to that institution, the incidence of neuroleptic drug use was reduced to 23% of the then 1,300 residents, and polypharmacy was eradicated altogether. Tu (1979) surveyed psychotropic drug usage in five regional centers for retarded persons in eastern Canada and found that 47% of the population of 2,238 residents was on psychotropic drugs. Little indication of beneficial effect, polypharmacy, and poor supervision of drug use were noticed.

The following conclusions can be drawn from these surveys:

1. Psychotropic agents have come into widespread, poorly controlled, and poorly reviewed use in institutions for mentally retarded persons.
2. Polypharmacy is practiced widely in institutions.
3. The use of drugs is often the measure of the lack of alternative approaches to unacceptable behavior and programmatic shortcomings in most institutions for retarded persons.
4. Psychotropic agents can effectively be *part* of the responsible treatment and habilitative programs for some institutionalized retarded persons.

Studies of the effect of psychotropic agents on the functioning of *noninstitutionalized* retarded patients are rare or inconclusive; there is a need for such studies.

PSYCHOTROPIC MEDICATION AND
COGNITIVE PERFORMANCE OF RETARDED PATIENTS

The intellectual and cognitive performance of retarded individuals is rarely improved by any of the major groups of psychotropic agents. The exceptions appear to be when a psychiatric syndrome is present that is responsive to a psychotropic agent, and when the mentally retarded child with a short attention span (sometimes hyperactive) improves in intellectual performance and function with the use of the stimulants (Lipman et al., 1978). The following two cases illustrate these points.

Case 1:   A 28-year-old woman with a full-scale IQ of 52 resided in a state institution for retarded people. She worked successfully as a laundry aide and attended school for 1½ hours a day. She had been able to master simple reading material at the second grade level and was able to calculate change for purchases up to a dollar. She had been noted to have mood swings since the age of 22, characterized by elevation of mood, giggling, and disorganization lasting 1 to 2 weeks, followed by vegetative depression lasting months. This had happened on at least three occasions from the age of 22 to 28 but had gone untreated. Similar symptoms at age 28 resulted in her losing her job and inability to read in school and make change at the canteen for simple purchases. Her aunt had had a history of depressive disorder and the family requested psychiatric consultation. As part of a total treatment program involving occupational therapy and intensive efforts to mobilize the patient from her general apathy, a tricyclic antidepressant at therapeutic doses was added to her regimen. Within 2 weeks, she was back at school and her job. Those staff members who had known her for years exclaimed, "Mary never pulled out of it as fast as this!" During previous episodes, she apparently had been out of work for months and usually lost her ability to read and calculate for over a year.

Case 2:   An 8-year-old hyperactive retarded boy with impaired attention and concentration but with a full scale IQ of 68 was considered by his family and school to be untrainable. He showed little aptitude for learning and was a constant source of disruption and disturbance in his resource room at school. He was both enuretic and encopretic. As part of a total program of rehabilitation, in which his family underwent psychotherapy, he received a new educational plan with more intensive input and he was required to join a play therapy group. Methylphenidate was added to his regimen at gradually increasing doses until a behavioral improvement was noted. Within a month, he was fully toilet trained, had learned the alphabet in school, and, on retesting, earned a full-scale IQ of 76. The family, formerly at their wit's end, was ready to consider keeping the boy rather than resorting to foster placement. These improvements were sustained for over a year. At the end of the academic year, the drug was discontinued for summer vacation. Within days, there was a relapse in the symptoms of enuresis, soiling, disruptive hyperactivity, and loss of the academic skills he had gained. Reinstitution of the drug returned him to the previous levels of improvement within a week.

REVIEW OF EFFECTS OF MAJOR DRUG GROUPS

The Neuroleptics

The neuroleptic drugs are divided for the sake of this review into the phenothiazine and nonphenothiazine compounds. The *Rauwolfia* alkaloids (particularly reserpine) are outdated antipsychotic agents and are not discussed here.

Phenothiazines Phenothiazines refer to those agents containing a tricyclic nucleus of two benzene rings joined by a sulfur-containing ring and a nitrogen atom, to which is attached either a carbon side chain or ring ending in a tertiary amine. Differences in the phenothiazines relate to differences in this latter side chain or ring. The aliphatics include chlorpromazine (Thorazine), the piperidines include thioridazine (Mellaril), and the piperazines include trifluoperazine (Stelazine) and fluphenazine (Prolixin). Piperazine compounds are more potent (but not necessarily more clinically effective) and less likely to produce sedation and hypotension, but they cause increased incidence of extrapyramidal reactions.

Aliphatics Of the aliphatic compounds, chlorpromazine (Thorazine) has been the most extensively studied. The majority of these studies, however, are not placebo controlled, randomized, or double blind. Nor do most of these studies assess long-term effects on intelligence and behavior in retarded patients. The results of the best of the studies of chlorpromazine with mentally retarded patients can be summarized as follows:

1. Short-term usage of chlorpromazine appears to have minimal effect (either positive or negative) on routine IQ test performance in the retarded person (Ison, 1957; Adamson et al., 1958; Freeman, 1970), although the effects of this class of drug by more sophisticated neuropsychological tests have not been assessed.
2. Chlorpromazine generally has been shown to lessen hyperactive, self-destructive, and assaultive behaviors significantly compared with control groups and placebo groups (Craft, 1957; Adamson et al., 1958; Hunter and Stephenson, 1963; Hollis, 1968; Freeman, 1970; Sprague and Werry, 1971; Hollis and St. Omer, 1972; Lipman et al., 1978). In many of these studies, however, there was a significant similar short-term symptomatic improvement in those treated with placebo, casting some doubt on the absolute value of chlorpromazine.

Piperazines Trifluoperazine (Stelazine) has been studied in retarded subjects, but most of the studies were not methodically sound.

Studies using adequate methods found no alterations in IQ, but significant improvement in clinical measures of behavior and sociability (Sharpe, 1962; Hunter and Stephenson, 1963) over controls.

Fluphenazine (Prolixin, Permitil) has been studied in six clinical studies, only one (LaVeck et al., 1960) of which used placebo control and double blind assessment. Although the noncontrolled studies suggested clinical improvement, the one placebo-controlled study rating institutionalized patients suggested that the need for isolation and restraints and degree of aggressiveness was not significantly changed with the use of fluphenazine (La Veck, de la Cruz, and Simondson, 1960). Fluphenazine is the only compound that has the advantage of being available as a long-acting depot injection. This is particularly useful for those retarded subjects needing neuroleptic drugs who do not wish to or cannot be relied on to take oral medication.

Perphenazine has been studied in four clinical noncontrolled trials, and short-term behavioral improvement was generally noted in retarded subjects.

Prochlorperazine (Compazine) has been studied in a number of adequate trials. One study (Craft, 1959b) reported significant improvement in behavioral symptoms of overactivity but no improvement over the placebo group in socialization or aggressive outbursts. One well-controlled 6 month study (Mitchell et al., 1959) did not show drug-placebo differences. Another (Rosenblum, Buoniconto, and Graham, 1960) showed significant behavioral improvement with placebo over prochlorperazine.

Piperidines Of the piperidine compounds, thioridazine (Mellaril) has been the most extensively studied. In general, the quality of the most recent studies is high. Of the important studies of institutionalized patients using this drug (Allen, Shannon, and Rose, 1963; Alexandris and Lundell, 1968; Davis, Sprague, and Werry, 1969; Davis, 1971; Le Vann, 1970), the following conclusions can be drawn: 1) thioridazine appears in most studies to offer short-term improvement in clinical measures of hyperkinesis, concentration, attention, sociability, mood, work capacity, interpersonal relationships, aggressiveness, appetite, and sleep disturbances (Allen et al., 1963; Alexandris and Lundell, 1968; Davis et al., 1969; Davis, 1971); and 2) measures of intelligence in short-term assessment are generally not impaired with this drug (Alexandris and Lundell, 1968), although some measures of visual motor function may be impaired (Sprague and Werry, 1971; Sprague and Boxley, 1979).

Nonphenothiazines

Butyrophenones The butyrophenones share with the piperazine phenothiazines high potency and a strong tendency to produce acute extrapyramidal side effects, but have less tendency to produce sedation, hypotension, and anticholinergic effects (Baldessarini, 1977). Haloperidol (Haldol) is the most commonly used drug in this class. Of the nine reviewed studies evaluating haloperidol in retarded patients, two used a double-blind, placebo-controlled design and three used drug control (Burk and Menolascino, 1968; Cunningham, Pillai, and Blackford-Rogers, 1968; Claghorn, 1969; Ucer and Kreger, 1969; Le Vann, 1971). The following conclusions can be drawn:

1. In the placebo-controlled studies, haloperidol caused a significant short-term improvement over placebo in measures of hyperactivity, assaultiveness, impulsivity, and self-injurious behavior. One of the studies showed that response rates to learning tasks were impaired more with the haloperidol than the placebo group (Cunningham et al., 1968).
2. In the drug comparison studies, one showed significant benefits of haloperidol over chlorpromazine in ratings of impulsiveness, aggressiveness, and hostility (Ucer and Kreger, 1969). No significant differences between haloperidol and thioridazine (Mellaril) could be shown in two studies that reported reliable improvement in measures of anxiety, aggressiveness, impulsivity, self-injurious behavior, concentration and attention span, and learning with the drug-taking patients as opposed to the controls (Le Vann, 1971; Ucer and Kreger, 1969).

Pipamperone (Dipiperon), a butyrophenone, was assessed in a 6-week, double-blind crossover study with placebo and was found to significantly improve the behavior of 20 female institutionalized retarded subjects in 6 of 10 behavioral and management measures (Van Hemert, 1975). More studies are needed with this drug.

Thioxanthenes Only one controlled study of the thioxanthenes in retarded subjects was reviewed (Le Vann, 1970). That study conclusively demonstrated a significant behavioral improvement in institutionalized retarded subjects over nondrug states. However, no significant advantage over the control drug thioridazine was demonstrated.

Dibenzodiazepines (Clozapine) The dibenzodiazepine clozapine (Leponex) was evaluated in an open study and was found to significantly improve behavioral symptoms in one study (Vynke, 1974). Controlled studies are needed to assess better this class of drug.

Other Drugs (Methylperon, Sulpiride) A study comparing the new drug methylperon (Eunerpan) did not demonstrate differences between it and equivalent doses of various phenothiazines, but it did demonstrate significant improvements in aggressive and self-injurious behavior in retarded subjects over untreated retarded controls in a double-blind study (Hacke, Bussing, and Jungen, 1978). This drug deserves more study.

Sulpiride, a benzamide structurally differing from existing psychotropic drugs, has been shown in a placebo double-blind crossover study to significantly improve the restless, aggressive, and self-injurious behavior of 10 retarded subjects when compared to placebo but not when compared to chlorpromazine (Vaisanen et al., 1975). This drug also is deserving of further study in retarded patients.

Side Effects of Neuroleptic Drugs

The acute and chronic side effects of neuroleptic drugs are well reviewed elsewhere (Shader and Di Mascio, 1970; The Medical Letter, 1976; Baldessarini, 1977). Retarded patients are often the victims of undiscovered acute and chronic side effects for two reasons: first, because of their inability to communicate discomfort and distress, and second, because of the institutional and medical neglect often present, which predisposes them to poor observation and infrequent review of drug regimens. The acute or chronic movement disorders caused by neuroleptic drugs often go undiagnosed or are often mistaken for chronic neurological symptoms, which frequently are associated with mental retardation and developmental handicap (Paulson, Rizvi, and Crance, 1975). Chronic use, multiple neuroleptic drug usage, sex (females more than males), and age predispose to the appearance of tardive dyskinesia, the often irreversible result of neuroleptic drug use. This iatrogenic condition should be a potent reminder of the need for periodic review of patients taking these drugs and that they be used chronically only when all other measures fail (Bell and Smith, 1978). Our experience and that of others (Blumer, 1975) is that the neuroleptic drugs rarely can potentiate seizures in the retarded patient, with or without a previous history of epilepsy. This is not a contraindication to their use when needed, but is a caution.

Diphenylmethane Derivatives

The diphenylmethane derivatives, which include diphenhydramine (Benadryl) and hydroxyzine (Atarax, Vistaril), have been widely prescribed in children and retarded patients for reducing anxiety states, sleep induction, sedation, hyperactivity, controlling aggressive symptoms, and as an antienuretic (Freeman, 1970). They are generally considered to be safe drugs and are occasionally effective in treating these symptoms. However, their use is discouraged except in the treatment of phenothiazine overdosage. They are rarely optimally effective in achieving symptom relief when symptoms are serious. Moreover, as anticholinergics, they occasionally produce an acute toxic delirium resembling "atropine psychosis" in certain retarded patients, particularly those with demonstrable acute or chronic organic brain syndromes (Greenblatt and Shader, 1975).

Stimulants

The indications for, and often successful use of, stimulants for the symptoms of hyperactivity, poor attention, and concentration and for the enhancement of certain types of learning in the learning-impaired and retarded child are reviewed elsewhere (Gittelman-Klein, 1975). In the author's experience and in that of others (Campbell, 1975), all of the stimulants have the capacity of producing stereotypic, disturbed, or psychotic behavior in retarded subjects and should be used with caution.

Amphetamine   A review of the adequately executed clinical trials of amphetamine on mentally retarded subjects (Craft, 1959a, b; Alexandris and Lundell, 1968) suggests that amphetamine did not significantly improve the behavior and cognitive performance of the mentally retarded subjects studied.

Dextroamphetamine (Dexedrine)   Five studies using dextroamphetamine in retarded subjects were reviewed and found to have experimental design adequate for clinical conclusions (Zrull et al., 1963; McConnell et al., 1964; Sprague and Werry, 1971). The same conclusions can be drawn for dextroamphetamine as for methylphenidate, namely: 1) that symptoms of poor concentration and hyperactivity are improved in some subjects, but not significantly so in large groups of patients studied, 2) that no other behavioral symptoms are significantly improved by dextroamphetamine, and 3) that in some cases, behavioral symptoms can be worsened and new untoward symptoms may appear as a result of the administration of dextroamphetamine to retarded subjects.

Deanol (Deaner)   Deanol was reviewed recently and found to have properties in addressing symptoms of overactivity and learning problems comparable to the other stimulant drugs (Oettinger, 1977). However, no therapeutic value for the use of this drug was found in seven studies of adequate design on mentally retarded subjects conducted before 1971 (Sprague and Werry, 1971).

Methylphenidate (Ritalin)   A review of adequately controlled studies employing methylphenidate in retarded subjects (Levy, Jones, and Croley, 1957; Blue, Lytton, and Miller, 1960; Davis et al., 1969; Blackridge and Ekblad, 1971; Davis, 1971; Sprague and Werry, 1971) suggests that this drug improves alertness and decreases hyperactivity in some subjects but does not have significant effects (except in some isolated cases) in reducing aggressive stereotypic or self-injurious behavior in mentally retarded groups when compared to placebo. No significant improvement in the cognitive function could be attributed in these subjects to methylphenidate. Baxley (1973) and Christensen (1975) have demonstrated that methylphenidate was better than placebo but poorer than a behavior modification program for improving behavior and cognitive performance in retarded subjects. In some cases, methylphenidate exacerbated behavioral symptoms and even produced psychosis in retarded subjects (Campbell, 1975). This reaction may be related to the amphetamine psychosis noted in normal individuals and, more commonly, in individuals predisposed to psychosis (Connell, 1958).

Antidepressants

Antidepressants (tricyclic antidepressants and the monoamine oxidase inhibitors) have been reviewed by Freeman (1970), Sprague and Werry (1971), and Lipman et al. (1978) and found, when not in association with clear-cut depressive disorder, to have no beneficial effects per se in retarded persons. However, recent reports of the minimal brain dysfunction syndrome in mildly retarded adults (Rybak, 1977) may necessitate a revision of this conclusion. Rybak (1977) found in an uncontrolled study of mentally retarded subjects that aggressiveness was lessened and learning and working were improved with judicious use of imipramine.

Conclusions Regarding Stimulants and Antidepressants

Although no conclusive evidence has been shown in studies of large groups of retarded subjects that stimulants or antidepressants are beneficial, it may be that they benefit certain subgroups, such as the hyperaccial (besides use of the latter in treatment of depression), it may be that they benefit certain subgroups, such as the hyperactive, poorly concentrating retarded patients, enough to warrant their cautious use in selected subjects. The benefits must be weighed against their known side effects (Baldessarini, 1977) and their propensity for causing worsening of preexisting symptoms or of stimulating new psychiatric symptoms or syndromes (Campbell, 1975).

Lithium Carbonate

The antimanic drug lithium carbonate has been shown to be of use in the prophylaxis of manic episodes and possibly of recurrent depression in subjects with an affective disorder (Baldessarini, 1977; Van Praag, 1978). In retarded patients, affective disorder can be identified successfully and treated with lithium carbonate (Naylor, Donald, and Le Poidevin, 1974; Rivinus and Harmatz, 1979).

Lithium carbonate also has been shown to be effective in controlling hyperactive, aggressive, and self-injurious behavior in retarded subjects in well-controlled trials (Dostal and Zvolsky, 1970; Campbell, Fish, and Korein, 1972; Micev and Lynch, 1974; Itil and Wadud, 1975; Goetzl, Grunberg, and Berkowitz, 1977). This drug shows unusual promise in difficult-to-manage mentally retarded subjects, particularly in those with demonstrable organic brain syndromes and hard neurological signs (Rosenbaum and Barry, 1975; Goetzl et al., 1977). Unusual caution needs to be exercised, however, with retarded subjects who are unable to report the untoward symptoms of toxicity in this drug, which has a low threshold for toxicity. Frequent blood lithium level measurements are most helpful in this regard.

Barbiturates, Benzodiazepines, and Meprobamate

The barbiturates, especially phenobarbital, are noted for their untoward behavioral effects in children, the elderly, and brain damaged patients (Reynolds, 1975; Rivinus, in press). The barbiturates are indicated for anticonvulsant and anesthetic purposes only (Greenblatt and Shader, 1975). Use of the barbiturates, in particular the rapidly acting preparations (e.g., sodium amytal), in the retarded patient for behavioral "control" leads to a pernicious situation, characterized by drug-induced behavioral changes escalating drug misuse (Kirman, 1975).

The benzodiazepines have not been well evaluated in retarded subjects. Two studies suggest that short-term anxiety-relieving effects can be achieved by use of chlordiazepoxide (La Veck and Buckley, 1961) and diazepam (Galambos, 1965). No further systematic investigations have been done.

Meprobamate is an obsolescent drug that has been shown, in those few studies that are methodologically adequate, to have no uses in the management of mentally retarded subjects (Craft, 1958; Freeman, 1970; Sprague and Baxley, 1979).

PSYCHOTROPIC DRUGS AND SPECIFIC PSYCHIATRIC AND MEDICAL DISORDERS IN RETARDED PATIENTS

Schizophrenic Disorders in Retarded Patients

One of the common myths about retarded people is that they are not like other people. This is certainly not true with regard to their susceptibility to the well-defined psychiatric syndromes. Disturbed behavior in retarded persons is usually not caused by limited intellectual capacity but by delayed and disordered personality functions, disturbed interpersonal relationships, and inappropriate environmental responses. Examinations of populations of retarded persons indicate that the usual psychiatric syndromes are, if anything, more common in them than in a normal population (Philips, 1967; Philips and Williams, 1975). Childhood and adult schizophrenic disorders exist in retarded persons. The symptoms of chronic childhood schizophrenic disorder respond poorly to the neuroleptic drugs. The acute-onset schizophrenic disorders in retarded adults are frequently dramatically responsive to the neuroleptic drugs and are optimally treated with a combination of a neuroleptic drug and individual and milieu therapy. There are no indications for the use of one neuroleptic drug instead of another in a mentally retarded patient; the appearance or nonappearance of untoward side effects may be the most helpful guide in the choice of a neuroleptic drug. However, the following points should be remembered:

Chlorpromazine (Thorazine), thioridazine (Mellaril), and haloperidol (Haldol) are the drugs that have been most widely tested in psychotic retarded subjects (although other neuroleptic drugs may be equally as good or more effective in any individual patient).

The retarded subject must be observed with rigorous care when a neuroleptic drug is prescribed, particularly if he is unable to report side effects.

Thioridazine retards or retrogrades ejaculation in males.

The aliphatic and piperazine compounds appear to be more sedating, in general, in retarded patients than the piperidines and butyrophenones in equivalent doses (Lipman, 1971).

The piperazines may be more effective in older retarded patients or those having "core" or "nonparanoid" schizophrenic disorders (Hollister et al., 1974).

Patients with organic neurological symptoms relating to impaired basal ganglia function and movement disorders probably should be treated with the piperidine phenothiazines, which have less tendency to exacerbate such symptoms.

The use of anticholinergic agents should be limited to those patients who are experiencing extrapyramidal reactions that are acute or uncontrollable without anticholinergic agent use. The drugs should be tapered and stopped at the earliest opportunity.

Drug holidays and trials off the neuroleptic drugs are standard for the prophylaxis of tardive dyskinesia. This is also true for the mentally retarded patient, particularly because tardive dyskinesia may be more common in the retarded or organically impaired patient (Paulson et al., 1975).

Some mentally retarded patients with or without signs of organic impairment are extremely sensitive to the entire gamut of side effects related to the neuroleptic drugs. In such cases, very small doses are necessary and often achieve the desired effect. The following is a case illustration of this:

A. B. is a 28-year-old institutionalized, profoundly retarded male known for his psychotic rampages, during which he destroys sheets and mattresses. He had been given intensive environmental supervision and therapies, but when left on his own he would rip and tear hundreds of dollars worth of sheets in a few minutes. Three neuroleptic drugs were tried without success. Finally, haloperidol was prescribed at a dose of 2.5 mg twice daily, but A. B. had incapacitating acute dystonic reactions to that dose that were unrelieved by anticholinergics. When the dose was reduced by trial increments to 0.5 mg twice daily, no extrapyramidal reactions occurred and the destruction stopped. When the drug was stopped, the destructive symptoms recurred dramatically; but when the drug was reintroduced at the same dose, the symptoms disappeared.

The depot preparations of fluphenazine (Prolixin) may be particularly useful in those retarded patients who resist the oral ingestion of medications or who are without someone reliable to administer oral medication. The following case is an illustration of this:

B. D. is a 49-year-old moderately retarded male with a chronic paranoid schizophrenic disorder. On low-dose oral fluphenazine (with drug holidays), he is maintained during the winter at a state school without paranoia or behavioral disturbance. He spends summers with his 80-year-old mother, who is unwilling to administer oral medication to him. Each September, he would return to the institution in a paranoid and violent state, requiring mental hospitalization for a month or more. A visiting nurse was engaged to pay 2 weekly visits to his summer home and administer fluphenazine injections. Four Septembers have since come and gone without paranoid decompensation or mental hospitalization for this patient.

Affective Disorder in the Retarded Patient

Reid (1972) has reviewed the literature and documented that affective disorder of manic, depressive, and bipolar type occurs in retarded persons at least as often as in the general population. There may be difficulty in differentiating the symptoms of major affective disorder from environmentally produced symptomatology or organic illness. Careful history taking and ruling out of organic illness by examination and special studies can be of help in these situations. The following case is an example:

> C. D. is a 31-year-old mildly retarded female with a positive family history of affective disorder and a clear (although difficult-to-obtain) history of cyclic mood changes, with both hyperactive and lethargic states lasting weeks, sometimes months, occurring once every 1–2 years since the age of 26. She was hospitalized for evaluation of extreme lethargy. She was awake and responsive to pain but otherwise inert, with no focal neurological signs. Repeated blood studies, spinal taps, and computerized tomography scan were normal. She was tube fed and unable to get out of bed for 2 weeks before she began to slowly regain eating habits and shuffle about the hospital. A week later, she was overactive and shouted, swore, and assaulted staff members. A psychiatrist was consulted; he obtained the essential family and past psychiatric history and made the presumptive diagnosis of bipolar affective disorder. He prescribed haloperidol until the patient's mood was stabilized and then substituted lithium carbonate. The patient has remained essentially stable in mood (with slight but hardly noticeable mood swings lasting days) for 2 years since the institution of lithium carbonate.

According to Rivinus and Harmatz (1979), the diagnosis of manic and depressive disorder requires careful behavioral observation and recording, with strict attention to the established diagnostic criteria for these disorders (DSM III, 1980). Affective disorder in the retarded patient can be successfully treated with lithium carbonate, as has been demonstrated in double-blind, placebo-controlled trials (Naylor et al., 1974; Rivinus and Harmatz, 1979). The tricyclic antidepressants have also been shown to be helpful and effective in the treatment of depression in retarded patients (Reid, 1972).

Epilepsy and Anticonvulsants in Retarded Patients

The common association of epilepsy, mental retardation, and behavior disorder has been shown in many studies (e.g., Guerrant et al., 1962; Rutter, Tizard, and Whitmore, 1970). The behavioral effects of the anticonvulsants, both positive and negative, have been reviewed comprehensively elsewhere (Rivinus, in press). However, the following important observations regarding these drugs should be made:

The anticonvulsants are often potent, psychotropic agents and can have at times subtle and insidious or dramatic positive or negative effects on the behavior of the epileptic patient (Rivinus, in press).

Often the poorly controlled epileptic patient shows disturbed behavior, which should be treated with more optimal control by the skilled administration of the proper anticonvulsant(s).

On rare occasions, behavioral symptoms of the epileptic patient are worsened when seizure control improves (the "alternating psychosis" phenomenon) (Flor-Henry, 1969). In such cases, substitution of one anticonvulsant for another, judicious use of a neuroleptic drug, or, as a last resort, allowing the occasional seizure to occur will improve this situation (Blumer, 1975).

Some anticonvulsants are known to produce behavioral syndromes. Most notable are the hyperactivity and confusion produced in children and the elderly with phenobarbital (and, more rarely, methylphenobarbital and primidone) and the insidious organic brain syndrome with dementia produced in some patients taking phenytoin (Dilantin, diphenylhydantoin). The reader is referred to Rivinus (in press) for a more complete review of such effects.

Some anticonvulsants are thought to have beneficial effects on behavior. A recent addition to the anticonvulsant drugs, carbamazepine (Tegretol) is an example of these. Carbamazepine is closely related in structure to the tricyclic antidepressants and phenothiazines (Gagneux, 1976) and may exercise its positive effects for this reason. Sulthiame, as yet uncleared by the Federal Drug Administration, has also been shown to be useful in the behaviorally disturbed epileptic patient (Grant, 1974). These considerations should be kept in mind by those clinicians prescribing to behaviorally disordered epileptic patients.

The "episodic dyscontrol" syndrome (behavioral outbursts), thought to be related to seizure activity (Maletsky and Klotter, 1974), seems to be extremely rare (Monroe, 1970). Episodic violence or self-injurious behavior in the retarded patient is much more commonly related to environmental deprivation or attention-getting contingencies and should be first treated as such. In intractable cases of episodic violence of self-injury, neurological investigation and cautious trial of an anticonvulsant are justified and occasionally helpful. Substitution of one previously administered anticonvulsant for another is also occasionally helpful.

Infantile Autism

The drug treatment of infantile autism, which is often associated with varying degrees of mental retardation, was reviewed extensively by Campbell (1975). She concluded that psychotropic drugs, particularly the neuroleptic drugs, are useful in treating specific symptoms (such as stereotypic behavior) but are not specific for the syndrome of autism in general. More recent reports have not changed this general conclusion.

Down's Syndrome

Share (1976) reviewed the use of psychotropic drugs in patients with Down's syndrome. No studies demonstrated cognitive or intellectual improvement in such patients as a result of a specific medication. Specific behaviors (i.e., self-injurious or stereotypic behavior) have been helped by psychotropic agents. These effects are nonspecific, however, and other treatments are often easier and produce more lasting effects.

Gilles de la Tourette Syndrome

Gilles de la Tourette syndrome involves involuntary, tic-like movements and vocalizations often associated with signs of organic brain syndrome or mental retardation; it has been described thoroughly by Connell et al., (1967) and Shapiro, Shapiro, and Wayne (1973). These authors have demonstrated that the movements and behavior disorders can often be relieved dramatically by the butyrophenone haloperidol (Haldol). It is agreed, however, that the drug is most effective when part of a total therapy approach.

NOTES ON VARIOUS SYMPTOMS
COMMONLY FOUND IN RETARDED PATIENTS

Aggressive and Assaultive Behavior   Pathological aggression in retarded patients is responsive to treatment with the phenothiazines (Kaplan, 1969; Le Vann, 1969, 1970; Freeman, 1970; Zaleski, 1970; Tischler et al., 1972; Lacny, 1973), butyrophenone haloperidol (Haldol) (Barker and Fraser, 1968; Ucer and Kreger, 1969; Freeman, 1970; Le Vann, 1971; Grabowski, 1973), lithium, and a new benzodiazepine preparation— SCH-12679 (Itil and Wadud, 1975). Epileptiform "episodic dyscontrol" seems to be rare in mentally retarded individuals, but in carefully investigated cases anticonvulsants may be tried (Maletsky and Klotter, 1974; Monroe, 1975).

Barbiturates, including the rapidly acting preparations used acutely as a "chemical restraint" (e.g., sodium amytal), can themselves produce, as they do in epileptic subjects, a behavioral syndrome of irritability, lability, and, sometimes, assaultiveness in the retarded patient (Kirman, 1975; Reynolds, 1975). Therefore, it is strongly suggested that barbiturates *not* be used for "chemical restraint" in assaultive patients. The benzodiazepines can produce a syndrome of irritability and aggressive states in some patients (Greenblatt and Shader, 1975). In some cases, aggressiveness and assaultiveness are associated with schizophrenic or affective disorder. Such cases are helped dramatically by pharmacological approaches. However, most pathological aggression and assaultiveness is rarely responsive to pharmacological treatment alone. Environmental causes should be carefully sought out and altered, behavior should be shaped by reward and limit setting, and safety for patient and personnel needs to be assured. Such management requires a comprehensive team approach, although it is often the psychiatrist who is called upon to direct the management of the acutely or chronically aggressive patient.

Anorexia   No controlled drug trials have been done for anorexia in retarded subjects. Cyproheptadine has been studied in subjects of normal intelligence with anorexia nervosa in a controlled trial and was found to be minimally effective in assisting weight gain (Goldberg et al., 1979). Anorexia in the retarded subject is sometimes related to environmental variables, such as inappropriate diet and struggles over food with caregivers, and often responds to an environmental or management change. In other cases, anorexia as a symptom may be related to a schizophrenic or affective disorder and may respond to a drug appropriate for those disorders (Rivinus and Harmatz, 1979). Where the symptom is life-threatening, a trial of a neuroleptic drug, a tricyclic antidepressant, or lithium carbonate in therapeutic range may be warranted.

Anxiety States   Acute anxiety and panic states are not infrequent in the retarded individual and usually occur because of the subject's limited cognitive ability to comprehend or prepare for environmental events or changes. Such reactions are best approached prophylactically and behaviorally. If drugs are necessary, the order of choice the author recommends is: 1) a benzodiazepine or 2) a neuroleptic.

Although the benzodiazepines remain the drugs of choice for panic and anxiety states (Greenblatt and Shader, 1974), they are frequently ineffective in the agitated epileptic patient in the usual doses, and occasionally cause paradoxical reactions in the organically brain-injured or hyperactive retarded patient (Walters, Singh, and Beale, 1977). Neuroleptics, with the usual precautions, are a useful second choice in the psychotically agitated or dangerously out-of-control subject. The use of the older drug sodium amytal, traditionally used for acute agitation in institutions, is strongly discouraged by this author. Sodium amytal is habituating, is a cause of worsened behavior (Kirman, 1975), and is subject to insidious overuse. Patients with repeated panic or anxiety states require a total approach that fully evaluates environmental and behavioral factors and approaches.

Attention and Concentration Problems   Attention and concentration problems can occasionally be related to schizophrenic or affective disorder or pathological anxiety in a retarded patient. These deficits should be treated with the appropriate agents related to those syndromes. The stimulants offer occasional hope of pharmacological treatment of the attention and concentration deficits sometimes associated with hyperactivity in retarded children. Morris, MacGillivray, and Mathieson (1955), Sprague, Werry, and Scott (1967), Alexandris and Lundell (1968), and Anton and Greer (1969) have adequately demonstrated this for the amphetamines; Zimmerman and Burgemeister (1958), Blue et al. (1960), and Blackridge and Ekblad (1971) have demonstrated the same for methylphenidate (Ritalin). The associated improvements in measures of memory and cognitive performance appear to be specifically related to the common denominator of improvement of attention in these studies (Shaffer, 1977).

Enuresis   Day- and nighttime enuresis is commonly found in the retarded subject and almost certainly is symptomatic of the neurodevelopmental delays experienced to varying degrees in this group. It often responds to behavior modification techniques. Although imipramine and nortriptyline have been found to be superior to placebo in a controlled trial in controlling enuresis in mentally retarded patients (Fisher et al., 1963; Smith and Gonzales, 1967), environmental and behavior modification, when possible, prove more effective in the long run (Drew, 1967; Ferber and Rivinus, 1979).

Hyperactivity   The pharmacological treatment of hyperactivity in the retarded patient depends on the definition of pathological hyperactivity. Environmental causes of hyperactivity must be ruled out or treated appropriately first. Hyperactivity with decreased concentration and attention in a retarded patient can be approached pharmacologically, but should be done so in a carefully measured and systematic way. Sprague et al. (1967) have shown that with high doses of stimulant medication, learning performance can decrease with activity level; they suggest that there are dose curves for individual patients. Activity level can often be reduced by stimulants but close attention should be paid to learning and attention (Levy, Jones, and Croley, 1957; Blue et al., 1960; Alexandris and Lundell, 1968; Anton and Greer, 1969; Blackridge and Ekblad, 1971). The neuroleptic drugs can often reduce hyperactive behavior in the retarded patient, but at what cost? Family members and school and institutional personnel need to be consulted and serial measures of cognitive performance need to be arranged when pharmacological treatment of hyperactivity is undertaken (Hutt and Hutt, 1970).

Self-Abusive and Self-Injurious Behavior   Pathological self-abuse, such as head banging, face slapping, scratching, eye gouging, and rectal manipulation ("digging"), is often encountered in the more severely and profoundly retarded subject. These symptoms are sometimes, although rarely, related to schizophrenic or affective disorders. As such, they can sometimes be helped with appropriate psychopharmacological approaches (Cooper and Fowlie, 1973; Rivinus and Harmatz, 1979). More often, they are a result of a combination of internal forces with environmentally reinforcing factors, such as general isolation with increased attention for the retarded individual at the time of the behavior. Psychopharmacological agents are rarely, if ever, successful in such situations.

Sleep Problems Sleep problems in retarded individuals are sometimes related to psychiatric illness, such as schizophrenic or affective disorders. Appropriate treatment includes neuroleptics or antidepressants, respectively. Sleep problems more often relate to the common scheduling and management difficulties in this group of patients. The hypnotics, flurazepam (Dalmane) and chloral hydrate, in accepted dosages can be used temporarily to reestablish broken routines but should not be allowed to become part of the patterns of chronic misuse of hypnotics seen in nonretarded patients.

Social Withdrawal Decreased socialization in retarded persons can be related to schizophrenic or affective disorder and should be diagnosed and treated appropriately. Some studies (e.g., Alexandris and Lundell, 1968) have demonstrated that a neuroleptic drug may improve socialization in retarded subjects. However, a significant study by Paul, Tobias, and Holly (1972) showed that the use of a drug in an unsocialized retarded subject actually appeared to inhibit socialization when active behavioral programs were instituted. Thus, caution should be exercised in the use of psychotropic agents to improve socialization, and they should be compared carefully with environmental treatment approaches. Scales developed by Balthazar and Phillips (1976) should prove useful in the measurement of changes in socialization in retarded subjects.

Stereotypic Behavior Stereotypic behavior is defined by Baumeister and Forehand (1973) as "repetitious, topographically invariant motor behaviors or action sequences...which [are] regarded as pathological" and includes body rocking, head rolling, head banging, twirling and spinning objects, and complex face and hand movements. It has been suggested (Hollis, 1968; Davis et al., 1969; Davis, 1971; Hollis and St. Omer, 1972; Baumeister and Forehand, 1973; Rivinus, 1979) that the neuroleptic drugs can significantly reduce the number and frequency of stereotypic behaviors in retarded patients. However, it is generally agreed that increased environmental input, stimulation, and program planning are more effective over time and are preferable to the pharmacological treatment of stereotypic behaviors. Neuroleptic drugs can be useful as *temporary adjunctive* measures to such total management programs.

Vomiting Pathological vomiting and rumination without demonstrable organic cause can sometimes produce life-threatening dehydration and, when chronic, cachexia in retarded subjects. Although there are no controlled studies of efficacy, the phenothiazines and related compounds and lithium (Reid and Leonard, 1977) can be important agents in reversing such a pernicious symptom trend.

LEGAL IMPLICATIONS OF PSYCHOTROPIC
DRUG USE IN MENTALLY RETARDED PATIENTS

Wyatt v. *Aderholt,* 503 F. 2d 1305 (1974), presents a widely recognized legal statement governing the habilitation of the mentally retarded patient in its document, "Minimum Constitutional Standards for Adequate Habilitation of the Mentally Retarded," and specifically states that:

a. No medication shall be administered unless at the written order of a physician.
b. Notation of each individual's medication shall be kept in his medical record....At least weekly the attending physician shall review the drug regimen of each resident under his care. All prescriptions shall be written with a termination date, which shall not exceed 30 days.
c. Residents shall have a right to be free from unnecessary or excessive medication....
d. Medication shall not be used as punishment, for the convenience of the staff, as a substitute for a habilitation program, or in quantities that interfere with the resident's habilitation program.
e. Pharmacy services at the institution shall be directed by a professionally competent pharmacist....

It also specifies that only trained staff members shall be allowed to administer psychotropic drugs and that a comprehensive individualized plan for each patient be employed, accounting for medical, educational, social, and psychological needs. In the case of *New York State ARC* v. *Rockefeller* (1973), a class action suit against the state of New York in behalf of the residents of the Willowbrook State School also ruled that limitations on medication and individual treatment plans be established for each patient.

Federal Drug Administration (FDA) guidelines are indicated on the package inserts of all FDA-approved drugs and should be heeded to avoid legal liability. Most states have specific guidelines for the use of drugs in institutions for mentally retarded persons. These should be adhered to by clinicians working in those settings. Michigan has a widely respected set of such guidelines (Sprague and Baxley, 1979), available from the State of Michigan Department of Mental Health.[1]

SUMMARY AND CONCLUSIONS

A survey of the literature makes it clear that psychotropic drugs are still greatly overused in institutionalized mentally retarded patients. Polypharmacy, overdosage, and inappropriate use are the most common problems in the use of psychotropic drugs. The reasons for overusage and misusage probably relates to the frustrations encountered by institutional personnel and families working with them, and the lack of comprehensive

[1]State of Michigan, Department of Mental Health, Lewis Cass Building, 6th floor, Lansing, Michigan 48926.

habilitative programs for retarded persons in institutions and in society at large (Kirman, 1975).

Retarded people have the same capacity for psychopathology as do nonretarded people. Psychotropic drugs, particularly the neuroleptics and antidepressants and lithium carbonate, are effective in treating documented schizophrenic and affective disorders in the retarded patients.

Specific symptoms in retarded subjects, such as hyperactivity, cyclical vomiting, anxiety states, aggressive and assaultive conduct, and self-injurious and sterotypic behavior, can sometimes be ameliorated by the judicious use of psychotropic agents. However, such use should only be part of a total habilitative or rehabilitative program. Other treatment modalities should always include environmental, occupational, and educational improvements, efforts to improve the quality of habilitative care, and behavioral techniques. Drugs used without such an approach can become a *faute de mieux,* when behavioral or environmental measures would be more appropriate.

Except when a specific psychiatric disorder or syndrome in the retarded patient is treatable by psychotropic drugs, there is no evidence that psychotropic medication can change the cognitive or adaptive level of a retarded subject.

Because of common misconceptions and magical expectations of psychotropic drugs, the psychiatrist as a medical member of a treatment team is in the crucial position of interpreter and demystifier to patients, families, other professionals and institutional staff concerning matters of psychotropic medication.

When psychotropic drugs are used as part of the total approach to patients, careful observations must be designed to 1) measure the validity of the treatment (Does the drug do what it is hoped it will do?), 2) measure target symptom reduction, 3) monitor for side effects, and 4) assure that other measures of patient function, such as cognitive function, are not compromised as a result of psychotropic medication. The example of the "quieted" patient who can no longer think or function is pertinent.

Apart from a few specific conditions, the use of psychotropic drugs in retarded persons should be viewed as a temporary, facilitating, and adjunctive measure to be monitored carefully for positive effects and to be stopped if ill effects are uncovered, if no positive benefits can be shown, or if they have outlived their usefulness.

State and federal legislation in the United States increasingly supports the position that the retarded person has the right to respectful and comprehensive medical care, which includes the careful and considered use of psychotropic medication (Bayh, 1977).

With regard to attempts to habilitate, maximize independent functioning, and facilitate integration of the retarded person into accepted social groups, drugs need to be much more carefully and scientifically compared to nonorganic measures than heretofore (Christensen and Sprague, 1973).

In all cases, psychotropic drugs should not be used to obfuscate society's obligation to provide services and offer social acceptance to retarded people.

REFERENCES

Adamson, W. D., Nellis, B. P., Runge, G., Cleland, C., and Killian, E. 1958. Use of tranquilizers for mentally deficient patients. J. Dis. Child. 96:159–164.

Alexandris, A., and Lundell, F. 1968. Effect of thioridazine, amphetamine, and placebo on hyperkinetic syndrome and cognitive area in mentally deficient children. Can. Med. Assoc. J. 98:92–96.

Allen, M., Shannon, G., and Rose, D. 1963. Thioridazine hydrochloride in the behavior disturbance of retarded children. Am. J. Ment. Defic. 68:63–68.

Anton, A. H., and Greer, M. 1969. Dextroamphetamine, catecholamines, and behavior: The effect of dextroamphetamine in retarded children. Arch. Neurol. 21:248–252.

Baldessarini, R. J. 1977. Antipsychotic agents. In: R. J. Baldessarini, Chemotherapy in Psychiatry, pp. 12–56. Harvard University Press, Cambridge, Mass.

Balthazar, E. E., and Phillips, J. L. 1976. Social adjustment in more severely retarded institutionalized individuals: The sum of adjusted behavior. Am. J. Ment. Defic. 80:454–459.

Barker, P., and Fraser, I. A. 1968. A controlled trial of haloperidol in children. Br. J. Psychiatry 114:855–857.

Baumeister, A. A., and Forehand, R. 1973. Stereotyped acts. In: N. R. Ellis (ed.), International Review of Research in Mental Retardation, Vol. 6, pp. 55–96. Academic Press, New York.

Baxley, G. B. 1973. Effects of psychotropic drugs on the short-term memory of retarded children. Unpublished doctoral dissertation. University of Illinois, Urbana.

Bayh, B. 1977. The abuse and misuse of controlled drugs in institutions. In: Hearings before the Subcommittee to Investigate Juvenile Delinquency of the United States Senate, 3 vols. U.S. Government Printing Office, Washington, D.C.

Bell, A., and Zubek, J. P. 1961. Effects of Deanol on the intellectual performance of mental defectives. Can. J. Psychol. 15:172–175.

Bell, R. C. H., and Smith, R. C. 1978. Tardive dyskinesia: Characterization and presence in a statewide system. J. Clin. Psychiatry 39:39–47.

Blackridge, V. Y., and Ekblad, R. L. 1971. The effectiveness of methylphenidate hydrochloride (Ritalin) on learning and behavior in public school educable mentally retarded children. Pediatrics 47:923–926.

Blue, A. W., Lytton, G. J., and Miller, O. W. 1960. The effect of methylphenidate on intellectually handicapped children. Am. Psychologist 15:393.

Blumer, D. 1975. Temporal lobe epilepsy and its psychiatric significance. In: D. F. Benson and D. Blumer (eds.), Psychiatric Aspects of Neurologic Disease, pp. 171–198. Grune & Stratton, New York.

Burk, H. W., and Menolascino, F. J. 1968. Haloperidol in emotionally disturbed mentally retarded individuals. Am. J. Psychiatry 124:1589–1591.

Campbell, M. 1975. Pharmacotherapy in early infantile autism. Biol. Psychiatry 10:399–423.

Campbell, M., Fish, B., and Korein, J. 1972. Lithium and chlorpromazine: A controlled crossover study of hyperactive severely disturbed young children. J. Autism Child Schizophr. 2:234–236.

Christensen, D. E. 1975. Effects of combining methylphenidate and a classroom token system in modifying hyperactive behavior. Am. J. Ment. Defic. 80:266–276.

Christensen, D. E., and Sprague, R. L. 1973. Reduction of hyperactive behaviors by conditioning procedures alone and combined with methylphenidate (Ritalin). Behav. Res. Ther. 11:331–334.

Claghorn, J. L. 1969. Drug treatment of mental subnormality. In: G. Farrell (ed.), Congenital Mental Retardation, pp. 289–301. University of Texas Press, Austin.

Cohen, M. N., and Sprague, R. L. 1977. Survey of drug usage in two midwestern institutions for the retarded. Paper presented at the Gatlinburg Conference on Research in Mental Retardation, March, Gatlinburg, Tenn.

Connell, P. H. 1958. Amphetamine Psychosis. Chapman & Hall, London.

Connell, P. H., Corbett, J. A., Horne, D. J., and Mathews, A. M. 1967. Drug treatment of adolescent tiqueurs: A double-blind trial of diazepam and haloperidol. Br. J. Psychiatry 113:375–381.

Conners, C. K. 1972. Psychological effects of stimulant drugs in children with minimal brain dysfunction. Pediatrics 49:702–708.

Cooper, A. F., and Fowlie, H. C. 1973. Control of gross self-multilation with lithium carbonate. Br. J. Psychiatry 122:370–371.

Craft, M. 1957. Tranquilizers in mental deficiency: Chlorpromazine. Am. J. Ment. Defic. Res. 109:91–95.

Craft, M. 1958. Tranquilizers in mental deficiency. Meprobamate. Am. J. Ment. Defic. Res. 2:17.

Craft, M. 1959a. Mental disorder in the defective: A psychiatry survey among in-patients. Am. J. Ment. Defic. 63:829–834.

Craft, M. 1959b. Tranquilizers, a Latin square trial. J. Ment. Sci. 105:482–488.

Cunningham, M. A., Pillai, V., Blackford-Rogers, W. J. 1968. Haloperidol in the treatment of children with severe behavior disorders. Br. J. Psychiatry 114: 845–854.

Davis, K. V. 1971. The effect of drugs on stereotyped and nonstereotyped operant behaviors in retardates. Psychopharmacologia 22:195–213.

Davis, K. V., Sprague, R. L., and Werry, J. S. 1969. Stereotyped behavior and activity level in severe retardates: The effect of drugs. Am. J. Ment. Defic. 73:721–727.

Diagnostic and Statistical Manual of Mental Disorders (DSM III). 1980. American Psychiatric Association, Washington, D.C.

DiMascio, A. 1975. An examination of actual medication usage in retardation institutions: A study of 2,000 cases. Paper presented at the Workshop on Psychotropic Drugs and the Mentally Retarded, American Association on Mental Deficiency meeting, March, Portland, Ore.

Dostal, T., and Zvolsky, P. 1970. Antiaggressive effect of lithium salts in severe mentally retarded adolescents. Int. Pharmacopsychiatry 5:203–207.

Drew, L. R. H. 1967. Drug control of incontinence in adult mental defectives. Med. J. Australia 2:202–207.

Ferber, R., and Rivinus, T. M. 1979. Sleep disorders in children. Hosp. Times 107: 71–80.

Fisher, G. W., Murray, F., Walley, M. R., and Kiloh, L. G. 1963. A controlled trial of imipramine in the treatment of nocturnal enuresis in mentally subnormal patients. Am. J. Psychiatry 67:536–538.

Flor-Henry, P. 1969. Psychosis and temporal lobe epilepsy. Epilepsia 10:363–395.

Freeman, R. D. 1970. Use of psychoactive drugs for intellectually handicapped children. In: N. R. Bernstein (ed.), Diminished People: Problems and Care of the Mentally Retarded, pp. 277–304. Little, Brown & Co., Boston.

Freeman, R. D. 1970. Psychopharmacology and the retarded child. In: F. J. Menolascino (ed.), Psychiatric Approaches to Mental Retardation, pp. 294–368. Basic Books, New York.

Gagneux, A. R. 1976. The chemistry of carbamazepine. In: W. Birkmayer (ed.), Epileptic Seizures—Behavior—Pain. University Park Press, Baltimore.

Galambos, M. 1965. Long-term clinical trial with diazepam on adult mentally retarded persons. Dis. Nerv. Syst. 26:305–309.

Gittelman-Klein, R. 1975. Review of clinical psychopharmacological treatment of hyperkinesis. In: D. F. Klein and R. Gittelman-Klein (eds.), Progress in Psychiatric Drug Treatment, Vol. 2, pp. 661–674. Brunner/Mazel, New York.

Goetzl, U., Grunberg, F., and Berkowitz, B. 1977. Lithium carbonate in the management of hyperactive aggressive behavior of the mentally retarded. Comp. Psychiatry 18(6):599–606.

Goldberg, S. C., Halmi, K. A., Eckert, E. D., Casper, R. C., and Davis, J. M. 1979. Cyproheptadine in anorexia nervosa. Br. J. Psychiatry 134:67–70.

Grabowski, S. W. 1973. Safety and effectiveness of haloperidol for mentally retarded behaviorally disordered and hyperkinetic patients. Curr. Ther. Res. 15:856–861.

Grant, R. H. E. 1974. Sulthiame and behavior. Dev. Med. Child Neurol. 16:821–831.

Greenblatt, D. J., and Shader, R. I. 1974. Benzodiazepines in Clinical Practice. Raven Press, New York.

Greenblatt, D., and Shader, R. I. 1975. Psychotropic drugs in the general hospital. In: R. I. Shader (ed.), Manual of Psychiatric Therapeutics, pp. 1–26. Little, Brown & Co., Boston.

Guerrant, J., Anderson, W. W., Fischer, A., Weinstein, M. R., Jaros, R. M., and Deskins, A. 1962. Personality in Epilepsy. Charles C Thomas Publisher, Springfield, Ill.

Hacke, W., Bussing, A., and Jungen, K. 1978. Die Wirkung von methylperon (Eunerpan) auf aggressives and auto-aggressives verhatlten bei geistigbehinderten. [Effects of methylperon (Eunerpan) on aggressive and self-injurious behavior of retarded subjects.] Pharmakopsychiatr. Neuropsychopharmakol. 11:86–96.

Hollis, J. H. 1968. Chlorpromazine: Direct measurement of differential behavioral effect. Science 159:1487–1489.

Hollis, J. H., and St. Omer, V. V. 1972. Direct measurement of psychopharmacologic response: Effects of chlorpromazine on motor behavior of retarded children. Am. J. Ment. Defic. 76:397–407.

Hollister, L. E., Overall, J. E., Kinbell, I., and Pokorny, A. 1974. Specific indications for different classes of phenothiazines. Arch. Gen. Psychiatry 30:94–99.

Hunter, H., and Stephenson, G. M. 1963. Chlorpromazine and trifluoperazine in the treatment of behavioral abnormalities in the severely subnormal child. Br. J. Psychiatry 109:411–417.

Hutt, S. J., and Hutt, C. 1970. Direct Observation and Measurement of Behavior. Charles C Thomas Publisher, Springfield, Ill.

Ison, M. G. 1957. The effect of "Thorazine" on Wechsler scores. Am. J. Ment. Defic. 62:543–547.

Itil, T. M., and Wadud, A. 1975. Human aggression with major tranquilizers, antidepressants and newer psychotropic drugs. J. Nerv. Ment. Dis. 160:83–99.

Kaplan, S. 1969. Double blind study at state institution using thioridazine in program simulating out-patient clinic practice. Penn. Psychiatry Quart. 9:24–34.

Kirman, B. 1975. Drug therapy in mental handicapped. Br. J. Psychiatry 127: 545–549.

Lacny, J. 1973. Mesoridazine in the care of disturbed mentally retarded patients. Can. Psychiatry Assoc. J. 18:389–391.

La Veck, G. D., and Buckley, P. 1961. The use of psychopharmacological agents in retarded children with behavior disorders. J. Chron. Dis. 13:174–183.

La Veck, G. D., de la Cruz, F., and Simondson, E. 1960. Fluophenazine in the treatment of mentally retarded children with behavior disorders. Dis. Nerv. Syst. 21:1–4.

Le Vann, L. J. 1969. Haloperidol in the treatment of behavioral disorders in children and adolescents. Can. Psychiatry Assoc. J. 14:217–220.

Le Vann, L. J. 1970. Clinical experience with Tarasan and thioridazine in mentally retarded children. Appl. Ther. 12:30–33.

Le Vann, L. J. 1971. Clinical comparison of haloperidol with chlorpromazine in mentally retarded children. Am. J. Ment. Defic. 75:719–723.

Levy, J. M., Jones, B. E., and Croley, H. T. 1957. Effects of methylphenidate (Ritalin) on drug-induced drowsiness in mentally retarded patients. Am. J. Ment. Defic. 75:719–723.

Lipman, R. S. 1970. The use of psychopharmacological agents in residential facilities for the retarded. In: F. J. Menolascino (ed.), Psychiatric Approaches to Mental Retardation, pp. 387–398. Basic Books, New York.

Lipman, R. S., DiMascio, A., Reatig, N., and Kirson, T. 1978. Drugs and mentally retarded children. In: M. A. Lipton, A. DiMascio, and K. F. Killam (eds.), Psychopharmacology: A Generation of Progress, pp. 1437–1449. Raven Press, New York.

McConnell, T. R., Jr., Cromwell, R. L., Bialer, I., and Son, C. D. 1964. Studies in activity level. VII. Effects of amphetamine drug administration on the activity level of retarded children. Am. J. Ment. Defic. 68:647–651.

Maletsky, B. M., and Klotter, J. 1974. Episodic control: A controlled replication. Dis. Nerv. Syst. 35:175–179.

Marker, G. 1975. Legal restrictions on the use of phenothiazines. Unpublished manuscript. (Available from the Mental Health Law Project, 1751 N Street, N.W., Washington, D.C. 20036.)

Medical Letter. 1976. Editorial. 18(22):89–96.

Micev, V., and Lynch, D. M. 1974. Effect of lithium on disturbed severely mentally retarded patients. Br. J. Psychiatry 125:110.

Mitchell, A. C., Hargis, C. H., McCarry, F., and Powers, C. 1959. Effects of prochlorperazine therapy on educability in disturbed mentally retarded adolescents. Am. J. Ment. Defic. 63:57–62.

Monroe, R. 1970. Episodic Behavioral Disorders. Harvard University Press, Cambridge, Mass.

Monroe, R. 1975. Anticonvulsants in the treatment of aggression. J. Nerv. Dis. 160:119–126.

Morris, J. V., MacGillivray, R. C., and Mathieson, C. M. 1955. The results of the experimental administration of amphetamine sulphate in oligophrenia. J. Ment. Sci. 101:131–140.

Mosher, L. 1975. Pawns in a pill game. The National Observer, Jan. 11.

Naylor, G. J., Donald, J. M., and Le Poidevin, D. 1974. A double blind trial of long-term lithium therapy in mental defectives. Br. J. Psychiatry 124:52–57.

New York State ARC v. Rockefeller. E.D.N.Y. 1973. 357 F. Suppl. 752.

O'Connor, N. 1951. Neuroticism and emotional instability in high-grade male defectives. J. Neurol. Neurosurg. Psychiatry 14:226–230.

Oettinger, L. 1977. Pediatric psychopharmacology: A review with special reference to Deanol. Dis. Nerv. Syst. 38(12):25–31.

Paul, G. L., Tobias, L. L., and Holly, B. L. 1972. Maintenance psychotropic drugs in the presence of active treatment programs: "Triple-blind" withdrawal study with long-term mental patients. Arch. Gen. Psychiatry 27:106–115.

Paulson, G. W., Rizvi, C. A., and Crance, G. E. 1975. Tardive dyskinesia as a possible sequel of long-term therapy with phenothiazines. Clin. Pediatr. 10:953–955.

Philips, I. 1967. Psychopathology and mental retardation. Am. J. Psychiatry 124:29–35.

Philips, I., and Williams, N. 1975. Psychopathology and mental retardation: A study of 100 mentally retarded children. I. Psychopathology. Am. J. Psychiatry 132:1265–1271.

Reid, A. H. 1972. Psychoses in adult mental defectives. I. Manic depressive psychosis. Br. J. Psychiatry 120:205–212.

Reid, A. H., and Leonard, A. 1977. Lithium treatment of cyclical vomiting in a mentally defective patient. Br. J. Psychiatry 130:316.

Reynolds, E. J. 1975. Antiepileptic toxicity: A review. Epilepsia 16:319–352.

Rivinus, T. M. 1978. Clinical aspects of consultation to a state school for the mentally retarded. Unpublished manuscript. (Available from author.)

Rivinus, T. M. 1979. Effect of various environmental inputs and pharmacological trials on rhythmic stereotypies in retarded subjects. Unpublished data. (Available from author.)

Rivinus, T. M. Psychiatric effects of the anticonvulsant regimens. In: R. I. Shader (ed.), Psychiatric Complications of Medical Drugs. Raven Press, New York. In press.

Rivinus, T. M., and Harmatz, J. S. 1979. Diagnosis and lithium treatment of affective disorder in the retarded: Five case studies. Am. J. Psychiatry 136:551–554.

Rosenbaum, A. H., and Barry, M. J. 1975. Positive therapeutic response to lithium in hypomania secondary to organic brain syndrome. Am. J. Psychiatry 132:1072–1073.

Rosenblum, S. 1962. Practices and problems in the use of tranquilizers with exceptional children. In: E. Trapp and P. Himmelstein (eds.), Readings on the Exceptional Child, pp. 339–357. Appleton-Century-Crofts, New York.

Rosenblum, S., Buoniconto, P., and Graham, B. D. 1960. "Comprazine" vs. placebo: A controlled study with educable, emotionally disturbed children. Am. J. Ment. Defic. 64:713–717.

Rutter, M., Tizard, T., and Whitmore, K. 1970. Education, Health, and Behavior. Longmans Green & Co., Ltd., London. pp. 318–319.

Rybak, W. S. 1977. More adult brain dysfunction. Am. J. Psychiatry 134:96–97.

Shader, R. I., and DiMascio, A. 1970. Psychotropic Drug Side Effects. Williams & Wilkins Co., Baltimore.

Shaffer, D. 1977. Drug treatment. In: M. Rutter and L. Hersov (eds.), Child Psychiatry, pp. 901–922. Blackwell Scientific Publications, London.

Shapiro, A., Shapiro, E., and Wayne, H. 1973. Treatment of Tourette's syndrome with haloperidol. Arch. Gen. Psychiatry 28:92–97.

Share, J. B. 1976. Review of drug treatment for Down's syndrome persons. Am. J. Ment. Defic. 80:388–393.

Sharpe, D. S. 1962. A controlled study of trifluoperazine in the treatment of the mentally subnormal patient. J. Ment. Sci. 108:220–224.

Smith, E. H., and Gonzalez, R. 1967. Nortriptyline hydrochloride in the treatment of enuresis in mentally retarded boys. Am. J. Ment. Defic. 71:825-827.

Sprague, R. L. 1975. Research findings and their impact on the FDA Pediatric Advisory Panel. Paper presented at the American Association on Mental Deficiency annual meeting, March, Portland, Ore.

Sprague, R. L., and Baxley, G. B. 1979. Drugs used for the management of behavior in mental retardation. In: N. R. Ellis (ed.), Handbook of Mental Deficiency. 2nd Ed. Erlbaum Associates, New York.

Sprague, R. L., and Werry, J. S. 1971. Methodology of psychopharmacological studies with the retarded. In: N. R. Ellis (ed.), International Review of Research in Mental Retardation, Vol. 5, pp. 147-219. Academic Press, New York.

Sprague, R. L., Werry, J. S., and Scott, K. C. 1967. Effects of dextroamphetamine on activity level and learning in retarded children. Paper presented at the Midwestern Psychological Association meeting, May 5, Chicago, Ill.

Tischler, B., Patriasz, K., Beresford, J., and Bunting, R. 1972. Experience with pericyazine in profoundly and severely retarded children. Can. Med. Assoc. J. 106:136-141.

Tu, J-B. 1979. A survey of psychotropic medication in mental retardation facilities. J. Clin. Psychiatry 40:125-129.

Ucer, E., and Kreger, K. C. 1969. A double blind study comparing haloperidol with thioridazine in emotionally disturbed, mentally retarded children. Curr. Ther. Res. 11:278-283.

Vaisanen, K., Kainulainen, P., Paavilainen, M. T., and Viukari, M. 1975. Sulpiride versus chlorpromazine and placebo in the treatment of restless mentally subnormal patients—A double blind cross-over study. Curr. Ther. Res. 17(2):202-205.

Van Hemert, J. C. J. 1975. Pipamperone (Dipiperon, R3345) in troublesome mental retardates: A double blind placebo controlled cross-over study with long-term follow-up. Acta Psychiatry Scand. 52:237-245.

Van Praag, H. M. 1978. Psychotropic Drugs. Brunner/Mazel, New York.

Vynke, J. 1974. The treatment of behavior disorders in idiocy and imbecility with Clozapine. Pharmakopsychiatr. Neuropsychopharmakol. 7:225-229.

Walters, A. Singh, N., and Beale, I. L. 1977. Effects of Lorazepam on hyperactivity in retarded children. N. Z. Med. J. 86:473-475.

Wolfensberger, W., and Menolascino, F. 1968. Basic considerations in evaluating ability of drugs to stimulate cognitive development in retardates. Am. J. Ment. Defic. 73:414-423.

Zaleski, W. 1970. A clinical evaluation of mesoridazine in mentally retarded patients. Can. Psychiatry Assoc. J. 15:319-322.

Zimmerman, F. T., and Burgemeister, B. B. 1958. Action of methyl-phenidylacetate (Ritalin) and reserpine in behavior disorders in children and adults. Am. J. Psychiatry 115:323-328.

Zrull, J. P., Westman, J. C., Arthur, B., and Bell, W. A. 1963. A comparison of chlordiazepoxide, d-amphetamine, and placebo in the treatment of the hyperkinetic syndrome in children. Am. J. Psychiatry 120:590-591.

BASIC PRINCIPLES OF BEHAVIOR THERAPY WITH RETARDED PERSONS

Chapter 14

Paul E. Jansen

The behavior therapies are a family of psychotherapeutic techniques that have become prominent in contemporary clinical work. In current professional usage, the terms *behavior therapy, behavior modification, contingency management,* and *applied behavior analysis* are often used interchangeably to describe this particular field of endeavor. All of these terms refer to the systematic use of principles and procedures derived from the experimental study of learning in clinical psychological practice. Throughout this chapter, *behavior therapy* is used as a single umbrella term that includes all these current usages. (See glossary at the end of this chapter for additional behavioral terminology.)

Before behavior therapy can be defined adequately, the technical meaning of the term *behavior* must be understood. Today, in behavioral psychology, the term *behavior* is broadly defined as any overt or covert act that can be measured or counted. Behavior, therefore, includes the traditionally accepted behavioral categories, such as muscular and glandular responses, as well as cognitive events, which can, in principle, be measured and counted by the person experiencing them. Behavior, then, involves anything a person does, says, thinks, or feels. Using this definition of behavior as a starting point, it is now possible to offer a clear definition of what is meant by *behavior therapy.*

Behavior therapy is best conceived as a technology of behavior change. The approach is characterized by an emphasis on discovering and altering the relationship between measurable behaviors (responses, feelings, cognition) and antecedent and subsequent environmental events. In marked contrast to more traditional forms of psychotherapy, behavior therapy assumes that deviant (and normal) behavior is learned, and that the current environmental context is more relevant in affecting an individual's ongoing behavior than personality structure, intrapsychic conflict, or the residual effects of early life experiences.

In behavioral psychology, the acquisition and maintenance of learned behavior is viewed in terms of two distinct arrangements of environmental events: 1) Reflex-like learned behavior is elicited by antecedent stimuli (this is known as respondent, or Pavlovian, conditioning). This kind of conditioning has often been referred to as stimulus-response (S-R) learning. 2) Voluntary, nonreflexive behavior is spontaneously emitted and maintained because of its consequences (rewards or punishments: this is known as operant conditioning). Experimental research on respondent and operant conditioning has provided the scientific basis of the contemporary behavior therapies.

BEHAVIOR THERAPY IN MENTAL RETARDATION

History

In 1949, the first operant behavioral intervention was attempted with a mentally retarded client (Fuller, 1949). In the report, the author described how he used sugar milk as a reward to teach a profoundly retarded, bed-ridden 18-year-old man to perform a single, voluntary response—raising his arm. Although arm raising had no clinical utility, the author speculated that, given time, a range of potentially adaptive responses might be conditioned in an individual who was generally considered to be incapable of learning anything.

From this modest beginning, behavior therapy has grown into a major therapeutic vehicle for habilitating mentally retarded clients. In the 1950s and 1960s there was a rapid expansion of clinical applications of behavior therapy to solving the problems of retarded persons, principally those in closed institutional settings. Behavior therapists typically began by attacking the behavior problems defined as most disturbing by the direct-care staff who worked with the institutionalized retarded clients daily. Self-feeding (Bensberg, 1965) and toilet training (Ellis, 1963) were common targets of early intervention efforts, since it was generally agreed that a neat, toilet-trained child or adult would more often gain access to other professional services, such as education and vocational training. The early self-help training programs were typically successful, and these positive results in turn led behavior therapists to develop intervention programs for the most difficult retarded clients—the self-injurious (Tate and Baroff, 1966) and the assaultive/destructive (Hamilton, Stephens, and Allen, 1967). Promising behavioral treatments were developed for each of these client categories and, by the late 1960s, grants totalling many millions of dollars were being channeled into research and demonstration projects showing the utility of behavior therapy with all levels of retarded children.

Function

Based on the results generated by early behavior therapy projects, it is now known that properly designed behavioral programs can reliably accomplish four clinical objectives for mentally retarded clients. First, behavior therapy programs can teach or increase new behaviors for mentally retarded children and adults (e.g., a self-feeding training program for a severely retarded child). Second, behavioral programs can be used to maintain previously learned behavior in retarded clients (e.g., token economy programs in sheltered workshops to maintain ongoing work behavior in retarded clients). Third, behavioral programs can be used to reduce the frequency or intensity of unwanted or maladaptive behaviors (e.g., using timeout procedures to weaken self-injurious behavior). Fourth, behavioral programs allow staff to redistribute client behavior in space and time to make it more socially acceptable (e.g., toilet training, which teaches a retarded client where and when to eliminate).

Development of Individual Behavioral Programs

As noted in Chapter 1, interdisciplinary team evaluation has become the model approach for generating appropriate services for mentally retarded people. However, this comprehensive team evaluation process is only the first step in the development of an individualized plan of care for each retarded client. Plans of care are written to incorporate two critical design features. First, the plans must be comprehensive, addressing medical, psychological, social, and educational domains. Second, the plans must be objective and quantified, so that progress or lack of progress can be assessed reliably over time. This second feature, the need for objectivity, has been the main avenue for behavioral thinking to enter into the interdisciplinary evaluation process. Today, virtually all treatment plans for retarded clients are written in terms of behavioral objectives or goals.

After the interdisciplinary team generates a set of behavioral objectives for a particular client, appropriate intervention strategies must be constructed to achieve each stated objective. Typically, an interdisciplinary evaluation does not go into great detail in specifying the behavioral intervention(s) needed to achieve a particular behavioral objective. Instead, the evaluation team produces target behavioral objectives (e.g., child X will be toilet-trained in 6 weeks) and then proposes a generic behavior modification program to meet this objective. At this point it becomes necessary for someone to take responsibility for creating and monitoring the behavioral program proposed by the team. As a rule, a psychologist will be assigned this responsibility, but this is not an automatic decision. For reasons that go beyond the scope of this presentation, some psychologists may be unfamiliar or uncomfortable with behavioral psychology and behavioral programming. Other professionals, such as nurses and psychiatrists, may possess considerable behavioral expertise. Whoever is ultimately selected to implement a particular behavioral intervention must, in the judgment of the team, have sufficient training and experience in behavioral programming to achieve the stated goals. Only a properly designed behavior therapy program can reach the therapeutic objectives developed by the interdisciplinary team. Poorly designed and managed programs inevitably lead to staff frustration, client regression, and failure.

BEHAVIORAL PROGRAMS FOR MENTALLY RETARDED CLIENTS

As a rule, behavior therapy programs for mentally retarded clients are implemented by direct-service staff workers rather than by psychologists, psychiatrists, social workers, or other professional staff members. However, professional staff members typically supervise, monitor, and evaluate these programs, and so it is vital that all involved professionals understand the true potential and limitations of behavior therapy with mentally retarded clients. To be genuinely effective, behavior therapy programs written for retarded clients must be behaviorally comprehensive, in the sense that behaviors-to-be-eliminated and behaviors-to-be-developed must be addressed concurrently. It is pointless to try to reduce or eliminate a maladaptive behavior, such as tantrums, without replacing it with an alternative response. Since maladaptive behavior, like all learned behavior, is maintained by its consequences, it therefore serves some utilitarian function in the life of a retarded person. For instance, tantrums may be intended to gain attention from others or exert social influence over others (parents or staff). If tantrums are targeted for elimination, the retarded client must be taught socially appropriate behaviors that can also gain attention and exert social influence. If one attempts to reduce or eliminate a retarded client's maladaptive behavior without developing a functional substitute for that behavior, it is likely that the maladaptive behavior will reappear in a very short time. Therefore, well-designed behavior therapy programs develop contingencies to extinguish maladaptive responses, as well as simultaneously build adaptive responses to replace the behaviors being eliminated.

Programs to Build New Behaviors

The details of any behavior therapy program to build new skills and behaviors for retarded clients vary with the level of retardation of the clients being served. Regardless of the specifics, the general behavioral format for all skill development programs follows a series of clearly defined steps. First, a task analysis will be developed for each skill to be learned, and the number of discrete steps required to achieve a terminal behavioral objective will be specified. For example, the behavioral objective of hand-washing might be task analyzed. Although handwashing may seem to be a simple enough behavior to teach, task analysis shows that as many as 22 separate steps must be learned before the terminal performance is mastered. When we say to a retarded child, "Go wash your hands," we are really telling him to: 1) turn on cold water faucet, 2) turn on hot water faucet, 3) test water temperature, 4) wet hands, 5) pick up soap, 6) rub soap on left hand, 7) rub soap on right hand, 8) put down soap, 9) rub hands together, 10) rinse hands, 11) pick up soap again, 12) rub soap on left hand, 13) rub soap on right hand, 14) put down soap, 15) rub hands together, 16) rinse hands, 17) turn off hot water, 18) turn off cold water, 19) pick up towel, 20) dry left hand, 21) dry right hand, and 22) put down towel.

A task analysis must be conducted for each behavior being taught in a behavior therapy program. For higher functioning clients, community-relevant behaviors like riding public transportation are also broken down in the same fashion and are then taught in graded steps. The size and complexity of the discrete behavioral units being taught will vary for different behaviors and different clients, and, as a general rule, the more severely retarded the client, the smaller the steps that will be needed to achieve a particular behavioral objective.

The target behavior being taught is termed a *chain,* and the subunits of the chain are termed *links.* Chains of behavior are usually taught backward, with the last link (the link closest to reinforcement) taught first. In the case of handwashing, the last link, hand drying, is first modeled for the client, and then the client is manually guided to imitate the hand-drying behavior. Positive reinforcement in the form of concrete rewards and social praise is provided to the client at the end of the hand-drying behavior, and the training is repeated until the client can perform the appropriate behavior when requested to do so. Once the terminal link of the hand-drying chain is mastered, the next-to-last link, turning off the water, is taught in the same manner. Reinforcement is then provided at the end of the two-link sequence: 1) turn off water, 2) dry hands, and 3) reinforcement delivery. Other links are added to the chain until the client is able to perform the whole sequence of steps required to wash one's hands.

With higher functioning clients, community-relevant skills are taught in the same way as basic self-help skills. For example, a client living in a group home might need to be taught to buy a quart of milk. This target behavior is broken down into smaller units, modeled, and reinforced in the same way that hand washing is approached. Prompts and other assistance provided by the teacher are faded, until the client reaches a point where he is able to self-initiate the "buy a quart of milk" sequence, cued only by his observation that there is no milk in the refrigerator. Using these chaining and positive reinforcement procedures, it is possible to teach a tremendous variety of adaptive behaviors to retarded persons who could not learn them in traditional teaching situations.

Programs to Maintain Previously Learned Behaviors

Once a behavior is learned, positive reinforcement is still necessary to ensure that the client will continue to perform the learned behavior. Although the density (amount and frequency) of reinforcement is gradually decreased as training proceeds, some level of reinforcement will still be required to maintain the ongoing behavior. Ideally, the learned behaviors eventually will be maintained by their natural, response-produced consequences. For example, if a client in a group home is taught how to initiate a conversation with other group home residents, the positive social feedback from the others may be sufficient to maintain behavioral performance in the absence of external reinforcement. In a sheltered workshop setting, the client will usually require ongoing social and token (money) reinforcement to maintain work performance. Failure to provide necessary maintenance contingencies has often resulted in the breakdown of well-learned behaviors in retarded clients. This finding is not surprising, since even highly skilled professionals will stop performing their jobs if reinforcement (pay) is terminated. Mentally retarded persons are just as susceptible to behavioral deterioration as those with normal intelligence if positive reinforcement is weak or absent.

Behavioral Programs to Decrease Maladaptive Behaviors

Eliminating a retarded person's maladaptive behavior is especially difficult, for practical and ethical reasons. All learned behavior, adaptive or maladaptive, is maintained because it achieves some rewarding objective for the person exhibiting the behavior. If a severely retarded child wants attention and has no normal behaviors available that can function to gain attention, the child is likely to develop attention-getting behaviors that an observer would label maladaptive. Thus, assaultive, destructive, and self-injurious behaviors serve a meaningful purpose in the life of a severely retarded person, and any programs that are developed solely to eliminate these behaviors will probably not succeed. Thus, if a retarded child is banging his head in order to gain attention, an alternative means of gaining attention must be taught concurrently with efforts to reduce head banging. Without such behavior substitution, the maladaptive behavior is sure to recur the next time the child wants attention.

Ethical difficulties may also arise when programs are developed to eliminate maladaptive behaviors, since punishment is usually seen as the best means of rapidly suppressing undesirable behavior. In the standard punishment paradigm, whenever a maladaptive behavior is exhibited, it is immediately followed by the application of an aversive event or stimulus (a reprimand, a slap, loss of attention, loss of a token). Punishment is very effective in suppressing behavior for a short time, and it is this effectiveness that necessitates an exploration of the values and attitudes of the person proposing punishment contingencies. Even a totally unsophisticated person can effectively employ punishment contingencies in ways that will reliably alter the behavior of others. Unfortunately, this can prove to be highly rewarding or self-reinforcing to the punishing agent, which can easily cause that person to feel powerful and effective while administering punishment, but weak and ineffectual when not employing punishment. If the person in a position to administer punishment to others does not understand how to use positive reinforcement to alter behavior, it is likely that that person will resort immediately to punishment contingencies whenever a behavior problem arises. In this case, the punishment is being administered because its use is rewarding to the punisher, rather than serving a necessary therapeutic objective for the punished individual.

Before punishment is used with mentally retarded clients, a broad, interdisciplinary consensus must be achieved on the behaviors that will be punished and the mode of punishment that will be employed. Punishment as a teaching technique has several inherent flaws, and these should be explicated before punishment is used in a clinical context. First, to be effective, a particular punishing stimulus must be truly aversive or unpleasant to the client. The operationally effective level of punishment may be so severe that it generates negative emotional states in the client (fear, anger) that are incompatible with learning. A second problem is that the person administering punishment may be a poor role model for the individual being punished. Any person who is repeatedly punished soon learns that he can control others with punishment, and this can lead to the punished individual becoming a tyrant with those weaker than himself. A final problem with punishment is that its effects do not readily generalize to new situations. Thus, a retarded person whose deviant behavior is punished in one environment by one particular person is likely to exhibit the behavior again as soon as the environment or the punisher changes.

Thus, punishment as a treatment technique should be a last resort. In practice, punishment is usually reserved for those behaviors that prove to be unresponsive to positive reinforcement. However, it should be noted that evidence is now accumulating that suggests that the sophisticated use of positive reinforcement may obviate the necessity of ever using more than the mildest form of conditioned social punishment (loss of attention) to alter the behavior of retarded people. An interesting case in point is the behavioral treatment of the self-mutilating behaviors that are characteristic of the Lesch-Nyhan syndrome. Lesch-Nyhan disease is a rare, X-linked recessive disorder, characterized by mild to severe mental retardation, spasticity, choreoathetosis, stunting of growth, and dramatically self-mutilative behavior. The self-mutilation typically includes biting of the lips and fingers, and past "therapy" for this disorder has meant reliance on tubular arm splints, restraints, and extraction of teeth. Not surprisingly, physical punishment has been found to be totally ineffective in reducing the self-mutilation seen in Lesch-Nyhan patients, since the self-inflicted pain of the mutilative behavior does not decrease the frequency of the behavior. Recently, five Lesch-Nyhan patients were treated with a combination of mild social punishment (withdrawal of adult attention) contingent on self-mutilative behavior and social positive reinforcement (attention, praise) contingent on talking, playing, or any other noninjurious behavior (Anderson, Dancis, and Alpert, 1978). This treatment approach was evaluated in a 2-year follow up, and all five children showed significant improvement in total time spent in physical restraints. If the results of this study can be replicated, it would seem to indicate that by providing sufficient positive reinforcement for behavior that is incompatible with the behavior to be eliminated, only the mildest form of concurrent social punishment would be necessary to eliminate virtually all maladaptive behavior. If this eventually proves to be the case, most of the debates about the practical and ethical ramifications of using physical punishment in behavior therapy programs for retarded clients may end.

Behavioral Programs to Redistribute Behavior in Space and Time

In addition to building, maintaining, and reducing specific behaviors, clinical necessity may sometimes dictate that a portion of a client's ongoing behavior must be temporally or spatially reallocated, to make it more socially acceptable. Technically, this is termed the *alteration of stimulus control of behavior*. The behaviors that are typically selected for this type of intervention are biologically based but can be expressed in a wide variety of social situations. Sexual and excretory behaviors have been most frequently selected for treatment by stimulus control procedures.

In recent years, a gradual shift has occurred in society's global perception of mentally retarded people. Emblematic of this change has been the National Association for Retarded Children's recent adoption of a new name, the National Association for Retarded Citizens. A comprehensive list of the basic legal rights of retarded citizens is still being developed, but one area where change is evident is in the emergence of a consensus that responsible sexual expression is a right for retarded citizens, just as it is a right for nonretarded citizens. Historically, the sexual behavior of institutionalized persons has tended to be deviant, as judged by community norms, and concern has been expressed that retarded persons who move from institutions into community-based group homes will be unable to adjust to society's standards governing sexual conduct.

In the therapeutic use of stimulus-control procedures, behavior is differentially reinforced under one particular set of environmental circumstances and is ignored or mildly punished in all other contexts. After training, the behavior being brought under stimulus control typically occurs only in the presence of those cues that signal reinforcement or the absence of punishment. An interesting example of the use of stimulus-control procedures occurred in a behavior therapy program for severely retarded boys who were being prepared for community placement. The boys had all recently reached puberty and were beginning to masturbate in socially inappropriate and disruptive situations, such as in classrooms and group activities. Although masturbation is usually tolerated in institutional settings, masturbation in the community can lead to severe censure of a retarded individual, including the possibility of arrest for indecent exposure. Since the boys' behavioral program was based on a system of token reinforcement, the program supervisor intervened by incorporating an opportunity to masturbate into the overall program. The opportunity to masturbate was made freely available in privacy during all nonprogram times. If, however, a boy began to masturbate in a classroom or other social situation, he was removed from the group, placed in a private room, and charged a number of tokens for engaging in this behavior. The "price" for the behavior was then systematically raised, and in a short time the boys recognized the significance of these new contingencies. As a result, masturbation disappeared from classrooms and other program environments. Naturally, it continued in private situations, but under these circumstances the behavior did not upset the staff, nor did it interfere with successful placement of the boys into a community residence that continued to use the token reinforcement approach. Creative solutions to behavior problems like inappropriate masturbation suggest that stimulus control procedures can be used to help facilitate the community placement of many retarded persons who would otherwise be confined in institutions because of socially unacceptable behavior.

To summarize, anyone beginning a behavior therapy program for mentally retarded clients should start by consulting available training manuals appropriate to the specific level of programming desired. Behaviorally oriented training manuals are usually broken down into Basic Self-Help Skills, Intermediate Self-Help Skills, Advanced Self-Help Skills (community-relevant skills), and Behavior Problems. Recently Bernal and North (1978) reviewed 26 commercially available behavior therapy training manuals and evaluated them by appropriate target populations, readability levels, use of technical language, organization and format, and the availability of supplementary training materials. Few of these manuals have been subjected to empirical evaluation, and so Bernal and North contended that research (pretraining, posttraining comparison studies) is needed to assess accurately their relative utility in clinical practice.

Although professional staff would not be expected to implement these training programs, they should read about and observe ongoing behavior therapy programs in order to be able to effectively evaluate day-to-day client progress or emergent problems. A qualified behavior therapist should be given the ultimate responsibility for ensuring the integrity of any behavior therapy program written for a mentally retarded client.

BEHAVIORAL PSYCHOLOGY AND THE PSYCHODYNAMIC THERAPIES

Behavioral and dynamic therapists have been drawn together by a common understanding of the appropriate goals of therapy for mentally (especially severely) retarded clients. The behavior of severely and profoundly retarded persons can be characterized as presenting obvious behavioral deficiencies (no self-help skills, no social skills) and behavioral excesses (hyperactivity, self-abuse) that must be remediated somehow. Since dynamic therapy is geared to serving the needs of relatively intellectually intact clients, severely retarded persons have become, by consensus, an appropriate clinical population for behavioral interventions. Since behavioral and psychodynamic interventions are not mutually exclusive, clear opportunities exist for conjoint behavioral/dynamic treatment approaches being developed to serve the complex needs of retarded clients.

BEHAVIORAL AND PSYCHOPHARMACOLOGICAL THERAPIES

There is much to be gained from the establishment of a positive, collaborative working relationship between behaviorally oriented psychologists and psychiatrists who are treating retarded clients. In the past, behavior therapy programs have proved to be most effective with retarded clients in isolated research and demonstration projects. Similarly, medical-psychiatric interventions such as use of psychoactive drugs have also proved to be most effective with retarded clients in controlled clinical trials. However, both therapeutic modalities have sometimes experienced serious difficulties when used jointly in clinical contexts with retarded clients.

The first problem shared by behavioral psychologists and psychiatrists working with mentally retarded clients has been the tendency for administrators in the mental retardation service-delivery system to try to co-opt members of both professions, in an effort to pacify and/or control unruly individuals. In this instance, behavior therapists leave themselves vulnerable to charges that they are using their intervention techniques to produce lock-step conformity among retarded persons, for the ultimate benefit of the "system," rather than to enhance client capacities. Similarly, psychiatrists have sometimes been accused of employing drug therapy as a chemical straightjacket for the benefit of the service-delivery system, rather than to assist individual clients. Members of both professions must be sensitive to the potential for misuse of their services, and an open dialogue on these issues seems to be the best avenue toward reducing the use of unwarranted interventions with mentally retarded persons.

Unquestionably, psychologically structured behavior therapy programs for severely retarded clients can be aided substantially by the cooperative efforts of psychiatrists. Ambulatory, severely disturbed/retarded individuals probably represent the most problematical clinical population confronting contemporary clinical psychology and psychiatry. In the past, behavior therapy programs for these clients have often been severely compromised by unpredictable and uncontrollable mood swings and behavioral outbursts by the clients. Psychiatric assistance in stabilizing the "inner" environment of these disturbed and disruptive persons with drugs can be extremely helpful to behavior therapists who are attempting to ameliorate behavior problems by systematically changing elements of the client's "outer" environment.

Just as the use of medical-psychiatric interventions can be of major clinical significance to a behavior therapy program, a well-run behavioral program can also be quite valuable to psychiatrists who are attempting to evaluate the effects of psychotropic medication with disturbed/retarded clients. In the past, psychiatrists working in mental retardation facilities have often been placed in the uncomfortable position of prescribing drugs and then evaluating their effects through anecdotal reports from direct-care staff. Behavior therapy programs emphasize the on-line collection of behavioral data, and these data can serve as a reliable check on the success or failure of a particular psychiatric intervention. Without a stable external environment, it is difficult, if not impossible, to evaluate the effects of psychoactive drugs with retarded clients. In the context of a behavior therapy program, however, psychiatric therapy can be as precise as medical interventions in medical facilities, where the physician has access to reliable feedback of concrete physiological data from his patients.

ETHICS OF BEHAVIOR THERAPY WITH RETARDED CLIENTS

Over the past 10 years, behavior therapy has been the most intensely scrutinized modality of psychotherapy being practiced (Golddiamond, 1975). Many states and federal agencies now have legal guidelines for behavior therapy programs, but no guidelines that deal with potential abuses of encounter groups, gestalt therapy, transactional analysis, psychodynamic therapy, and the like. A number of reasons exist for this. One is the public confusion that still surrounds the definition of what is and what is not behavior therapy. A second reason is that behavior therapy is the most clearcut, explicit, and understandable mode of psychological therapy being practiced. This openness renders behavior therapy susceptible to many pressures and constraints originating outside of professional psychological circles. A third reason is that behavior therapy is a very personal and philosophically existential therapy. A working hypothesis of behavior therapy is that all behavior, including human behavior, is lawful, predictable, and controllable—essentially a determinist position. The word *control* is used in a probabilistic sense, but many people react negatively when control in any way appears as an element of a therapy program. Since free will is not seen by behavior therapy as the ultimate determinant of human behavior, a therapy modality that excludes free will and willpower as explanatory concepts is automatically rejected by many people. A fourth and final reason for behavior therapy's special status is that, in the past, a number of projects that were labeled behavior therapy or behavior modification by their creators were actually textbook examples of programs that grossly abused the civil rights of the individuals on whom they were practiced. As a rule, behavioral programs in which there could be any question of ethical violations, and all programs involving aversive stimuli, should be reviewed carefully by an independent human rights committee, and an advocate or legal guardian for the client in question should be available to represent his interests. In addition, the informed consent of the client's guardian should be obtained in writing before any punishment procedures are used. In the latter instance, the behavior to be suppressed or eliminated must be of such magnitude as to constitute a clear and present danger to the client or those around him. Violent, persistent self-mutilation would be an example of a behavior that might be selected for elimination by means of punishment contingencies. It must be thoroughly documented that all conceivable behavioral interventions based on positive reinforcement have failed to solve the problem. This is a variation of the principle of least restrictive alternative, which states that a retarded client's problems must be remediated under the least intrusive and restrictive set of conditions that are compatible with solving the problem.

There is a final ethical caveat on behavior therapy programs for mentally retarded clients. In a functional sense, a behavior therapy program is a prosthetic device, and like other prostheses, once it is in place, provisions must be made to ensure its indefinite continuance. If a severely retarded client is being served by a behavior therapy program and that program suddenly changes or stops, the learned behavior of the client immediately undergoes a process called *extinction*. The extinction process has been studied extensively, and it is known to lead to the subjective psychological state commonly termed *frustration*. In objective terms, extinction causes marked variability in ongoing client behavior. Thus, extinction leads to inevitable client regression, including acting-out episodes. Therefore, anyone who is contemplating beginning a behavior therapy program for mentally retarded clients must face the ethical implications of starting a program that will necessitate long-range commitments of time, money, and resources. If such commitments cannot be made, complex behavioral programs for retarded clients should not be initiated.

SUMMARY

Behavior therapy represents a technology of behavior change, a technology that is still in its relative infancy. Like all technologies, behavioral psychology can be used or abused, depending on the value systems of the people who control the technology. Society's best protection against abuses of behavior therapy is public education about, and understanding of, the realities and limitations of behavior therapy. The potential risks and benefits of this and other emerging technologies should be the focus of continuing public scrutiny.

GLOSSARY

aversive event A stimulus that suppresses a behavior that it follows, or that increases a behavior, resulting in termination of an aversive event. A noxious or unpleasant stimulus.

avoidance Performance of a behavior that postpones or averts the presentation of an aversive event. Avoidance behavior is maintained by negative reinforcement.

backup reinforcer An object, activity, or event (primary or secondary reinforcer) that can be purchased with tokens. (See **token reinforcement.**)

baseline The frequency at which a behavior is performed before the initiation of a behavior therapy program. The baseline is used to evaluate the effects of the behavioral program. Also termed the *free operant rate* of the behavior.

behavior Any observable and measurable response or act of an individual. Categories of behavior include operants, respondents, and coverants.

chain A sequence of behaviors that occur in a fixed order. Each behavior in the chain serves as a discriminative stimulus (S^D) for the next response. Also, each behavioral unit or link in the chain (except the first one) serves as a conditioned reinforcer for the previous link. Reinforcement is provided at the end of the entire chain.

chaining Developing a sequence of responses in a backward order. The terminal response in the chain, the response closest to reinforcement, is developed first. The next to the last response is trained second. The remaining responses are trained in the reverse order of their eventual performance.

classical (or respondent) conditioning A type of learning in which a conditioned stimulus (CS) is paired with an unconditioned stimulus (UCS), which already automatically elicits an unlearned, reflexive response. After repeated pairings of the conditioned stimulus with the unconditioned stimulus, the conditioned stimulus alone will elicit a reflex-like response. In classical conditioning, new stimuli gain the power to elicit respondent behavior. Also termed *Pavlovian conditioning*.

conditioned aversive stimulus An event that is initially neutral may acquire aversive properties by virtue of being paired with other aversive events, or by serving as a signal that no reinforcement will be forthcoming. Verbal reprimands serve as conditioned aversive stimuli.

conditioned reinforcer See **secondary reinforcer.**

conditioned response A reflex-like response elicited by a conditioned stimulus (CS) alone, in the absence of the unconditioned stimulus. The conditioned response (CR) resembles, but is not identical to, the unconditioned response.

conditioned stimulus A previously neutral stimulus which, through repeated associations with an unconditioned stimulus, can eventually elicit a reflex-like response.

contingency The relationship between a behavior (the response to be changed) and the events (consequences) that follow the behavior. Sometimes events that precede the behavior are also specified by a contingency. An if...then relationship between events or stimuli.

differential reinforcement Reinforcing a response in the presence of one discriminative stimulus (S^D) and simultaneously extinguishing the response in the presence of other stimuli (S^Δs). Eventually, the response is consistently performed in the presence of the S^D, but not in the presence of S^Δ.

differential reinforcement of other behavior (DRO) Delivery of a reinforcer after any response except the target response. The individual is reinforced for not performing the target response. All behaviors other than the target response are reinforced. The effect of a DRO contingency is to decrease the rate of the target response, which is not reinforced.

discrimination Responding differently in the presence of different cues or antecedent events. Control of behavior by specific discriminative stimuli (S^Ds). (See **stimulus control.**)

discriminative stimulus (S^D) An antecedent event or stimulus that signals that a certain response will be reinforced. A response is reinforced in the presence of an S^D. After an event becomes an S^D by being paired with reinforcement, its presence can increase the probability that the response will occur.

elicit To automatically bring about a response. Respondent or reflex behaviors are elicited by unconditioned stimuli. Contrast with **emit** and **operant behavior;** see also **classical conditioning.**

emit To perform a response spontaneously. An emitted response is not automatically controlled by stimuli that precede it. Operant behaviors are emitted. They are controlled primarily by the consequences that follow them. (See **operant conditioning.**)

escape Performance of a behavior that terminates an aversive event. Escape behavior is maintained by negative reinforcement.

extinction A procedure in which the reinforcer is no longer delivered for a previously learned response. Extinction induces immediate variability in behavior. The rate of an extinguished response gradually decreases over time.

fading The gradual removal of discriminative stimuli (S^Ds), including prompts like instructions or physical guidance. The development of new behavior is usually facilitated by the use of prompts. The prompts are later faded out in most teaching situations. Fading can also refer to the gradual removal of reinforcement, as in the progressive thinning of a schedule of reinforcement over time.

generalized conditioned reinforcer A conditioned reinforcer that has acquired reinforcing value by being associated or paired with a variety of other reinforcers. Tokens (in token economies) and money are examples of generalized conditioned reinforcers.

high-probability behavior A response that is performed with a relatively high frequency when the individual is given the opportunity to select among alternative behaviors. (See **Premack principle.**)

incompatible behavior Behavior that cannot be performed at the same time as, or that interferes with, another behavior.

intermittent reinforcement A schedule of reinforcement in which a response is not reinforced every time it is performed. Only some occurrences of the response are reinforced.

modeling See **observational learning.**

naturally occurring reinforcers Reinforcing events in the environment that are not contrived, but are usually available as part of the setting. Attention, praise, completion of an activity, and mastery of a task are naturally occurring reinforcers.

negative reinforcement An increase in the frequency of a response, which is followed by the termination or removal of an aversive event. Escape and avoidance behaviors are maintained by negative reinforcement.

observational learning Learning by observing another individual (a model) engage in a behavior. To learn from a model, the observer need not perform the behavior nor receive direct consequences for his performance.

operant behavior Emitted behavior that is controlled by its consequences; voluntary behavior. The term *operant* is derived from the observation that specifiable groups of responses operate on the environment to produce consequences for the operator.

operant conditioning A type of learning in which behaviors are altered primarily by regulating the consequences that follow time. The frequency of operant behaviors may be increased or decreased, depending on the consequences they produce.

positive reinforcement An increase in the frequency of a response that is followed by a rewarding stimulus or event.

Premack principle A principle that states, that for any pair of responses or activities in which an individual freely engages, the more frequently performed one can be used to reinforce the less frequent one.

primary reinforcer A reinforcing event that does not depend on learning to achieve its reinforcing properties. Food, water, sleep, and sex are examples of primary reinforcers. Contrast with **secondary reinforcer.**

prompt An antecedent event that helps initiate a response. A discriminative stimulus (S^D) that sets the occasion for a response. Instructions, gestures, physical guidance, and modeling cues can serve as prompts with retarded clients.

reinforcement An increase in the strength or frequency of a response when the response is immediately followed by a particular consequence. The consequence can be either the presentation of a positive reinforcer or the removal of a negative reinforcer.

respondent behavior Behavior that is elicited or automatically controlled by antecedent stimuli. Reflexes are respondents because their performance automatically follows certain stimuli. The connection between unconditioned respondents and the antecedent events that control them is unlearned. Respondents may come under the control of otherwise neutral stimuli through classical or Pavlovian conditioning.

response cost A punishment procedure in which a positive reinforcer is lost, or some penalty is invoked, contingent upon the occurrence of an undesirable behavior. Unlike **timeout,** there is no specified time limit to the withdrawal of the reinforcer. Fines in token economies represent a common form of response cost.

response generalization Reinforcement of a particular target response, which increases the probability of occurrence of other responses which are similar to the target response or which belong to the same response class. Contrast with **stimulus generalization.**

S^Δ An antecedent event or stimulus that signals that a certain response will not be reinforced. A reciprocal of an S^D.

satiation Providing an excessive amount of a reinforcer. A loss of reinforcing effectiveness that occurs after a large amount of the reinforcer has been delivered.

secondary (or conditioned) reinforcer An event that becomes reinforcing through learning. An event becomes a secondary reinforcer by being paired with other events (primary or conditioned) that are already reinforcing. Praise and attention are examples of secondary reinforcers. Contrast with **primary reinforcer.**

shaping Developing a new behavior by reinforcing **successive approximations** toward the terminal response.

social reinforcers Reinforcers that result from interpersonal interactions. Examples include attention, praise, approval, smiles, and physical contact.

stimulus A measurable event that may have an effect upon the behavior of an individual.

stimulus control The presence of a particular antecedent stimulus serves as an occasion for a particular response to occur. A response is performed while in the presence of a stimulus, but not in its absence. (See **discriminative stimulus.**)

stimulus generalization Transfer of a learned response to situations or stimulus conditions other than those in which learning has taken place. The learned behavior generalizes to other environments. Contrast with **response generalization.**

successive approximations Responses that increasingly resemble the terminal behavior that is being shaped. (See **shaping.**)

target behavior The behavior to be altered or focused upon during a behavior therapy program. The behavior subjected to baseline assessment and proposed for change.

timeout Time out from positive reinforcement. A mild punishment technique where an individual is removed from the opportunity to earn positive reinforcement, contingent on the occurrence of disruptive behavior. Timeout is typically employed for relatively brief, fixed time periods.

token economy A closed-ended economic system, governed by rules that specify behaviors to be reinforced, numbers of tokens to be provided for each behavior, and exchange rates of tokens for backup reinforcers.

token reinforcement A process whereby a desired behavior is immediately followed by the presentation of a generalized conditioned reinforcer (token). Tokens are later exchanged for a variety of backup reinforcers.

REFERENCES

Anderson, L., Dancis, J., and Alpert, M. 1978. Behavioral contingencies and self-mutilation in Lesch-Nyhan disease. J. Consult. Clin. Psychol. 46:529–536.

Bensberg, G. J. 1965. Teaching the Mentally Retarded. Southern Regional Educational Board, Atlanta.

Bernal, M. E., and North, J. A. 1978. A survey of parent training manuals. J. Appl. Behav. Anal. 11:533–544.

240   Jansen

Ellis, N. R. 1963. Toilet training the severely defective patient: An S-R reinforcement analysis. Am. J. Ment. Defic. 68:98–103.
Fuller, P. 1949. Operant conditioning of a vegetative human organism. Am. J. Psychol. 62:587–590.
Golddiamond, I. 1975. Singling out behavior modification for legal regulation: Some effects on patient care, psychotherapy and research. Arizona Law Rev. 17:105–126.
Hamilton, J., Stephens, L., and Allen, P. 1967. Controlling aggressive and destructive behavior in severely retarded institutionalized residents. Am. J. Ment. Defic. 71:825–856.
Tate, B. G., and Baroff, G. S. 1966. Aversive control of self-injurious behavior in a psychotic boy. Behav. Res. Ther. 4:281–287.

SUGGESTED READINGS

Baker, B. L., and Heifetz, L. J. 1976. The Read project: Teaching manuals for parents of retarded children. In T. D. Tjossem (ed.), Intervention Strategies for High Risk Infants and Young Children, pp. 351–370. University Park Press, Baltimore.
Guidelines for the Use of Behavioral Procedures in State Programs for Retarded Persons. 1976. NARC Research Advisory Committee. East Arlington, Tex.
Individual Rights and the Federal Role in Behavior Modification. 1974. U.S. Government Printing Office, Washington, D.C.
Kazdin, A. 1973. Issues in behavior modification with mentally retarded persons. Am. J. Ment. Def. 78:134–140.
Leitenberg, H. 1976. Handbook of Behavior Modification and Behavior Therapy. Prentice-Hall, Englewood Cliffs. N.J.
Lovaas, I. O., and Bucher, B. D. 1974. Perspectives in Behavior Modification with Deviant Children. Prentice-Hall, Englewood Cliffs, N.J.
Skinner, B. F. 1953. Science and Human Behavior. Macmillan Publishing Co., New York.
Skinner, B. F. 1974. About behaviorism. Alfred A. Knopf, New York.
Watson J. B. 1924. Behaviorism. University of Chicago Press, Chicago.

CONSULTATION

Over the past 15 years, humanistic concerns within the field of mental retardation and developmental disability have led to a resurgence of interest in such concepts as mainstreaming and the least restrictive environment for handicapped persons. Translation of these concepts into policy has not been easy, but retarded and developmentally disabled persons increasingly have ceased to reside in large institutions and have come to be cared for in the community. Because the number of mental health professionals on the staffs of schools and small residential facilities is usually limited, the need for mental health consultation services has increased greatly. As anyone who has attempted it will testify, the role of the consultant is vastly different from the role of one who provides direct clinical service. The two chapters in this section describe the goals of mental health consultation and provide some practical examples of successful approaches. Ideally, the consultant should be helpful to both the institution and to the individual client, ultimately increasing the likelihood that the mentally retarded person will be able to function optimally in the least restrictive environment.

MENTAL HEALTH CONSULTATIONS TO EDUCATIONAL PROGRAMS FOR RETARDED PERSONS

*Ludwik S. Szymanski
and David R. Leaverton*

Chapter 15

Mental health consultations to programs for retarded students in public school systems are becoming more frequent with the advent of laws such as PL 94-142 (Education for All Handicapped Children Act) and Massachusetts Chapter 766 (pertaining to education of children with special needs). These mandate a full range of services for special needs children, to be provided as part of their comprehensive educational plans. A disturbed retarded student cannot be rejected from public school classes unless it is absolutely impossible to provide for him there. Indeed, the school must provide him with integration into the regular program to the maximum degree feasible. The mainstreaming of such students may create a degree of stress for the regular class teachers, as well as for the special educators, who may request help in managing the students. These developments have, in recent years, led to increased demands for mental health consultations by public school systems.

These demands depend also on factors like the sophistication of the school administration, financial constraints, and the availability of trained and willing consultants. A psychiatrist to whom several referrals of retarded and disturbed children have been made by a school system may sometimes suggest that having a regular consultant may be more efficient than sending every case to an outside clinic.

THE CONSULTATION MODELS

Mental health consultation in general has been discussed in the literature (Caplan, 1970). The role of the consultant can be seen as occurring along the continuum between two extremes: 1) a specialist, passively waiting until he is asked to help with the problem, and then leading the consultees to arrive at their own solutions, particularly through helping them to overcome their own resistances; and 2) the specialist sending the school a written summary after seeing the child in his clinic. The authors prefer a more eclectic and pragmatic model of the consultant as a part of an interdisciplinary team (including the school personnel and the parents), who visits the schools regularly, observes and/or interviews children, helps the educators to select appropriate cases for consultation (both leading them to their own solutions and giving direct recommendations), follows their progress, and generally is co-responsible for the children's (and teachers') progress. He may participate in conferences and interviews with the parents. If he has medical training he may serve as a liaison with local medical facilities where the children may be seen and as interpreter to the teacher of the medical findings. He may lead teachers' groups and didactic courses on mental health topics. Generally, because of time constraints, confidentiality, and role confusion, he will not provide ongoing treatment to the children.

Thus, the consultant's roles are flexibly adapted to the school's and the child's needs. Unfortunately, some school systems may be uncomfortable with such a model. They may prefer a consultant who labels the children according to administrative demands, who does not expect the teachers to work with him, but who relieves them of the responsibility for the disturbed child. Some mental health professionals may feel more comfortable in such a role.

ISSUES BROUGHT UP FOR CONSULTATION

General Considerations

The problems presented for consultation in most cases will involve individual children. The consultant is less often asked directly about problems that primarily affect the teachers, such as their anxiety or lack of knowledge about handling or relating to retarded/disturbed children. This picture changes, however, if one classifies the presenting problems into manifest and latent. Manifest problems are usually verbalized directly by the consultees and refer to disturbed behavior of the child, his family, and his lack of progress. Latent problems, which exist in almost every case, are not verbalized and may be conscious or unconscious for the consultee. They may include anger at the uncontrollable nonprogressing child, a wish to have the child removed or diagnosed as incurable or uneducable, or disturbed because of the family situation, thus exonerating the teacher. They may also include the teachers' ego-dystonic perceptions of self, such as low self-image, depression, or anxiety. This hidden agenda is usually heavily emotionally invested and anxiety provoking to the consultee. It must be recognized and dealt with by the consultant. Thus, at the beginning and throughout each consultation, the consultant must ask himself why a particular problem is brought to him and what it might mean to the consultee.

The choice of presenting problems depends on other factors, such as resources available at the school and the teachers' sophistication, training, personality features, and even prejudices. For instance, in a white suburban school, black children bused from the inner city were brought up for consultation as aggressive because of their boisterous behavior and language, contrasting with the controlled behavior of their upper middle class peers.

Children's Behavior as Presenting Problem

The increased frequency of behavioral disorders in retarded children has been described in the literature and is discussed elsewhere in this book (Chapter 6). It should be kept in mind that a mildly retarded child may be first recognized at school because of his behavior, which is a reaction to his educational failure, which is in turn caused by undiagnosed retardation. Conversely, as pointed out by Dunn (1958), it had been common practice to place socially deprived children, those from broken homes, and other "misfits" in classes for retarded children. Lax and Carter (1976) pointed out that a child's disruptive behavior, rather than his competence, may determine whether he is labeled retarded and whether he is placed in a regular or special class.

Disruptive and Disturbing Behaviors   Children's disturbing behaviors are the prime cause for asking for a consultation, especially aggression directed toward others or themselves or more diffuse aggression, such as temper tantrums; the teachers feel responsible for safety in the classroom. Noisy behavior, overactivity, attentional disorder, negativism, and general unruliness distract other children and disturb the class and the teacher. However, when nonretarded children manifest similar behaviors, the teacher often deals with them confidently. With retarded children—particularly nonverbal ones—such behaviors may appear to be much more threatening and dangerous, perhaps because of lack of understanding of the child by the teacher.

Wehman and McLaughlin (1979) surveyed 18 teachers of 145 severely and profoundly retarded children. They identified as most difficult-to-manage stereotypic behaviors, temper tantrums, noncompliance, self-abuse, and aggression toward others. Lack of skills, such as independent toileting, were considered far less important. Szymanski (un-published data) surveyed a sample of 83 students in special education programs of a public school system, all of whom functioned on a sub-average level. Aggressive behavior was the most frequent cause of refer-ring the boys for consultation (43%), and inappropriate social behavior was the second most frequent (18%). This was reversed for the girls (20% and 30%, respectively).

Inappropriate Behaviors Inappropriate behaviors are often a source of confusion to teachers who do not know what standards to use in judging inappropriateness. For instance, the question may arise whether encopresis is caused by general developmental delay, medical problems, a child's inability to learn, desire to get attention, or unconscious conflicts. Poor frustration tolerance, clowning in the classroom, bizarre behaviors, and self-stimulation are affected by similar factors. Teachers and admin-istration are very sensitive to any behaviors with sexual connotations (e.g., masturbation and exhibitionism), and these are brought to the con-sultant's attention immediately, often on an emergency basis. Much rarer are instances of retarded youngsters' direct sexual advances to their peers. There are frequent episodes of retarded students being sexually exploited by nonretarded peers, but the latter rarely become the subjects of consul-tation.

Children's Level of Functioning as Presenting Problem in the Con-sultation It is a good indicator of the teacher's sensitivity to his students' problems if he becomes concerned about a student who is not aggressively disrupting the class but is maladjusted otherwise (for instance, depressed, anxious, has low self-esteem, dependent, passive, fearful, or has other symptoms, e.g., school phobia). However, many teachers have lower ex-pectations of a retarded child (Dunn, 1958) and may see his maladapta-tion as inevitable.

The teacher may also become concerned not because of the child's behavior but because of the child-parent relationship, if he perceives it as pathological (e.g., if the parents are extremely overprotective).

Consultants are being asked increasingly to advise on a child who un-derachieves, even in relation to his retarded cognitive capability, and whose underachievement is suspected to be caused by emotional con-cerns. In sophisticated (and well funded) school systems, the consultant may be asked to become a regular member of an interdisciplinary team evaluating children with special needs in order to help in spotting this group of underachievers.

The child's social inadequacy may also be a subject of consultation. This may include children who are withdrawn and do not reach out to peers. Sometimes teachers, on their own initiative or in response to the consultant's inquiry, may bring up the issue of the nonretarded child's cruel, rejecting, or teasing behavior toward his retarded peer.

ISSUES RELATED TO MAINSTREAMING

Issues related to mainstreaming may prompt requests for consultation. The consultant should be familiar with the concept and the practice of mainstreaming. MacMillan, Jones, and Meyers (1976), in their detailed discussion of mainstreaming, pointed out the confusion in defining mainstreaming; in some systems, mainstreaming only means that a retarded child should spend 50% or more of his time in the regular class with nonretarded peers. These authors stressed the importance of having an ongoing assessment of a child's educational needs, coordinated planning, and programming.

There has been a long-standing discussion among educators and researchers about the merits of mainstreaming (and the consultant may often be asked his opinion). These have been reviewed in the literature (Sheare, 1974; Lax and Carter, 1976). Earlier studies tended to show that social adjustment of mildly retarded children was better when they were placed in segregated special classes. More recently, it has been felt that such placement may have no specific effect. Gottlieb and Davis (1973) found that both integrated and segregated retarded children were chosen less often as playmates than nonretarded children by their nonretarded peers. They pointed out that their nonacceptance was a function of their behavior. Bruininks, Rynders, and Gross (1974) pointed out that social acceptance of retarded children may be better in inner city schools than in suburban ones. Gampel, Gottlieb, and Harrison (1974) and Sheare (1974) reported that integration of retarded children may be associated with better social behavior and acceptance. These studies, however, did not resolve the question of whether children who behave better are those who are chosen for mainstreaming. Budoff and Gottlieb (1976) answered this partially in a study in which children were assigned at random to segregated and integrated classes. They found that at 1-year follow-up integrated children had better self-image, more positive attitudes toward the school, and internalized controls. Their sample was small, however. Clearly, more research in this field is necessary, based not only on use of tests and questionnaires but also on comprehensive clinical assessment.

From the consultant's point of view, it is important to clarify to the teachers that the child's adjustment to special versus integrated classes involves complex factors, such as the child's competence, social skills and experience, psychopathology, frustration tolerance, and the attitudes of nonretarded peers, teachers, and families. These will have to be assessed comprehensively in order to give valid predictions.

Teachers' feelings about mainstreaming may be verbalized frequently. Generally, special education teachers have positive feelings. Other teachers may oppose it. These attitudes can be crucial in determining the success of mainstreaming (MacMillan et al., 1976).

Negative feelings may reflect the teachers' concerns about their inability to teach the special children and, particularly, to control their behavior (which is often expected to be disruptive). Concerns may also be voiced that they will monopolize the teacher's time and be dangerous. One of the authors was once told, in the course of a consultation, "How can we let him in the home economics class—there are knives and stoves around!" Fear of narcissistic injury may be expressed ("What does it do to us when we try to cope with him?").

The consultant can prevent and alleviate these feelings through teacher education, e.g., dispelling the myths of dangerous retardates, helping teachers overcome fears that they cannot manage retarded children or teach them effectively. Organizing peer support groups for the teachers is very helpful, as is consultant availability, regular ongoing support, and child-oriented services, as necessary.

TEACHERS' DIFFICULTIES AS PRESENTING PROBLEMS

One of the most important issues in consultation is teachers' emotional reactions to their students' problems (and retardation) and the interdependence of these reactions with the teachers' professional performance. However, these issues are rarely brought up directly; they usually become latent complaints. Latent problems may be suspected if complaints about the child are vague and unrealistic, or if the teacher's emotional investment in the complaints seems to be inappropriate. It is wise to explore tactfully, in every case, the teacher's own feelings about and reactions to the difficult child he brings up for consultation. Just as physicians want to "cure" their patients, teachers want to educate their students. Working with a retarded learner can be frustrating, especially if the child is uncooperative, aggressive, and disturbing to the class. The teacher may question his professional competence in teaching and in controlling his students. Such concerns are usually expressed with more ease by teachers of regular classes where the retarded child is mainstreamed, since they have an ego-syntonic explanation: they have not been trained in special education. These concerns may also relate to a "rescue fantasy" or wish to "cure" the retarded child. There may be pressure from the administration to have no "problem" students. Teachers' psychological defenses may further aggravate the situation, if their anxiety is conveyed to the students or parents, or if the defenses reduce the teachers' effectiveness. Projection is frequent. Teachers may accuse the parents of being responsible for the child's behavior, the administrators of understaffing the school, and the physicians of not medicating the child. Teachers may see the child's behavior as the result of brain damage and thus as not the teacher's responsibility. In extreme situations, the child may be disliked (and feared) to the point that demands are put on the consultant to recommend sending the child to a residential treatment facility. Some teachers may become extremely overprotective of their retarded students, to the point of holding back their development.

TECHNIQUES OF INTERVENTION

The first task of the consultant is to assess the territory. He must know the administrative structure of the school, the school's economic realities, and the interrelationship between administration and teachers. Simply asking various people he comes into contact with about these issues may provide a wealth of information. In order to avoid future misunderstandings, a clear contract is necessary with the teachers (usually verbal) and the system's administration (preferably written). This should specify the amount of time the consultant is expected to spend at the school and his responsibilities (e.g., whether he agrees to provide direct services, such as diagnostic and treatment interviews with the child and prescribing medication, or whose responsibility it is to contact the parents, if necessary). It is wise to review these commitments with each teacher involved in consultation.

Building the relationship with teachers is essential. They should see the consultant as a concerned professional, empathetic but objective, not subject to manipulation, and one who respects them as professional co-workers. It is important to be available to each teacher through regular visits to the classroom, as well as to respond to emergency phone calls, even if it is not a real emergency. In these cases, the teacher usually does not want the consultant to come immediately to the school and take charge of a disturbed child; rather, the teacher usually needs empathy, promises to visit the class at the nearest opportunity, or a referral to a local mental health resource.

Depending on the teachers' experience in mental retardation and mental health issues, the consultant may need to provide them with some training in the initial stages of his consultation. This is usually done indirectly and informally, through discussion of individual cases. Sometimes, depending on the teachers' motivation and on the administrators' interest, he may be asked to conduct formal didactic seminars.

Educating the teacher about the reality of a child's abilities and medical condition is often necessary. For instance, is the child's bizarre way of talking caused by psychosis or language disorder? Are his mannerisms the result of psychosis or an expression of situational anxiety? Is his inability to understand the teacher caused by stubbornness or a need to get more concrete explanation? Interpreting medical diagnoses (e.g., "Does a diagnosis of congenital idiopathic encephalopathy mean that his brain is severely damaged?'') and the effects of psychotropic medication are important. Referring the child to appropriate medical specialists and serving as liaison with them should be done, if necessary.

Comprehensive psychiatric diagnostic assessment should be done whenever appropriate. This can be performed by the consultant or by an outside clinic, depending on the family's wishes and the consultant's contract with the administration. Clear diagnosis may have important programmatic implications. For example, a retarded child's stereotypic mannerisms may be seen by some teachers as evidence of craziness, autistic tendencies, and uneducability. Similar symptoms in a genuinely psychotic child or a child with Gilles de la Tourette syndrome may be interpreted as simple behavior disorders and treated with increasingly desperate behavior modification, which is frustrating for the child and teacher alike.

The consultant must lead the teacher to see a child's presenting problem not as an isolated entity but in light of his total adjustment and abilities. He may have to explain it clearly at the beginning of the consultative meeting and then review with the teachers available material and/or establish what additional information should be obtained. The teachers must be helped to see the issue from the point of view of the child's development and past experiences.

> A severely retarded, nonverbal 8-year-old boy would "spit," or rather blow air and saliva at his teachers, who naturally assumed that it meant anger. Closer observation established that this happened in any situation of happy or unhappy excitation. It was learned from the history that the child's foster mother had taught him to do it while an infant, thus making this behavior a means of communicating emotion. The teachers were relieved, and implemented a behavior modification program suggested by the consultant, which was quite effective in eliminating the spitting.

Some dynamically oriented teachers will see all behaviors as expressing unconscious concerns that need psychotherapy. They may have to be taught to observe the contingency that perpetuates the behavior (e.g., attention given to the misbehaving child) and be helped to establish behavior modification programs. Other teachers, however, subscribe to strict limits and ignore a child's feelings.

> A 15-year-old girl with Down's syndrome wrote letters to her teacher, saying things like: "I am going to kill you; don't believe it-love-Jane." The teacher dealt with her with harsh discipline, but the consultation helped her to see the letters as an expression, albeit inappropriate, of the girl's anger and wish to get more love and attention.

Teachers often see the consultant as a sort of miracle worker who will cure the child. Their own guilt feelings for not handling the situation may surface as anger directed at the consultant. Thus, the consultant may find himself under angry pressure to do something immediately. It is important not to respond with angry defensiveness, but rather to maintain composure, express empathy, and state firmly the need to work as a team, since no one has a monopoly on a solution. Each consultative session should end with clear and concrete conclusions and plans for future next steps, as well as a timetable for follow-up.

Emphasis should be placed on the child's normalcy and not only on his deviancy; the retarded child has feelings that underlie his behavior, just as any other child has, and he needs experiences of success, not constant failure. Many teachers will focus on a child's learning problem, drilling him mercilessly and thus increasing his anxiety. They may need to be coaxed to devote adequate time to areas in which the child excels, thus giving him an opportunity to succeed.

Helping teachers to deal with their own reactions and feelings may be difficult. It should be done tactfully and indirectly. Rather than asking an anxious teacher, "How do you feel about this child's masturbation in the classroom?" the professional may ask, "What does this child think about your reaction to him?" It is helpful for professionals to relate their own or others' reactions in similar situations because it gives the teachers permission to admit their feelings. Group consultations may be very effective because of peer support. Teachers may have to be helped to find gratification in their work instead of irrational guilt.

> A teacher complained that an 8-year-old retarded child in first grade was still anxious and read poorly in spite of the pressure she applied in teaching him throughout the whole year. In answer to a question, she acknowledged that he couldn't read at all at the beginning of the year, and now read on a first grade level, representing 1 year's gain in 1 year of teaching. She was congratulated for achieving this with a retarded child, after which she exclaimed, "I hadn't realized this."

Under no circumstances should a teacher be treated as a patient. If the teacher brings up any personal problems and requests help, the professional may listen, of course, but should not press for details. If necessary, the professional may make a referral for a diagnostic consultation, explaining at the same time that, as a co-worker, he cannot provide such service himself.

Whenever possible, the consultant should have contact with the child's family. This will depend, however, on his interest and motivation, as well as on the families, the teachers, and the administration. Family contacts may be part of the diagnostic process or they may occur at the forum of the school's interdisciplinary team, to which the consultant belongs. In any case, it seems to be the parents' right to know what the consultant feels about their child and what his recommendations are.

Last, but not least, in all consultations, the child's and family's right for privacy and confidentiality should be observed. Efforts should be made to have the teacher and the parents discuss in advance their concerns about the child and to secure the parents' consent and cooperation for the consultation, thus making them members of the interdisciplinary team. Of course, no child can be examined without the parents' prior consent.

PREVENTIVE APPROACHES

The mental health professional who consults to schools has a rare opportunity to do preventive intervention. Based on his knowledge of the development of retarded persons and life crises faced by them, he may help teachers to teach these youngsters skills and improve their defenses and coping patterns, all of which will prepare them for later developmental challenges. For example, consultants to high school programs are typically asked how to handle inappropriate sexual behavior and acting-out of retarded adolescents, who use it to make friends. Much of this could be prevented by guiding teachers and parents in earlier years to provide the children with multiple opportunities to achieve appropriately in areas of their abilities, thus increasing their self-esteem; to teach them peer-relating skills; to provide them with opportunities to socialize with peers on their level who accept them; and to give them appropriate sex education, including skills of socializing with the opposite sex. A consultant who is not waiting passively for children to be sent to him may help to identify children at risk emotionally and organize appropriate intervention. Also, organizing didactic courses for the teachers on such subjects as child development, mental retardation, and sex education are important in prevention.

ADMINISTRATIVE ISSUES

The consultant will inevitably find himself faced with administrative controversy between teachers, parents, and administration, such as: Should the child be classified as retarded or disturbed for bureaucratic expediency? Should he be placed in a different class? Should the class be reduced or increased in size? It is easy for the professional to let himself be manipulated into taking sides; nevertheless, he should remain an objective clinician who states the child's needs in generic terms, and through tactful questioning leads all involved to make the best, most realistic decision. His intervention may be the catalyst necessary to start constructive dialogue between opposing parties.

ASSESSMENT OF THE EFFECTIVENESS OF CONSULTATIONS

Ascribing specific changes to a consultant's intervention is impossible, because his input is only part of a comprehensive approach by the interdisciplinary team. Trusting and friendly attitudes of the teachers are a useful indication, but the professional should not try to win a "popularity contest." It is useful to observe the increase in the professional effectiveness of the teachers, their confidence, their gratification, and empathy with the children. A decrease in "emergency" problems and an increase in asking the consultant to assess total functioning of the child (rather than focusing on his disturbing behavior) is a most gratifying sign.

SUMMARY

In summary, the mental health consultant is an important member of the educational team in programs for retarded students. To be effective, he must be well trained and experienced in the fields of mental health and mental retardation. He should be flexible, able to function in a variety of roles, and familiar with eclectic intervention techniques. Although his consultations may begin with handling behavioral emergencies, his long-term goals should be oriented toward mental health preventive approaches.

REFERENCES

Bruininks, R. H., Rynders, J. E., and Gross, J. C. 1974. Social acceptance of mildly retarded pupils in resource rooms and regular classes. Am. J. Ment. Defic. 78:377-383.

Budoff, M., and Gottlieb, J. 1976. Special-class mainstreamed: A study of an aptitude (learning potential) × treatment interaction. Am. J. Ment. Defic. 81:1-11.

Caplan, G. 1970. The Theory and Practice of Mental Health Consultation. Basic Books, New York.

Dunn, L. M. 1958. Special education for the mildly retarded—Is much of it justifiable? Except. Child. 35:5-22.

Gampel, D. H., Gottlieb, J., and Harrison, R. H. 1974. Comparison of classroom behavior of special class EMR, integrated EMR, low IQ and nonretarded children. Am. J. Ment. Defic. 79:16-21.

Gottlieb, J., and Davis, J. E. 1973. Social acceptance of EMR children during overt behavioral interactions. Am. J. Ment. Defic. 78:141-143.

Lax, B., and Carter, J. C. 1976. Social acceptance of the EMR in different educational placements. Ment. Retard. 14(2):10-13.

MacMillan, D. L., Jones, R. L., and Meyers, C. E. 1976. Mainstreaming the mildly retarded: Some questions, cautions, and guidelines. Ment. Retard. 14(1): 3-9.

Sheare, J. B. 1974. Social acceptance of EMR adolescents in integrated programs. Am. J. Ment. Defic. 78:678-682.

Wehman, P., and McLaughlin, P. J. 1979. Teachers' perceptions of behavior problems with severely and profoundly handicapped students. Ment. Retard. 17(1):20-21.

MENTAL HEALTH CONSULTATIONS TO RESIDENTIAL FACILITIES FOR RETARDED PERSONS

Ludwik S. Szymanski,
Bruce A. Eissner, and
Quinn B. Rosefsky

Chapter 16

Their removal from the community into institutions like the Massachusetts School for the Feeble-minded at Waltham and the Wrentham State School is not only helpful to the children themselves, but is of benefit to the community by removing those children who would there grow up in idleness and ignorance, and become a menace to the morals of the community where they live.
—1910 Yearly Report, Wrentham State School, Wrentham, Massachusetts

The above quotation epitomizes the origins and early goals of the institutional system in the last century. A cognitively subnormal person, previously accommodated by a largely agrarian and craftsmen-oriented economy, was out of place with the advent of industrialization and a competitive employment market. The work of Seguin and his followers emphasized education of retarded people by special techniques. As a result, residential schools for retarded people were constructed in order to teach them useful skills, usually farming.

In later years, with the progress in neuropathology, all mental malfunctioning was ascribed to brain pathology, emphasizing that retarded people were sick but incurable patients, to be kept in custodial hospitals. This, together with the "discovery" of the "morons" by mass intelligence testing at the beginning of the 20th century and the eugenics movement, linked socially deviant behaviors with mental retardation. Thus institutions gradually were transformed into custodial hospitals for retarded people as a means of protecting society. Therapeutic nihilism led to warehousing in conditions of overcrowding and hopelessness. The psychiatrist's role in these institutions was that of a neuropsychiatrist-diagnostician, or of an administrator, and one of his major functions was to control disturbed, unruly inmates.

Since 1960 there has been a gradual shift in attitudes toward mental retardation, called by Menolascino (1977) "a developmental model." The retarded person is seen as able to grow, learn, and develop. The underlying philosophy is *normalization,* a term first suggested by Nirje (1969) as "making available to the mentally retarded patterns and conditions of every day life which are as close as possible to the norms and patterns of the mainstream of society." This concept was further developed by Wolfensberger (1972). As a result, the following attitudes toward institutional care emerged:

1. Normalizing and otherwise improving the conditions in the institution. Class action suits, such as *Pennsylvania Association for Retarded Children (PARC)* v. *Commonwealth of Pennsylvania* (1972) and *Wyatt* v. *Stickney* (1972) spearheaded this process of change.
2. Transferring the residents to small, community-based, home-like residences. This deinstitutionalization was formalized in President Nixon's address of 1972. The population of public institutions for mentally retarded people has declined from a peak of 193,000 in 1967 to 168,000 in 1975, and the institutions have become smaller as well (Conroy, 1977).
3. Improving the conditions in the institutions, mainly in physical plant and available supplies, but without materially changing their custodial character and without deinstitutionalizing the residents.

There seems to be no question, however, that the thrust of the current policies is toward the second goal. Recent legal decisions, such as in the *Pennhurst* (1978) case in Pennsylvania, even cast doubt on the future legality of the system of large institutions. It is acknowledged, however, that some more severely handicapped persons will need more structured, specialized, and intensive services, and for them the so-called Intermediate Care Facilities (ICFs) are envisioned as an alternative to large institutions. (The reader who is interested in the subject of development of the institutional model of care is referred to Wolfensberger, 1975.)

MODELS OF MENTAL HEALTH CONSULTATION

Obviously, lumping all residential facilities under the single rubric of institution is as inappropriate as stereotyping all retarded persons as a homogeneous group. A range exists, from the old-fashioned, large, public custodial institution to the progressive, small community residence in a single-family house or cooperative apartment. Still, these facilities may have similar needs in the mental health area in addition to their unique concerns.

The delivery of mental health services in institutions can range from consultee-oriented consultation format to direct clinical service.

Classical mental health consultation has been defined by Caplan (1970) as "a type of professional interaction in which the consultant accepts no direct responsibility for implementing remedial action for the client." Instead, he provides to the consultee help in understanding the client, he may offer management suggestions, and he strives to increase the consultee's knowledge to enable better handling of similar cases in the future. He may also focus on the consultee's own problems in managing the case, as well as advise on the relevant programs in the consultee's institution. The drawback of this approach is that the mental health professional is not involved in the actual care of the patient, and thus he may be seen as an outsider who criticizes the institution's staff but leaves them to their own devices. This "hands off" attitude and uninvolvement historically has contributed to the negative image of the mental health professions among institutions' staffs.

At the other end of the spectrum, the consultant functions as a specialist to whom selected patients are referred with specific problems and whom he diagnoses, treats, and follows, much the same way as a surgeon would approach a patient with appendicitis. This model may be impractical, since enough professional time (especially that of a psychiatrist) is rarely available in an institution to deliver all these services personally.

Obviously, various health professionals will favor one model over another, depending on the institution's needs and their own attitudes, interests, and available time. Attitudes of the staff of institutions may be important as well.

The need for (child) psychiatric services by retarded persons, including those living in institutions, had been pointed out by Potter (1964). He suggested a case seminar format in which the psychiatric consultant would function as preceptor and teacher, aiding other staff members in using their skills for the stimulation, support, and self-realization of the retarded child. Beitenman (1970) described his 5 years of experience in implementing psychiatric services in an institution, based substantially on the case seminar model suggested by Potter. This led to improving communication among staff members as well as to initiation of attitudinal changes. He pointed out the role of the psychiatrist in leading the team to reassess its function. Beitenman's conclusions are still valid. However, the role of mental health consultants in institutions in the late 1970s and early 1980s has to be adapted to new approaches: mainly, deinstitutionalization, normalization, and interdisciplinary team principles.

A flexible, middle-of-the-road approach to consultation is considered optimal. For the sake of brevity, the term *consultant* is used in this chapter, although the meaning is different from that of Caplan (1970). In keeping with the modern philosophy of management of mental retardation by an interdisciplinary team, the mental health professional should see himself as a full member of such a team, with conceptually equal responsibilities and privileges, modified by the reality of time he can offer. This is most important because behavior disorders are a multicausal phenomenon. Since residents' lives in institutions are influenced by multiple caregivers and service providers, they must act in agreement and cooperation with the mental health consultant to ensure the success of the treatment program. Thus, the consultant should be a team member who comes regularly and frequently to each unit at the institution he is assigned to and participates in relevant team meetings. As does any other professional on the team, he consults often, within his area of competence, on issues of client management, program formulation, and others. Whenever clinically indicated, he sees patients referred to him by other team members, or he may suggest such a referral himself, e.g., after noticing a disturbed behavior of a particular individual or hearing about him during a consultation or routine review conference. He is expected to do diagnostic examinations and, in conjunction with the team, formulate treatment plans. In some cases, all or part of the treatment will be delivered by him; in others, through other team members whom he supervises or advises. In similar fashion, he will follow the patients' progress.

INITIATING THE CONSULTATION

The function of the mental health professional is affected by the reasons that led to hiring him. For instance, if the need for his services was perceived by the staff members themselves, his role will be much better accepted than it would be if he were hired after a court order mandating improvement in clinical services.

Social workers or psychologists joining institution staffs find, as a rule, an established department of their own discipline whose members help them with orientation. A psychiatrist (and perhaps a psychiatric nurse) usually enters as a "solo" consultant, who has to "fend" for himself. During the initial stage, the professional should become familiar with the structure of the institution (Caplan, 1970), key personnel, individual subdivisions, and the residents and their mental health needs. Attitudes toward, and expectations of, mental health professionals should be explored and understood. Direct contact with staff on the professional and direct-service levels and personal observations (e.g., spending a day in each unit) are helpful in achieving these goals. At the end of the orientation period, a sort of "contract" is made with responsible, key staff members delineating the allocation of the consultant's time and defining his duties.

INSTITUTIONAL STRUCTURE AND CONSULTANT'S ROLES

The organization of the institution and staff attitude influence the utilization of mental health consultation. Institutions vary. Most public institutions are under the legislated and/or court ordered mandate to reduce their population as one step toward normalization of residents' lives. An institution with which the authors have been associated has grown from 25 residents in 1900 to 2,010 in 1940, declining to about 1,100 in 1979, with a projected census of 725 in 1982 (Nelson and Crocker, 1978).

Heads of institutions are usually administrators with a background in education or social work but rarely, if ever, in medicine. They usually have considerable power over all aspects of institutional life but may be constrained by policies of the state office of mental retardation.

Most institutions are in the country rather than in larger population centers. Thus, for example, a psychiatrist associated with an urban university affiliated clinic might accept a part-time consulting position to be able to maintain his academic affiliation and professional stimulation. A novel approach is a contract between a university affiliated hospital and an institution whereby the former provides medical services (Nelson and Crocker, 1978) and furnishes the physician with a staff appointment in the university.

Institutions' residents are usually assigned to smaller administrative units, depending on such factors as age, type of handicap, degree of retardation, behavior, and participation in a specific program (e.g., preparation for discharge); however, considerable overlap may exist. Larger units may contain smaller, autonomous subunits in separate buildings. Larger, self-contained institutions may have their own hospital, theoretically for acutely ill patients, but it often houses chronically psychiatrically disturbed "undesirables." There may be considerable transfer of residents, particularly the disturbed ones, between various units, to the point that the consultant finds it difficult to ascertain who is responsible for a given individual. Units are headed by professionals of various disciplines, including administration, education, social service, and nursing, but rarely, if ever, medicine. Each unit, depending on its nature, staff, and director, may differ in its style of decision-making, problem-solving, intrateam relationships, and the like. It is essential for the consultant to become well acquainted with these factors.

This organization, while creating more manageable, smaller units, has led to a dual power system: units and professional departments. Thus, theoretically, a professional staff member is responsible administratively to a unit director and professionally to the head of his professional department. In practice, this distinction may be unclear, and power struggles readily develop between unit and department heads. Since there is rarely a formal department of psychiatry in an institution, the psychiatric consultant may have to cover a number of units, and he may have a considerable degree of independence, although administratively he may be assigned to the department of medicine.

Architecturally, most older facilities have an unmistakable institutional "stamp"; they are designed to care for a dehumanized group in a conveyor belt-like fashion (Menolascino, 1977). Residents may be housed in huge dormitory rooms that serve also as dayrooms. Increasingly, however, residents spend day hours in separate schools, workshops, or recreation facilities, either on the grounds or in neighboring communities. A visit to the living quarters permits quick assessment of the quality of residents' lives, such as the presence or absence of personal possessions and provisions for privacy. For instance, use of different colored bedcovers may testify that staff members view the residents as individuals, not as an amorphous group. Some newer institutions may follow a cottage system, with small groups of residents living family style with houseparents. In predischarge units, usually housed in smaller buildings, residents may be living in private or semiprivate rooms and may even run the house with appropriate supervision.

Allocations and manner of use of consultant's time depend on the amount of his time available, the institution's needs for his services, and his and the staff's attitudes. Ideally, he should frequently and regularly spend sufficient time in each unit to be able to participate in the staff's review meetings of individual residents, visit the unit on rounds, talk with relevant staff members, interview individual residents who need his attention, and review their progress. In this way he can function as a team member, being equally responsible for the residents, rather than as a specialist for episodic consultation. The specialist model is employed if the consultant can spend only a very short time on each unit, and if the staff sees him as a threatening person, to be used only in strictly limited fashion. He will be asked then to render only specific opinions in specific cases, and often only to prescribe psychoactive medication. Unfortunately, some psychiatrists like such a role because it is safer and less challenging, and they may have little interest in mental retardation. They will contribute to the image of the psychiatrist as an uninvolved pill pusher. Some prefer only to hold consultation conferences with the staff. Others see patients only in solitary interviews and rarely talk to the staff. The mark of the good consultant is the ability, and the willingness, to work flexibly with the staff on all levels; to deliver direct clinical service; to be a part of the team; to accept and share responsibilities; and not to hide behind the title of M.D.

Realistically, however, time utilization on a unit may require a compromise. The professional may have to focus on one or several units where the need for services is the greatest, and perhaps where the staff is most cooperative. Challenging the institutional hierarchy is not the best way to begin; rather, the consultant should meet the heads of the institution and familiarize himself with the units and the relevant professional departments. Spending an entire day or more in each unit is an excellent way of meeting the staff, observing the residents, and learning about the realities of their lives. The consultant should ask questions of the staff, but should be cautious lest he be critical or threatening. During this stage, on the basis of his own observations, requests by the staff members, and discussions with them, the consultant's time allocations may be established.

TECHNIQUES OF CONSULTATION

The consultant should keep in mind that he is primarily a clinical specialist, contributing clinical help to services-starved residents, and not a management consultant. Thus, his focus, and the best way to "sell" himself to the staff, is to start with service delivery. Usually, he is given oral or written requests to consult on a disturbed resident. (He should be aware that the first few cases may be a "test" and he should make it clear to the staff that no "miracle" can be expected and that certainly they have worked hard and tried their best before requesting the consultation.)

It is essential to meet directly with the staff member(s) who made the referral. The consultant should make it clear that they know the referred resident much better than he, and that detailed information from them is necessary for the success of the consultation. If professionals on the staff contact him first, he should make a point to invite direct-care staff to join as well, e.g., through asking questions about the resident's daily life, which only they can answer. Thus, he will create an interdisciplinary mini-team, which will review the resident's history, current status, and diagnostic assessment and will formulate recommendations, assign the responsibility for implementation, and follow-up on the case. With a consultant's tactful leadership, dissent between staff members concerning the resident will surface in the forum of this team and is likely to be resolved.

Interviewing the referred resident is, of course, a part of good clinical practice and, depending on the case and time constraints, may be done before or after the meeting with staff members. Sometimes the resident may be present at the staff meeting, making it a sort of a group interview, if it is not traumatic to the resident or does not violate his privacy, and if permission is given by him (if capable).

Frequently the staff members utilizing the consultant form a semipermanent group, meeting with him regularly in a behavior management conference for group consultation or didactic seminars; this may be a time-economic way of reaching many of them.

Staff members (especially direct-care workers) are essentially part-time parents, on whom the residents depend in all aspects of their lives and who have the power to implement or sabotage the consultant's recommendation. Their feelings about, and relationship with, the residents may be compared with those of natural parents and may be partly responsible both for the genesis of the residents' psychopathology and their progress. Thus, involving all these caregivers as allies in the mental health diagnostic and treatment process is imperative. Yet they should never be approached as patients needing help for themselves, even if they ostensibly present themselves as such. Support, respect for their work, treating them as colleagues, and empathy are all necessary. Whenever possible, the consultant should guide them to proper observations of residents' behaviors and of their own reactions to it, rather than confront them immediately and authoritatively with his own opinions.

THE CONSULTANT AS A CATALYST OF ATTITUDE CHANGE

Deindividualization (Wolfensberger, 1972) is a hallmark of an institution. The retarded residents are seen merely as part of a group, more similar to than different from one another. Deindividualization can be characterized by a low common denominator (gearing the environment to the needs of the lowest functioning residents), large residential groupings, reduced autonomy, and spending the day in one setting. Certain behaviors are seen as stereotyped and expected. More extremely, an ability to have and express emotions may be implicitly denied, and all behavior is seen as conditioned by external events rather than as expressing inner needs as well. Well-meaning concern for the residents' welfare may be transformed into overprotection. Perske (1970) spoke about "the dignity of risk" denied retarded people and the unexpected inner values a retarded person may demonstrate given the chance, even if it is an unorthodox, risky chance.

Mental health professionals can influence these attitudes because they are trained to relate to individuals. Thus they have a role in promoting an attitude of reindividualization, e.g., through acting as role models in addressing the residents as individuals and exploring and explaining their unique inner lives. They should promote the view of the retarded person as a "developing person" (Menolascino, 1977), capable of learning, whose behavior should be seen as part of developmental progression and not as an isolated phenomenon.

The second opportunity for attitude influencing is interdisciplinary cooperation. Mental health professionals promote it by relating to and respecting professional and direct-care personnel on all levels, as well as by creating an ad hoc mini-team, as described earlier.

FUNCTIONS OF THE CONSULTANT

For clinical service to be effective, the reasons for requesting psychiatric consultation must be understood. The discussion of manifest and latent complaints in the previous chapter applies here as well. The situation may be further complicated by different, even opposing, views of the resident in question by various staff members. These issues have to be elicited, dealt with, and reconciled by the consultant. It is well known that consultations are usually requested because the caregivers find certain behaviors disturbing to them. This is illustrated by the following list of chief complaints in 100 referrals for psychiatric consultation in a large public institution:

Assaultive behavior	24	Need for formal diagnosis	4
Bizarre behavior	20	Pica	3
Self-abuse	11	Work problems	2
Withdrawn behavior	8	Medication review	2
Hyperactivity	7	Seizures	2
Sexual problems	5	Regurgitation	2
Depression	4	Manipulative behavior	1
Placement problems	4	Suicidal behavior	1

Diagnostic Assessments

Formal psychiatric diagnosis is more than a label mandated by an annual review. For instance, realization that a resident is actively psychotic may relieve pressure on him to modify his "behavior disorder" and may permit conflict-free use of antipsychotic medication. Proper diagnosis of manic-depressive illness may lead to specific treatment with lithium. Conversely, delabeling an inappropriate diagnosis of psychosis may dispel the staff's fear of the resident and enable placing him in educational-habilitational programs. Thus, diagnostic assessment has an important role in planning of treatment programs. The psychiatric consultant's task is to help the staff to synthesize the resident's history, medical findings, and psychological development into a comprehensive and coherent picture.

Treatment Interventions

General Considerations Some staff members may oppose using more than one intervention approach at a time because it is "unscientific" and does not show which is the effective one. Others are concerned that if one modality (e.g., drugs) is used, the resident will be quieted but forgotten. Still others demand that the emotional disturbance must be cured before another intervention (e.g., education) can be started. These attitudes may be overt manifestations of ignorance, ideological training (e.g., as experimental psychologists), or power struggle (wish to control through using approaches identified with one's own discipline). The consultant has to overcome these attitudes in order to have the staff understand that the synergistic effect of several modalities is the most beneficial, and that one modality may actually make the patient more responsive to the other one.

Psychoactive Medications   Use of psychoactive agents may involve highly charged emotions of the staff; misconceptions about proper use are common. Drugs are often put in the same category as punishment and aversive conditioning (which happened in a 1979 proposal for Individual Service Plans of the Massachusetts Department of Mental Health); they are seen as chemical restraints or as miracle agents that produce normal behavior. Some staff members may insist on drug use in a particular case, whereas others may vehemently oppose it. Some direct-care workers may fear that if a resident is taken off drugs he will become violent and hurt them. Although it is true in some cases, in others the staff's anxiety is perceived by the resident and induces him to act out. Unfortunately, these views have a historical basis in the misuse of drugs in institutions. Review of literature documenting this is presented in Chapter 13.

The role of the consultant is to promote rational drug use rather than to attempt to eliminate it. Depending on the institution and how complicated the case is, he may prescribe and monitor the drugs himself; in less complicated cases, he may act as adviser to the unit's general physician, who will carry these responsibilities. Educating the staff members, eliciting their misgivings, and reconciling their views are necessary prerequisites to success. Expected results from the drug (including possible side effects) have to be stated clearly, monitored, and recorded regularly. Reviewing effects of drugs in meetings with the staff is most helpful.

Psychiatric Emergencies   Genuine emergencies can be expected, considering the concentration of individuals with poor ego strengths, primitive defenses, and poor internalized controls. Many of them are mentally disturbed as well. In an understaffed facility, acting out may be the only way of attracting attention. Emergencies may include acts of aggression, psychotic episodes, and, rarely (in our experience), suicidal attempts. Requests for emergency consultations are frequent, however. Institutional staff members are often accustomed to using crises as a means of obtaining services. Often the "emergency" reflects tensions among the unit staff members (communicated to the resident) or staff members' unwillingness to accept transfer of a troublesome resident to that unit (although they readily manage similar behaviors in other individuals). These factors have to be recognized and acknowledged by the consultant and followed-up through successful resolution. Empathy with the staff's plight, securing additional help for the staff, fostering interstaff and staff-administration communication, creating interdisciplinary crisis teams, and providing respite placement for disturbed residents are all helpful. The consultant has to be available and should not rebuff the emergency request on the phone, even if he knows that there is no genuine psychiatric emergency. As he becomes established in the unit and trusted by the staff, and when the process for preventive, regular mental health intervention is effected, such emergencies become rare.

Psychotherapy   Time constraints will usually make it impossible for the consultant to do individual psychotherapy, although he occasionally may engage in it to teach staff members (e.g., in continuous case seminars) or for his own interest. He may lead therapy groups, especially to train group leaders, and he may also train and supervise individual therapists chosen from the members of the mental health disciplines.

Teaching Responsibilities

Participation in staff training is an important function of the consultant. Every case conference should be used for this purpose, with efforts to ensure participation of both professional and direct-care staff. Professional staff relies more on theoretical concepts; direct care staff can contribute their intimate knowledge of the residents, and will press for concrete solutions as well as intellectual understanding. Thus, working with these two staff groups will be most helpful in progressing toward normalization. More formal, didactic teaching meetings may also be arranged at the request of the staff and/or the suggestion of the consultant. Some of the topics frequently requested are psychiatric nosology, use of psychotropic medications, and sex education. Whenever possible, such presentations should be done by an interdisciplinary group of mental health professionals to enrich their content and to further the cause of interdisciplinary cooperation.

Administrative Functions

Like any other staff member, the consultant may be asked to serve on relevant committees, such as drug utilization or human rights. An important role that borders the clinical, training, and administration spheres is staff support. The consultant supports staff daily on a direct level in individual and group meetings on clinical issues. He may have to express his support for the plight of staff members (particularly direct-care staff), recognize lack of resources, and lobby for them. He may lead staff members to recognize their own feelings concerning the resident in question or uncover interstaff hostilities and show how these affect the staff's clinical effectiveness. Under no circumstances should he permit himself to act as therapist for the staff, even if requested to do so. Sometimes he may be requested to lead staff groups on issues like their feelings of frustration or burnout, but he should act only as a catalyst and not as a therapist.

The consultant may be asked to advise administrators on staff management; this is an example of staff support on an indirect level. This is illustrated by a situation in which the unit director became aware of intrastaff tensions, particularly between professional and direct-care staff and between various shifts. Discussions with the consultant clarified that the day and night shifts saw their roles as opposing ones: the former strove to activate the residents and the latter, to keep them quiet. They had different resources available to them. Their primary means of communication was through written reports. On the consultant's suggestion, intershift training meetings focusing on clinical cases were instituted. Both direct-care and professional staff attended and became actively involved as a team in comprehensive planning and consistent implementation of treatment plans.

MENTAL HEALTH ASPECTS OF DEINSTITUTIONALIZATION

Public institutions, as a rule, are working toward discharging their residents into the community whenever possible. This poses mental health challenges on several levels.

The Resident

For the resident, the institution as a whole, and some staff members individually, represent parental figures on whom he depends. He often identifies with the staff's image of him (e.g., child-like, crazy) and with unwillingness to let him go. His skills may be adapted to institutional—not community—living. A higher functioning resident may be considered at the top of his group in the institution, but not in the community at large. He may realistically fear life on the outside. Thus, considerable ambivalence and resistance to breaking this dependent attachment may develop, similar to the ambivalence of nonretarded adolescents about becoming independent. It may be manifested by passivity, regression to a more dependent state, aggressive outbursts, or frank psychopathology (particularly clinical depression).

The Staff

Staff members may be equally threatened by separation from the resident. They may have made emotional investment in the particular resident and may fear he will be exploited and lost without the protection of the institution. They may be possessive, and see the resident as an eternal child on whom they can exercise their need to be parents. Other personal pathology may be projected onto the resident. On the other hand, staff members may overrate the resident's progress and take it as proof of their own professional adequacy, and the resident may be pressed into prema-

ture discharge. Last, but not least, staff members see deinstitutionalization as a step toward closing the institution and loss of their jobs, and it
has been opposed by groups of institutional employees (Santiestevan,
1975).

This resistance may take different forms. A double message to the
resident may encourage his dependency and regression. He may be overtly
overprotected, and discharge plans may be directly opposed or indirectly
sabotaged. For instance, plans for preparing the resident for the discharge
may not be put into effect and his subsequent failure to adapt to the outside taken as proof of his need to stay in the institution.

The Families

Resistance from the parents may be encountered, even if they had not
been involved much with the resident previously. Their guilt for institu-
tionalizing the child may be mobilized by the possibility that others may
succeed in keeping him in the community and thus be better parents. They
may fear that the child will be exploited without institutional protection.
They may fear having to take the child back home.

The Community

The prospective caregivers in the community may be very concerned
about accepting an individual who is "emotionally disturbed." They may
see normal reactions to separation as potentially dangerous. On the other
hand, they may exhibit rescue fantasy in wanting to accept a very disturbed resident without adequate preparation and provision for services,
believing that "good" placement will "cure" him.

Mental Health Interventions

As usual, prevention is the best treatment. Consultants' input into
periodic review processes and diagnostic assessments will help in assessing
residents' developmental readiness for separation. Group and individual
psychotherapy may be indicated for resolving conflicts around this issue
and for preparing a resident for leaving the institution. Psychoactive medication, particularly antidepressants, is a useful adjunct and helps relieve
the depression that may underly the apathy and lack of motivation.
Group meetings with staff members (preferably with clinical focus) may
help them in resolving their conflicts. Meetings with the family may be
similarly useful. The consultant may be actively involved with prospective
caregivers in the community and clarify for them the resident's behavior
and motivation. His input will be most important in planning for gradually increasing the challenges and responsibilities for the discharged resident, lest he be overwhelmed by stress. Cochran, Sran, and Varano (1977)
described "a relocation syndrome," a clinical depression, resulting from

transfer to a new facility. They suggested preventive measures, such as the resident visiting a prospective facility, his involvement in planning for the move, cooperation of the staff from the old and new facility, and appointment of a personal advocate for the resident. It is helpful if the consultant can provide the continuity of mental health care for the discharged resident, or at least serve as a liaison in securing it from a community-based clinic (although this may be difficult if few staff members of the clinic are motivated and trained to work with retarded patients). In one model of service delivery (Ziring, personal communication), an institution contracted and paid teams of mental health professionals in community mental health centers in its vicinity to provide services for discharged residents.

INSTITUTIONAL ROADBLOCKS TO MENTAL HEALTH INTERVENTIONS

Hostility to the medical model may be relevant if the consultant is a psychiatrist (see Chapter 1 and Dybwad, 1970; Wolfensberger, 1972). In institutional settings, the hostility often reflects a power struggle and concern about doctors taking over, especially since institutional administrators on all levels, as a rule, are not physicians. *Professional territoriality* may be a problem. In institutions, role definitions are usually drawn arbitrarily and the turf of the disciplines is guarded jealously. Also, realistically, lack of experience in working with a particular type of professional (e.g., psychiatrist) may underly confusion about his role, or perhaps the institutional staff had had a bad experience with incompetent consultants in the past. The consultant may be seen as an intruder on another's territory, or as someone who can only prescribe drugs (a pill pusher), or as an analyst who wants to analyze the staff. *Communication difficulties* may be considerable in an institution, both between various disciplines and between various administrative levels. It may be hard to obtain information, or information may be based on gossip, and the consultant may not know to whom to turn. A staff member may warn a consultant that, e.g., direct-care staff members know nothing and his attempts to talk with them may threaten an existing order. *Staff morale* may be low because of a low level of training, poor working conditions, isolation, or lack of recognition by administration. Staff members may fear that a new outside specialist, especially one with academic connections, will point out their ignorance. *Custodial mentality* is encountered, especially among older staff members. They are devoted to the residents, but they see them as dependent children to be protected, taken care of, and given love when they behave well. Mental health consultants may threaten this child-parent relationship through focusing on the resident's inner life, needs, strengths, and his "push" toward normalization.

Manifestation of these roadblocks may vary. In the most obvious form, the consultant may be told that the residents are not crazy and that his services are not needed. He may be told to whom of the staff he should talk. He may be asked to attend only to signing prescriptions. Meetings with him may be cancelled continuously. Gossip about him may circulate. He may be denied entrance to a unit without prior permission.

Prevention is the best way to manage roadblocks. The consultant's willingness from the beginning to meet all staff members, to recognize existing order, to learn from others, to be patient and not expect miracles, and not to criticize all serve as a message that he respects the staff members, their hard work, knowledge of the residents, and devotion to them. His focus on clinical approach through an ad hoc mini-team will demonstrate the benefits of interdisciplinary cooperation. His professional skills will prove him to be a useful addition to the staff (if his recommendations are in clear language and are realistic). His willingness to be available whenever needed and following up on his patients without being asked to do so will establish him as a concerned and devoted professional.

The consultant should always be aware that staff complaints about him may be realistic, and self-examination should be a first step if they occur. When he develops rapport with the staff, frank and open discussion of their complaints should be helpful.

MENTAL HEALTH ISSUES IN COMMUNITY RESIDENCES

A logical outcome of enabling retarded persons to reside in as close to normal as possible conditions (normalization) is living in the community. Care and supervision are provided as necessary, without creating an institutional atmosphere, and enabling maximally possible independent decision making. The setting most frequently utilized is a community residence—a house or group of apartments in which a small group (usually under 10) of retarded older adolescents or adults lives under supervision of trained workers working on shifts, perhaps with two houseparents living on the premises. The residents run the household to the extent permitted by their abilities. This model has been described in the literature (O'Connor, 1976; Baker, Seltzer, and Seltzer, 1977; Seltzer and Seltzer, 1978).

It has become increasingly known that behavioral disorders, rather than lack of skills, are a major roadblock to a resident's successful integration into community living (Nihira and Nihira, 1975; Seltzer and Seltzer, 1978; Sternlicht, 1978). In the community, deviant behavior is neither expected nor tolerated as it would be in the institution. Furthermore, normal stresses inherent in community living may create a high level of anxiety in an individual brought up in a protected institutional setting. For these reasons, community residences increasingly turn to mental health professionals for help.

Psychologically oriented consultations to community residence programs have been described by Parks (1978). He divides these programs into two types. In type A, the staff is relatively inexperienced and the consultant's primary role is to provide training for them and assistance in program development. In type B, where the staff is more experienced and trained, the consultant is concerned with strengthening staff cohesion and aiding in handling clients who pose serious management problems.

There are important differences between consultations in community residences and in large institutions, because of differences in setting, staffing, and residents, and these are examined separately.

The Setting

In a normalized environment, institutional deindividualization and deprivation are usually minimal or absent, although behaviors fostered by them in the past may persist, at least initially. External architectural limits (controls) are minimal, and for impulsive residents who tend to run away, supervision must be maintained. The consultant, together with the staff, has to evaluate these factors in light of the resident's skills, past history, and physical limitations, and has to design a system of priorities that will give exposure to new challenges. There may be problems with neighbors who fear the "crazy" newcomers or who overprotect them. The consultant can be most helpful in organizing informative meetings to resolve or prevent these.

The Staff

Generally, staff members are young, motivated, and without institutional mentality, but they may lack training and experience. Thus, inservice training on a variety of mental health issues may be necessary, especially in the first phases of the consultation (Parks, 1978). The enthusiasm is often translated into rescue fantasies and omnipotent feelings, leading to inappropriate expectations overwhelming the residents, over- or under-controls, and overprotection. The consultant has to help the staff resolve those feelings and yet learn to derive gratification from their work. The consultation technique focuses on leading staff members to realize these feelings by themselves, with the consultant acting as a catalyst and supporter (similar to his role described earlier). If staff members are very behaviorally oriented, they deny that anxiety and other feelings may be underlying the inappropriate behaviors of the residents that they try unsuccessfully to extinguish. Their own anger, depression, and rejection of the resident may ensue. These issues should and can be prevented through staff training, good initial mental health assessment of the residents, setting comprehensive and realistic programs, and ongoing group meetings with the consultant. If the later is a physician-psychiatrist, he will have important roles in assessing and interpreting for the staff the resident's medical-neurological status, serving as a liaison with other medical specialists, and securing necessary services in various clinics. Special situations arise when houseparents, usually a young couple, live on the premises and find it difficult to reconcile their needs for privacy with the residents' need for attention. Consultants' support then may be invaluable (Parks, 1978).

The Residents

Depending on the orientation of the residence, the individuals who are accepted are preselected by level of skills and age. Optimally, the consultant should participate in the selection process through doing a review of the past history and comprehensive diagnostic assessment, if indicated. The consultant may suggest to the prospective resident's caregivers to set up a preparatory program to ensure successful placement in the residence. These individuals are usually dependent on familiar environment, and sudden transfer to a residence may precipitate a relocation syndrome (Cochran et al., 1977), manifested by depressive symptoms. Residents who are on psychotropic medication may require follow-up unless supervised by their own physicians. Individual and group therapy may be indicated as well, the latter being particularly useful in such small and stable groups. Last, the consultant may learn much about the realities of the life in the residence and establish himself as a concerned and genuinely involved professional, if he spends some "unorthodox" time there (such as staying for dinner with the residents).

THE CONSULTANT'S REACTIONS TO THE INSTITUTION

For many professionals, especially psychiatrists, an institution may be a threatening place. It is not a safe mental health clinic with colleagues who speak the same jargon and do similar things. He has to prove himself to be useful to other staff and be ready to have his views challenged. The consultant's adaptation depends on many factors besides the institutional reality: his basic personality structure, training, experience, and expectations of his work. An overintellectualizing person, sensitive to criticism, concerned about power, and unable to share and work with the group, who sees work in the retardation field as unchallenging or primarily a way of making money or doing research but has no sense of broader commitment, will not do well. Some leave quickly; others persist, denying their maladaptation. Maladaptation may take different forms. Some defend professional territoriality and claim authority on the basis of their M.D. or Ph.D. alone or avoid involvement, emphasizing their role as detached observers, consultant-advisers to others. Some relate only to the patients and communicate minimally with the staff. Others meet with the staff only and do not see the patients at all, or briefly and rarely at best. They may focus on staff problems and interpret everything in terms of staff pathology. Some overtly advise the administration and take sides in power struggles within it. Another form of reaction is sterotyping all institutional staff into a negative mold as "they," thus virtually deindividualizing them.

Undoubtedly professional burnout does exist and may be justifiably based on institutional reality. To avoid it, the professional must be confident, capable of self-examination, realistic, able to relate to others, and to share. Support of colleagues is essential, both on an individual and group basis, as are alternate sources of professional gratification. For this reason, many prefer working part-time in an institution and part-time in another facility with different types of patients in order to obtain such support and to maintain a broad range of professional skills.

It should be stressed, however, that after an initial adjustment period, a devoted professional will find this field of work challenging, offering long-term gratification through contributing to bettering the lot of a very neglected segment of our society and providing experiences useful in other areas of his professional endeavors.

REFERENCES

Baker, B. L., Seltzer, G. B., and Seltzer, M. M. 1977. As Close As Possible: Community Residence for Retarded Adults. Little, Brown & Co., Boston.
Beitenman, E. T. 1970. The psychiatric consultant in the residential facility for the mentally retarded. In: F. J. Menolascino (ed.), Psychiatric Approaches to Mental Retardation. Basic Books, New York.
Caplan, G. 1970. The Theory and Practice of Mental Health Consultation. Basic Books, New York.
Cochran, W. E., Sran, P. K., and Varano, G. A. 1977. The relocation syndrome in mentally retarded individuals. Ment. Retard. 15(2):10–12.
Conroy, J. W. 1977. Trends in deinstitutionalization of the mentally retarded. Ment. Retard. 15(4):44–46.
Dybwad, G. 1970. Roadblocks to renewal of residential care. In: F. J. Menolascino (ed.), Psychiatric Approaches to Mental Retardation. Basic Books, New York.
Menolascino, F. J. 1977. Challenges in Mental Retardation: Progressive Ideology and Services. Human Sciences Press, New York.
Nelson, R. P., and Crocker, A. C. 1978. The medical care of mentally retarded persons in public residential facilities. N. Engl. J. Med. 299:1039–1044.
Nihira, L., and Nihira, K. 1975. Normalized behavior in community placement. Ment. Retard. 13(2):9–13.
Nirje, B. 1969. The normalization principle and its human management implications. In: R. Kugel and W. Wolfensberger (eds.), Changing Patterns in Residential Services for the Mentally Retarded. President's Committee on Mental Retardation, Washington, D.C.
O'Connor, G. 1976. Home Is a Good Place: A National Perspective of Community Residential Facilities for Developmentally Disabled Persons. Am. Assoc. Ment. Defic. Monogr. No. 2. Washington, D.C.
Parks, A. W. 1978. A model for psychological consultation to community residences—Pressures, problems, and program types. Ment. Retard. 16(2):149–152.

The *Pennhurst* case: Equal rights for the retarded. 1978. The Philadelphia Inquirer. Jan. 1.

Pennsylvania Association for Retarded Children (PARC) v. *Commonwealth of Pennsylvania,* 343 F. Supp. 279 (E.D. Pa., 1972).

Perske, R. 1970. The dignity of risk. In: W. Wolfensberger (ed.), The Principle of Normalization in Human Services. National Institute on Mental Retardation, Toronto.

Potter, H. W. 1964. The needs of mentally retarded children for child psychiatry services. J. Am. Acad. Child Psychiatry 3:352-374.

Santiestevan, H. 1975. Out of Their Beds and into the Streets. American Federation of State, County and Municipal Employees, Washington, D.C.

Seltzer, M. M., and Seltzer, G. 1978. Context for Competence. Educational Projects, Inc., Cambridge, Mass.

Sternlicht, M. 1978. Variables affecting foster care placement of institutionalized retarded residents. Ment. Retard. 16(1):25-28.

Wolfensberger, W. 1972. The Principle of Normalization in Human Services. National Institute on Mental Retardation, Toronto.

Wolfensberger, W. 1975. The Origin and Nature of Our Institutional Models. Human Policy Press, Syracuse, N.Y.

Wyatt v. *Stickney,* 344 F. Supp. 387, 395 (M.D. Ala., 1972).

INDEX